OHNNY ROBINSON · WARREN RABB · ROY "MOONIE" WINSTON

· GEORGE RICE · GEORGE BEVAN · MIKE AND

· WARREN CAPONE · A.J. DUHE · CHARLES ALEX

OOKS · JOE "NACHO" ALBERGAMO · WENDELL DAVIS · TOMMY HO

NY McFARLAND · BRADIE JAMES · STEPHEN PETERMAN · CHAD LA

ER · CRAIG STELTZ · HERMAN JOHNSON · SKIP BERTMAN · SAM

JOHNNY ROBINSON · WARREN RABB · ROY "MOONIE" WINSTON

· GEORGE RICE · GEORGE BEVAN · MIKE ANDERSON · RONNIE

· WARREN CAPONE · A.J. DUHE · CHARLES ALEXANDER · ROBERT

OOKS · JOE "NACHO" ALBERGAMO · WENDELL DAVIS · TOMMY HO

NY McFARLAND · BRADIE JAMES · STEPHEN PETERMAN · CHAD LA

ER · CRAIG STELTZ · HERMAN JOHNSON · SKIP BERTMAN · SAM

JOHNNY ROBINSON · WARREN RABB · ROY "MOONIE" WINSTON

· GEORGE RICE · GEORGE BEVAN · MIKE ANDERSON · RONNIE

· WARREN CAPONE · A.J. DUHE · CHARLES ALEXANDER · ROBERT

OOKS · JOE "NACHO" ALBERGAMO · WENDELL DAVIS · TOMMY HO

NY McFARLAND · BRADIE JAMES · STEPHEN PETERMAN · CHAD LA

ER · CRAIG STELTZ · HERMAN JOHNSON · SKIP BERTMAN · SAM

JOHNNY ROBINSON · WARREN RABB · ROY "MOONIE" WINSTON

WHAT IT MEANS TO BE A TIGER

WHAT IT MEANS TO BE A
TIGER

LES MILES
AND LSU'S GREATEST PLAYERS

RAY GLIER

LEE FEINSWOG, CONTRIBUTING EDITOR

TRIUMPH
B O O K S

Library of Congress Cataloging-in-Publication Data

Glier, Ray.
    What it means to be a Tiger: Les Miles and LSU's greatest players / Ray Glier.
        p. cm.
ISBN: 978-1-60078-209-1
    1. Louisiana State University (Baton Rouge, La.)—Football—History. 2. LSU Tigers (Football team)—History. 3. Football players—Louisiana—Baton Rouge—History. I. Title.
    GV958.L65G57 2009
    796.332'630976318—dc22

                                                                    2009017638

This book is available in quantity at special discounts for your group or organization. For further information, contact:

Triumph Books
542 South Dearborn Street
Suite 750
Chicago, Illinois 60605
(312) 939-3330
Fax (312) 663-3557
www.triumphbooks.com

Printed in U.S.A.
ISBN: 978-1-60078-209-1
Design by Nick Panos
Editorial production and layout by Prologue Publishing Services, LLC
All photos courtesy LSU Athletics Department unless otherwise specified

For Raymond and Alexander

CONTENTS

FOREWORD

What It Means to Be a Tiger

I THINK THE STYLE OF PLAYER who comes here is ambitious and has competitiveness. They want to compete in the SEC, and they want to get their degree, and that is what we call a full measure of success.

This is my fourth fall here [2008], and generally speaking, our players understand the quality it takes to be part of the program and work hard and understand doing the right thing. They stand for what is good and right about college football.

Football in this conference is awfully important, and I think it is societal. I think the people in the states that follow SEC football understand it to be awfully important. I think that those players from those areas, when they choose their school, realize that the commitment they made was a sincere one and will take great effort because of the passion surrounding football.

There is a responsibility to the traditions and to link the current players with players who have come before them. The teams that we have had the last several years have participated in a fashion to which LSU is accustomed.

We talk a lot about a process we go through here, which is very specific to what we do, and we take pride in that process. It is important to us because it is hard to do. We like to say that process is the reason we are having success. It is different than other schools and different than other places, but it is like the other great teams at LSU.

As a coach, there is a responsibility to display tradition and uphold what has been done before us. I cherish that opportunity. I enjoy that, and our staff and team enjoy the comparisons of other great teams. Coming from Michigan, I certainly understood traditions, and I understand the traditions here at

LSU. You look at the great rivalries with other schools, and you want to uphold those rivalries.

I heard about the passion at LSU routinely before I came here as head coach. My first fall here we had Hurricane Katrina. We went from the old administration building to the one we're in now in two moves—first with the players and then the coaches—so getting up to speed with the passion probably took me longer than it should have because there was so much going on on the perimeter of football. I did not have clean observation powers the first fall.

Then I realized throughout that first year that this is not a normal job, nor a normal football school, nor a normal school. This is a very rare opportunity in competition, surrounded by the most passionate fans in college football.

I work hard. I get up early in the morning, and I work a full day. I enjoy what I do, and I don't leave a stone unturned. My staff doesn't, either, nor do my players. You get to a game, it's time to celebrate, it's time to go have fun, you prepared hard, it's time to go see how we do. I allow myself to smile and embrace a passionate stadium. I really do enjoy those games and everything around them because it is an exciting time for people.

When it comes to being on the field, what it means to be a Tiger is to have a spirit, a contact with the past, and the pursuit of excellence that is rare and something a little deeper than a football game.

What it means to be a Tiger is cultural, something that is more important than the score. People around this state, around this program, find football is as important as a lot of work, their jobs. It ranks up there because it is so intertwined with the culture.

Families come together for the games, they listen on the radio. It's how they grew up. It is not a dispassionate love; it is an intimate piece of their lives. Off the field, it is awfully important, and I understand that.

The sound that reverberates through that stadium is so serious, and loud, and peaks at the right times. I have not been in a stadium like it. There are stadiums that have more fans, but no place makes as much noise as a 92,500, arrive-early, stay-late crowd in Tiger Stadium.

Going into Tiger Stadium is one of the great thrills in my life, and I enjoy it every time. My family is happy here, I love the people I work with, I love my team, coaches, and support staff. And, compared to Michigan, it is relatively warm here.

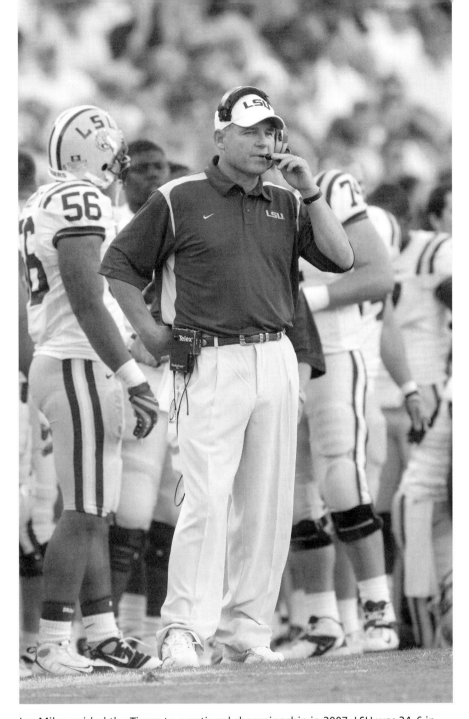

Les Miles guided the Tigers to a national championship in 2007. LSU was 34–6 in Miles' first three seasons and 8–5 in 2008. Miles is 4–0 in bowl games with the Tigers, which includes a 38–24 victory over Ohio State on January 7, 2008, in the BCS National Championship Game.

Coach Miles lifts up the Coaches' Trophy after LSU became BCS national champions with their victory over Ohio State in the 2008 BCS Championship Game.

The staff, the players, they expect excellence, and they will work to achieve it. I find there is a commitment to excellence here, and it's been that way for a long time.

I have my favorite traditions before a game. I see my family and give them a kiss before going into the stadium. I enjoy walking out and greeting the student section before our team goes out. I have a radio show that I do on the field before each game, so I like to go out there and see the students gathering in the student section.

One tradition I started when I got here was singing the alma mater after victories. Considering that I leave here at midnight, 12:30, or 1:00 AM, it is the best way to celebrate with the alumni and student section before you go to the locker room.

I don't know if you can count it as a tradition, but beating Florida, Auburn, and Alabama in the same year (2007) is a great tradition I would like to keep going.

Do they like my style? It is the job of the coach to give the team opportunities for victory. I am fortunate to have a talented team, and for me not to call some of those plays that our kids are able to make would be a mistake. I try and envision opportunities for success, and sometimes those are through some play calls.

There is so much here. There are so many different styles of people, so many different types of food, so many things to do. It is a wonderfully diverse community, the college, the town, and the state. The history of the state, the Cajuns that are here, the people make it a wonderful place. The port of New Orleans just opened up this state and helped create this diversity.

Players through the years have enjoyed adding their characteristics to the program. Great players have handed back to this football program. Kevin Faulk comes back. Michael Clayton comes back and has been heavily involved in this program. Billy Cannon and Jimmy Taylor come back, and I see Paul Dietzel weekly. Tommy Hodson stays involved.

Those people are always there for you, always there to lend a hand, show some guidance, and be a part of the program that they love.

—Les Miles

Les Miles became the LSU football coach in January 2005 and took the Tigers to a national championship in 2007. LSU finished in the top five three straight seasons under Miles, which had never happened at the school. LSU was 34–6 in Miles' first three seasons and 8–5 in 2008. Miles is 4–0 in bowl games with the Tigers, which includes a 38–24 victory over Ohio State on January 7, 2008, in the BCS National Championship Game. Miles, who was born November 10, 1953, in Elyria, Ohio, graduated from the University of Michigan in 1976 with a degree in economics. He was a two-year letterman at Michigan and played on two Big Ten championship teams. Miles has coached at Michigan, Colorado, Oklahoma State, and with the Dallas Cowboys.

ACKNOWLEDGMENTS

CHARLIE MCCLENDON WROTE the ultimate letter of acknowledgment. On his return from the Tangerine Bowl, his last game as coach of the LSU Tigers, he wrote a thank-you note to bowl officials and told them they had a splendid game and a "diamond in the rough."

Not long afterward, members of the Tangerine Bowl board showed up in Baton Rouge and offered him a job running their bowl. They were impressed by the grateful man and needed a hard worker.

In the spirit of Charlie McClendon, this is my thank-you note.

There are a lot of people to thank for the process of making this book a reality. One of the first to jump in was Bill Sharkey, who owns the Depeaux restaurant in Decatur, Georgia, my hometown. I walked in one day, laid an LSU media guide on a table, and asked, "What do you know about LSU football?"

Sharkey, who grew up in Baton Rouge, went to Baton Rouge High, and attended LSU, lit up. He tipped me off to Gene Sykes and the project rolled forward.

Sykes, a former player, jumped in with phone numbers of Paul Dietzel and Jerry Stovall. The ball was rolling. I called Gene a few times, and he dug up other numbers: Dalton Hilliard, Moonie Winston, Billy Truax, and others.

Sykes, who played from 1960 to 1962, holds the LSU traditions as close as anyone who has gone through the program. A draft pick of the Buffalo Bills in 1963, Sykes organizes reunions of his former teammates.

Bill Martin of the LSU Sports Information Department gathered the photos for the book, which were taken by Steve Franz. It was a big job and appreciated.

Jack Marucci, the LSU trainer, steered me toward several key players in the book, including All-American Bradie James, center Rudy Niswanger, and quarterback Matt Mauck.

Herb Vincent and Michael Bonnette in the LSU athletic department answered countless emails and phone calls. Lois Stuckey in the LSU football office also answered my calls, in between answering the hundreds of calls that come to her desk.

One regret is not hooking up with the great Glenn Dorsey, who was in his rookie season with the Kansas City Chiefs. We tried and tried. If there are some players of prominence you don't see in this book, it may be they did not respond to messages or passed away, or were simply overlooked. We had only a certain number of players we could include here.

The project rolled easier with the help of Les Miles, the 2007 national championship coach. In just a few short seasons, his personality seems to have the essence of what it means to be a Tiger: wide open, passionate. Thank you to Les for helping with the foreword for this book.

There is a special thanks to Dee Alberty, the daughter of Charlie McClendon. She has kept alive the Charles McClendon Scholarship Foundation (www.coachmac.org), which provides money to children of former players.

xv

"It is an appreciation of what their dads did to contribute to the LSU family," Dee Alberty said. "We have worked with almost 100 kids in 12 years, and they are so grateful."

Cholly Mac was all about being grateful. The winningest coach in LSU history had a credo, which are the character qualities he admired in people and strived for: responsibility, gratefulness, and respect for others.

For the purposes of this book, I underline <u>gratefulness</u>.

There is special thanks to Lee Feinswog, and his wife, Brenda LeBlanc, who shared their home with me several times as I tracked down former players. Lee, whom I have known 20 years, interviewed some of the LSU greats you will read about in this book.

A more special thanks goes to Alexander and Raymond, my boys. Some days, their dad could not go out and throw the football in the street or shoot the basketball because there was work to do on this book. They tried to be patient; they really did.

When I hear the stories of what it means to be a Tiger—the passion, the work, the dedication it takes—I make notes to pass on to my boys and let them share in some of the secrets.

INTRODUCTION

Y.A. TITTLE BEGAN HIS WALK near the goal line at Tiger Stadium and, by the time he got to the 50-yard line, the throng of fans had the 82-year-old man on the verge of tears with their applause. Tittle could only recall one other football moment that made him breathless, and that was his ride in the convertible in Canton, Ohio, at his enshrinement at the Pro Football Hall of Fame.

"I hadn't played for LSU in 60 years," Tittle said. "I just couldn't believe how they reacted to me. It was like Eisenhower coming home from the war."

Is that what it means to be a Tiger, to be wrapped in the arms of the faithful long after your playing days?

It has to be.

The passion of LSU fans has wrapped itself around Tiger football players for decades. The graybeards among the players can still walk through the tailgate crowd and get picked out by fans 40 years after their glory. The reminiscing begins until it has to break up for kickoff to watch the current Tigers.

The stories never lose their luster.

The goal-line stand that helped beat Ole Miss 14–0 in '58 and paved the way for the first national championship. It was a season of fortitude at the goal line for LSU as a goal-line stand against Alabama in Mobile gave birth to the Chinese Bandits.

Billy Cannon's Halloween night run to beat Ole Miss in '59.

LSU's defense throttling No. 4 Texas 13–0 in the Cotton Bowl to close the 1962 season.

The 1966 Cotton Bowl win over No. 2 Arkansas, 14–7, which kept the Razorbacks from the national title and earned McClendon a win over his home state team. It broke the Hogs' 22-game winning streak.

Bert Jones rallying the Tigers to a winning touchdown over Ole Miss on the final play in 1972.

LSU fighting No. 1 Southern Cal to the finish in Tiger Stadium in 1979, McClendon's last season as head coach. If Cholly Mac had won that game, could they have fired him?

Defensive tackle Leonard Marshall strong-arming No. 8 Alabama in a 20–10 victory in 1982.

The Blue Grass Miracle that beat Kentucky 33–30 in 2002.

The national title wins of the new era, both in New Orleans, to cap the 2003 and 2007 seasons.

The passion for LSU football is fueled by big moments, which usually came under the lights. You know night football was invented in Tiger Stadium, right?

The rest of the East Coast and the South would be headed for bed, except in Baton Rouge, where John Ferguson's voice came through the radio to provide the last sounds of football for a Saturday on this side of the Mississippi.

The lights are special to LSU fans. Billy Cannon knows.

When Hurricane Gustav swept through to delay the 2008 season, Cannon said the lights had to be readjusted to hit their spots on the field because the high winds had knocked the beams off line. When the lights came on, Cannon said, there were thousands of people in Tiger Stadium as witnesses.

"There wasn't a game, there wasn't even a practice, or a scrimmage, nothing," Cannon said. "The school engineers were seeing which lights were knocked off line by the winds of the hurricane, and they had to adjust them.

"People were there just to see what things were like inside their stadium. You don't think they love football down here?"

That must be what it means to be a Tiger.

Fifty years after he played his last game in Tiger Stadium as a college player, Cannon still can't help but gaze up and look around the upper rim of the stadium, then peer down the sidelines, or point to a spot on the field where a play was made, or mention something about the courage of a teammate.

"When I first started coming to this stadium as a kid, the north end did not go up this high," Cannon said and pointed to the scoreboard. "I have seen every building construction change that you can imagine. It has been a beautiful thing to follow."

It is the stadium's aura that gripped players consistently through the years, especially the ritual of running out between the goal posts. Most programs have the single stanchion goal posts, but LSU had the double posts to keep the tradition intact.

The ritual has been enlivened with the voice over the public address system:

"It's Saturday night in Death Valley and here come your Fighting Tigers of LSU."

Dan Borne' has given that call for 23 years over the dramatic drum cadence of the band.

Just before kickoff he will add to the passion with, "It's 62 degrees, relative humidity 40 percent, winds from the south at 3 miles per hour, chance of rain, never!"

If circumstances permit, there is more thrill added to the game that starts in the later afternoon, those 3:30 (ET) starts on CBS. Along about the end of the third quarter, the last sliver of sun will be in the sky, and Borne' will stir the crowd.

"Ladies and gentlemen, the sun has found its home in the western sky, and it is now Saturday night in Death Valley." The roar can shake the stadium.

"The atmosphere in Tiger Stadium [is that] it is not just a game, it is an institution," said Borne', who completed his 23rd year in 2008 as the PA announcer in Tiger Stadium.

There is some brutal honesty that goes with being a Tiger. A.J. Duhe, who went on to a fine NFL career with the Miami Dolphins, said LSU's downturn in the mid-1970s could have had something to do with the scarcity of black players. He did not accuse anyone of racism, he just said the program had half as many black players as other schools in the SEC, and LSU was not as athletically talented as those schools.

What does it mean to be a Tiger? Winning, that's what.

It didn't seem like Paul Dietzel was around LSU long enough to have a significant impact on the football program. He arrived in Baton Rouge in 1955 as a 30-year-old football coach and left just seven years later to become the head coach at Army, which was his lifelong dream.

Dietzel was around long enough to establish LSU as a national powerhouse and fans have not forgotten him. He won.

And if you don't win?

They throw shoes at you. David LaFleur, the former All-America tight end, remembers walking too close to Curley Hallman following the Tigers distressing 20–18 loss to Southern Miss on November 12, 1994, and a shoe bounced off the ground near Hallman as he left the field. He was fired not long after that loss.

What does it mean to be a Tiger?

Bert Jones, who may be the only consensus All-America quarterback to share playing time, gritted his teeth through a perplexing platoon system and stayed at LSU. He loved the school, its history, its people, and as competitive as he was, Jones did not transfer.

What does it mean to be a Tiger?

On his 60th birthday, Ronnie Estay was in the doctor's office in Saskatchewan when he found out the cancer had been removed from his body—for good. He called that day to talk about LSU football and broke into tears when he talked about getting a scholarship at LSU, which was just before his father died of bone cancer. It had been almost 40 years since he played football at LSU, and the emotion of how LSU football intertwined with his life left him deeply moved.

That's what it means to be a Tiger.

The FORTIES AND FIFTIES

Y.A. TITTLE

QUARTERBACK

1944–1947

DURING THE WAR, THEY LET FRESHMAN play on the varsity because of a shortage of players, so I got to play a lot of college football. I played left halfback on defense—*cornerback* is what they call it today. We played both ways, and I was a good tackler.

Bernie Moore was the head coach and a good coach. He was not a technician, not a detailed strategist. He relied on his assistant coaches for that. He was more a father figure, an organizer. He had good teams at LSU, even before I got there, so he had a handle on the program.

You knew he was a great organizer and coach because he also coached the track team, and they won the SEC 15 straight years. He would go to different LSU athletic programs, like football or basketball, get one athlete he thought could help him in track, and maybe get some points placing fourth in the shot put.

He was the grand old man of coaching at LSU, and a lot of people wanted to be an assistant coach for him because he was so well-respected. Coach Moore ended up with some great assistant coaches, and that makes a difference on a football team.

My first year at LSU, we were still running the single wing, but my sophomore year we went to the T formation—that was the new, inventive offense of college football in 1945. People used the single-wing or the double-wing

Y.A. Tittle played single-wing tailback and quarterback at LSU from 1944 to 1947. He was the first T formation quarterback at LSU.

offense, and we were the first to go to the T in the Southeastern Conference, one of the first in the country.

Coach Moore had recruited so many players that could run and be the main offensive player—the tailback in the single wing—that he decided we needed an offense where he could get them all on the field at the same time. We had all the same type talent. You had me, the single-wing left halfback; Jim Cason, single-wing left halfback; Ray Coates, single-wing left halfback; and Red Knight, left halfback. We had four outstanding talents on the team, all left halfbacks.

So when we put in the T formation, Red Knight played fullback, I played quarterback because I had the best arm, Ray Coates played left halfback, and

Jim Cason was playing right halfback. All four were now playing, and we had a good season in 1945, going 7–2.

I was surprised Bernie Moore did that. He was an old coach, and he used the old numbering system for plays in the single wing that he had used at Carson-Newman in Tennessee. He was old-fashioned, and then all of a sudden he came up with the T formation, which kind of shocked everybody.

He did have a creative, young assistant by the name of Slick Martin. He went on to coach Mississippi State, so maybe that was part of the reason we jumped ahead of everybody else with that offense.

You can imagine that first game with Rice, the opener of the 1945 season. We surprised them, and they didn't know what was going on. There was no swapping of film back then or instant information for scouting. Everybody was accustomed to the single wing, and we came out in this T formation. The Chicago Bears had a guy come down in spring training and install it for us to get us educated.

On one play when Cason went in motion, they thought he was running out of the game. Cason came back to the huddle and told me, "Just throw me the ball," because there was no one covering him or paying attention to him. I threw him the ball on the next play, and he went 44 yards for a touchdown, untouched.

So I had to go up under center, and we had some problems with the snap. That was hard for me to do. I was so old-fashioned. It was quite difficult at first because the center did not know what to do, either, as we had been in the shotgun. He would just throw it at you instead of snapping it right into your top hand.

All the tailbacks from the single wing were on the field, and we threw the ball more than most teams with this formation. We didn't have anywhere near the passing system they have today, but we threw it more than others. They had four or five passes that were traditional to the single wing, and we used them in the T formation.

We had success, and then a huge percentage of teams started changing to the T formation to follow us. Texas installed it in 1946, and they were the first from the old Southwest Conference.

My most memorable game was against Tulane my freshman year in 1944. They were a big rival of LSU's, and my brother, Jack, had just finished playing four years at Tulane. I had an offer from Tulane, but decided to go to LSU, which made the game with Tulane pretty big.

I was very sought after in recruiting. I was 180 pounds, which was good size, and I had an arm. I was also 4-F, which meant I did not go to the military. I was not physically able to go to the military. It's how they classified me. So we had a lot of 17- and 18-year-olds at LSU that first year I was there, and I played a lot.

People in my hometown had convinced me it was stupid to go to a Louisiana school when I was born and raised in Texas. They told me it was bad for my career in business after football. I agreed, my parents agreed. So I went to Austin, Texas, to attend the University of Texas, and they put me in a boarding house with other players. The Texas coaches had come and got me the day of my high school graduation and took me right off to Austin.

One of those players I was roomed with was the quarterback Bobby Layne. That was fortunate for LSU because Texas had told me that I was going to be the single-wing tailback and that Bobby Layne was going to be the fullback. But Layne told me he was there to be the single-wing tailback, and I asked myself, "What am I here for?"

While I was in Austin for two weeks before summer school opened at the university, I was around Bobby all day. He was 17 years old going on 35, and I was 17 going on 14. I was from a dry county and never tasted beer before; meanwhile Bobby Layne was out late at night, had girlfriends, and was living it up. I felt very inadequate to this guy. He was a man already and I wasn't.

Well, the LSU coaches came into Mrs. Poole's boarding house one Sunday morning in Austin, along about the time I was feeling inferior. I was disenchanted, and they asked me if I would change my mind. They were on their way to pick up Jim Cason in Houston, so we all went to breakfast. After breakfast, I went back, packed my bags, and went to Baton Rouge.

I did not want to go to Tulane like my brother because their players lived in boarding houses, and LSU players were in an athletic dorm, which I thought was better. I didn't want to live in somebody's house.

Anyway, I ended up at LSU, and in our game against Tulane I completed 19-of-24 passes and something like 10 or 12 passes in a row. My brother was at the game, and he rooted for me, not his school. He was my big brother, he rooted for me, no doubt about it.

In 1946 we had a 9–1–1 team, which was a great team. We should have gone all the way and won a national championship, but we had some morale problems, and that hurt us. Veterans were coming back from the war, and they wanted their positions back. They were older, had served their country, and now found a bunch of kids in their spots. We had freshmen and sopho-more 4-Fs who had not gone to war, and there was slight grumbling, some friction, and a lot of competition. Guys came back on the GI Bill or had scholarships, and there must have been 125 or 130 players going out for the football team. There was unbelievable competition.

We lost to Georgia Tech and then we tied Arkansas 0–0. We couldn't stand up in the ice on the field. It was −5, maybe −30 degrees with the wind chill. So those were the two games we didn't win but could have. Bernie Moore kept it together pretty well considering the circumstances. We had all-con-ference players who had come back sitting on the bench and not getting in the game. It was very difficult for the prewar players who were now married and older and found us there ahead of them on the team.

The older players had a scholarship and a right to be back in school play-ing football. There was rivalry and some bitterness that penetrated the team. Most of the veterans really came back for the 1947 season, and then it really made a difference in chemistry. There was also an age factor among players, with us 19-year-olds and these war veterans who were 23, 24, 25.

As far as LSU today, whoever that guy is that gets them on television so much is doing a great job, because I can see a lot of games out here in the San Francisco area. All my friends have become LSU fans because that's what we see out here.

I was back for the Ole Miss game [in 2008], and except for going into the Pro Football Hall of Fame, it was my greatest thrill in sports. My son, grand-son, and nephew were with me, and when I was introduced, you would have thought it was General Eisenhower back home from the war. It was noisy, and it brought tears to my eyes. I could hardly handle it. It was mind-boggling.

Y.A. Tittle played single-wing tailback and quarterback at LSU from 1944 to 1947 and then entered pro football, where he played from 1948 to 1964. His greatest success was near the end of his pro career, when he led the Giants to three division championships. Tittle's 36 touchdown passes in the 1963 season was NFL record until Dan Marino threw 48 touchdown passes in 1984. Tittle is an insurance man in the San Francisco area and resides in Atherton, California.

SID FOURNET

TACKLE

1951–1954

GAYNELL TINSLEY, MY HEAD COACH, was personable and well-liked. He was a good player himself, an All-American, which helped with his coaching. His problem as the head coach was he had no money for assistants. There was a lean budget back then, so he was doing a lot of it himself. That was part of our problem with trying to put good teams on the field. They didn't make the commitment to it like they do today with all the money.

The first two years I was there, it was a two-platoon system, so you could come off the field. The last two years, I played the whole game, there was no free substitution. That was 1953 and 1954. You had to play the whole game. I probably played 50-something minutes those last years.

I was about 230 pounds. I was probably one of the biggest ones on the team. I was always in good shape and was a good blocker, and, like I say, being 230, I was bigger than the rest of them. I was pretty strong, so that makes a difference.

I played right defensive tackle on a five-man front. So I played with some speed in that alignment and would chase a guy down from behind. They would run to their right, and I would try and get there to make a play from the backside. I was shooting in between the guard and tackle.

It was fun. You could tell when the guy was pulling. You watched his hand, watched his foot. I would fly through the hole. Sometimes I could get

Sid Fournet was All-SEC in 1953 and 1954 and was an All-American in 1954. He played seven years in the NFL.

the quarterback before he made the pitch out to the back. Teams would always run to the right side.

Back in those days, I was in really good shape. I was 6' tall. I didn't drink and was married at the time, so I kept my nose to the grindstone. I worked hard at practice. If you practiced hard, you were able to stay in shape. I didn't know what being single was like. I guess those single guys ran around and weren't in as good shape. I'm not sure. I went home to my wife every night.

We had a good season my freshman year [7–3–1], then not so good my second year [3–7], and got better my junior year [5–3–3].

One game that season we played Bart Starr and Alabama at Ladd Stadium in Mobile. They were ranked pretty good [No. 5], and we tied them [7–7].

The next season, my senior season, we had a losing season [5–6], and they fired Gaynell Tinsley.

As far as big plays, one of those games we tied my junior year was against Kentucky [6–6], and I intercepted a lateral. I followed the quarterback and thought he was going to pitch out. So I ran in front of the halfback, and he threw it to me. I didn't score. If I had scored, we would have won the game, but at least it kept them from winning because it was late and we ended in a tie.

The only thing I remember that really helped us win a game was when we played Georgia in Athens, between the hedges. I blocked a punt, and we won 7–0. They were at the 2-yard line. I was right in the middle and came through and blocked the punt.

It was a wild game. They had this big old quarterback, Zeke Bratkowski, and he could throw that ball. He kept throwing the ball to his ends, but they kept dropping it.

That season, 1951, I got to play a lot as a freshman because a lot of kids went off to the Korean War. They were drafting students as soon as you got out of high school. You either went to college or you went to Korea.

That senior season, 1954, we started off slow but finished pretty good. I forgot a lot of things from that season, except that first game my senior season when we played at Texas. It was 110 degrees on the field. They took me out of the game with a minute left before the half, and I didn't think I was going to make it to the locker room. Seemed like the summer time, but I guess it was September.

I played all but one minute of the first half, both ways. It was pretty tough in those conditions going offense, then defense. We lost the first four games and then ended up winning five games. I think I played over 500 minutes.

We weren't as big as they are now. Today, these guys that play my position, tackle, are 290 pounds. No way you could play both ways at that size and in the heat we played in. You couldn't keep up. We stayed in good shape by working out every day, but we were much lighter.

The thing about it, football was like a job, really. My being married, I was going to school, playing football, and going home. It was all work. School, football, and home and homework.

I had some favorite teammates. Joe Tuminello, he was right end, and I was right tackle. Al Doggett and I were friends. The thing I remember about Joe was he would want me to call timeout after the first four or five plays of the game. You would start the game all excited and lose your breath. You would need a timeout to get your second breath, and then you were okay. Doggett wasn't very tall, but he could throw the ball. He was just as good on defense.

Right after I left, they fired all the coaches and hired Paul Dietzel. Norman Cooper was the line coach, a guy from Alabama, and they fired him. They had some poor coaches in there working with Tinsley, which is one of the reasons we didn't do much, and they fired him.

I think the last year I was there they brought in Charlie McClendon as an assistant coach. He didn't like me, and I didn't like him. He must have changed his ways because people seemed to like him. I remember running wind sprits after practice and I was laying down. He came over and said, "Get your ass up." I said, "I'm not getting up, I'm tired. I have to get my breath." He treated you like you were a servant. He must have changed his ways.

They enlarged the stadium the last year I was there as a player (from 38,000 to 46,000), but we still couldn't fill it up. We would have 35,000 to 40,000 my senior season. Now they keep adding to it, and they fill it up.

LSU football is bigger now than it was then, and I'm happy and proud I was a part of it. My brother, Emile, played in the program, too, and was on the national championship team. He was on those Chinese Bandits.

When I left, Jim Taylor came in, and you could see what kind of player he was going to be. He showed up from junior college, and he was big and fast and he hit people. LSU had something in that guy because he was tougher to bring down as a freshman than the Tennessee backs we ran up against that season. That guy was tough. He could have gone right out of high school into the NFL.

LSU was starting to come together with players like Taylor coming along. Now look at them with all those players.

Sid Fournet was All-SEC in 1953 and 1954 and was an All-American in 1954. He played seven years in the NFL and then went to work for Johnson Wax. Fournet is retired and lives in Bogalusa.

JIM TAYLOR
RUNNING BACK/LINEBACKER
1956–1957

I WASN'T A GROOMED RUNNING BACK, one of those guys that comes out of high school and is supposed to be the star. I did not have that individual thing about me, I was just a guy who wanted to work hard and help the team win.

I went to Hinds Junior College my sophomore year and came back for my junior and senior seasons at LSU. Schooling wasn't my strong suit, so I went up there to Mississippi for a year and a half. I went out to Colorado and looked at that school after Hinds but then decided I would come back to LSU for my junior season.

I don't know if they were all that worried I would stay out there at Colorado because I had not shown I was going to be a dominant player, maybe just a little above average. I was on the bubble.

The best I remember, I was not even first-team until midway through my junior season. I did some extra-point kicking and some kicking off. I just wasn't chosen to run the ball and that was that. You just try and be the best player you can be for the LSU Tigers and learn how to compete.

The fullback position was tackle-to-tackle runs, not much of a sweep, not much passing, so when I played linebacker I liked that better. I liked the contact and was a middle linebacker for Cholly Mac, the defensive coordinator at the time.

They were just getting it going down there; it was Paul Dietzel's first coaching job, and he and Cholly Mac were laying the foundation. Dietzel knew what he wanted to do and was trying to get the right players and move to the next level.

We were playing both ways in the 1957 season. We started off well [4–1], and then it went downhill from there. I'm not sure what happened, except we played a lot of close games on the road and lost them.

I guess I developed what little bit of ability I had.

Of course, when I left LSU to go to Green Bay, I was the second draft pick for them. You just have to learn what's going on, try your hardest. I was the 15th pick in the whole country, so I guess I learned a little and improved at LSU from what I was in high school.

I grew up in Baton Rouge and went to Baton Rouge High School. I was a basketball player. I wasn't much of a football player. I went to a high school All-America game as a basketball player—the round ball was my sport. As a freshman, I was on the varsity and competing with the 17- and 18-year-olds.

I was a lightweight. I was 5′8″ as a freshman, but this was my sport, this was my game. I was kind of a frail kid. I went to Murray, Kentucky, for the high school All-America game. We won the state championship my senior year, so I was a 5′11″ guard and was All-State and All-America.

I had moved along in basketball achieving All-City and All-State and on and on. I got more offers to go to college in basketball than I did in football.

By the time I was a senior in high school, I was a pretty violent player in football. I got after it. I wasn't a running back, I was the guy taking the snap and making spins and throwing the ball. Basketball had helped make me a pretty good athlete. The hand-eye coordination and all the above came from basketball.

Of course, my scholastics were weak. I had to work because my dad had passed away when I was 10, so I was always throwing newspapers or hustling chips. You just grow up faster. I have two other brothers; I was the only dumb jock. One brother was a CPA; the other was an attorney.

I didn't take off in football and get any notice really until the start of my senior year when we put in the single wing. I took the direct snap, and I could run it, pass it, or kick it. You learned that it came down to how hard you wanted to work, how badly you wanted it. I was always in great shape and fit.

Jim Taylor was named All-America in 1957 by the Football Writers Association and was the MVP of the 1958 Senior Bowl. He was named MVP of the NFL in 1962 and was elected to the Pro Football Hall of Fame.

I never drank, never smoked. These are the things you needed to avoid to be the player you wanted to be. I loved the defense because I had better defensive games than offensive games. You had to outwork people.

When I got to Green Bay, I said that no one was going to outwork me. I knew I was going to carry the ball 20 to 25 times. I was the workhorse, and Paul Hornung was the tin carrier.

Today's ball carriers—well, you never would see me step out of bounds. These college and pro players will get out of bounds. You want the mentality of initiating the contact. You have to have the toughness to move the chains for the team.

LSU was starting to show some upward climb as a football program when I was a senior. We were starting to show some character and integrity and discipline and hard work. They had some players finally, like Billy Cannon, who could move the program to that next level.

They won some close games there in 1958 and showed an urgency of making plays, which is the difference between winning and losing. And there has to be some luck in it, too. But having the opportunities to win is part of it.

My senior season we lost a lot of those close games. We were competitive. We were in the games, we just didn't win all of them. I went on to the Senior Bowl and was the MVP, and then I ended up with the Packers.

The game itself lasts two and a half hours, but if you dissect it into four- or five-second intervals, you can see the explosion needed for the game. There is an urgency of the offensive line coming off the ball that lasts just four or five seconds. You have to comprehend that. Vince Lombardi had the philosophy that you should never be tired playing in that four- or five-second interval.

He wanted to get players with that real mental toughness who wanted to work through the week. You have certain players who really play the game and like to get in on every play. You have to represent yourself and have some urgency of being the best you can be.

You learned that if you saw a different color, you just wanted to get it on. *You ain't getting the best of me.* It was that type of thing.

The Packers kept giving me the ball because I wanted to hit people and move the chains. My goal when I left LSU was to make the team, make my contract, and be the best player I could be. The first year progresses, the second year, and you start getting better and better. Eventually I was gaining 1,000 yards, playing for the NFL title, and winning the championship.

LSU got back to the high level of discipline when Nick Saban was here. There is recruiting and getting good players, but there is a discipline you need to go along with the players. Saban moved it to another level by getting up in the face of these players and getting them to move to another level. Work hard, hit people.

What it means to play here is to maximize your ability. This game is 75 percent mental, and you have to compete. Guys were competing here at LSU when they won the two national championships. It is not about the end result, though, it has more to do with being competitive, not looking ahead to the trophies.

My advice to guys here is not to let the complacency set in. Some of it has to do with my background of growing up without a father after I was 10. You get some parenting from coaches. Cholly Mac was a hard-nosed guy who took care of you and showed you what it took. I got that parenting at LSU with guys like him.

I was selling concessions when I was in high school. That's what I had. I learned to work early, maybe when I was eight years old. Don't use the copouts, just work and be accountable for actions, and LSU helped me learn that.

I'm not a radical type in following the Tigers, but I support them. I go out there and see the folks and visit with them. It's like the National Football League here.

Jim Taylor is considered one of the greatest players in the history of LSU football. He was named All-America in 1957 by the Football Writers Association and was the MVP of the 1958 Senior Bowl. He went on to have an even better career in the NFL with the Green Bay Packers, named MVP of the league in 1962, and elected to the Pro Football Hall of Fame in 1976.

BILLY CANNON

HALFBACK

1957–1959

GOING INTO THAT 1958 SEASON, you could sit anywhere you wanted to in Tiger Stadium. You win, they'll come. We weren't winning—yet. The fans of Louisiana are the best fans in the world and they are behind you—win or tie. And I love them.

I knew we were going to be good in '58, so I bought up a bunch of tickets. It was resale. I wasn't the only one who did it, but I'm the only one who will tell you I did it. That was my section right up there [north end zone].

We were out here one day playing Ole Miss, which was a big game, and Johnny Robinson came up and said, "Billy, how you feeling? You okay?"

I looked up at my section and said, "Yeah, Johnny, I feel pretty good. My section is filling up pretty good." I sold them game by game. As we got better, they got more expensive. Whatever the market would bear.

I might have been the only one that thought, before the season, that we could win a national championship. I talked at the North Baton Rouge Lions Club, which met weekly, and they asked me to come out there to go to the Lions Club meeting. They had followed me from Istrouma High to LSU. And one of the questions they asked me one day was, "Billy, how many games do you think we're going to win?"

My answer to them was, "Right now, we haven't lost any, and I don't plan to lose any." These were the business leaders of North Baton Rouge, and every one that was there has recalled that to me a dozen times. We didn't lose any.

We came close to a loss one time, a 7–6 game at Mississippi State where it was horribly muddy. Their state legislature was so embarrassed by the field conditions, they built a stadium there the next year. I've never played in worse conditions, and I played pro football in the ice and in New York in mid-December.

They scored to go ahead 6–0. And then we came back and scored. Red Hendrix made a one-handed catch, and Tommy Davis kicked that extra point straight through there. He was a great kicker.

Here's a story about Tommy. We used to practice on the baseball field, so we would get dressed here and then go out the gate and hang out there outside the north end of the stadium. We were out there, looking up, and an argument started. Somebody said, "Cannon, can you kick the ball into the stadium?" I said, "No, but Davis can."

They said, "No way, he can't kick the ball that high." We used to get $7.50 laundry money every two weeks. Tommy came out. I said, "Tommy, we have a bet here, and I have booked 'em all. They said you can't kick the ball in that stadium."

Tommy asked me how much I had, and I said $30. He said, "I get half."

He shook his leg twice, kicked up in the air with his leg twice, shook his leg one more time, and punted the ball up. It shot off his foot and nosed up over into the stadium. If you go stand outside the north end of the stadium and look up, you'll see how high that is. You know it took a good kick to do it.

Well, then they said, "You can't do it twice." Now the betting was on. We could only raise $20 this time. Now we were playing with their money. He looked over at me and said, "I get half." He shook his leg twice, kicked it up in the air twice, shook his leg once, and kicked it into the stadium again. That's how good he was. Tommy kicked for 11 years with the 49ers as punter and place-kicker.

I remember practicing one day, and the ball went through the placeholder's hands. Tommy just grabbed it and drop-kicked the ball right through the uprights. The coaches were looking at each other. He did it the very first try. Not many people can do that.

I was 225 pounds my senior year. I was a big back and could run a little. I returned a kick in Lubbock against Texas Tech 100 yards. They would stop the clock right at the end of the score, and when I looked up, there were 10 seconds off the clock. And that's not running straight. The best I could do was a 9.4-second 100. The world record back then was a 9.3.

Billy Cannon charges through a hole during an 89-yard punt return for a touchdown that helped LSU beat No. 3 Ole Miss 7–3 in Baton Rouge on Halloween night in 1959. *Photo courtesy AP Images*

I ran track, the sprints and also threw the shot. You have to understand I had a brother who was four years older than me, and he ran track and he threw the shot. Throwing the shot is fun, but going down to get it is not fun, so he had me go down and get it and throw it back to him. I would retrieve for Harvey and throw it back.

Any Ole Miss game was a big game for us. People still talk about the Halloween night run versus Ole Miss in 1959, but I still remember the blocks I had. We trailed 3–0, and it was hot and muggy, and it was a wet field. Ole Miss had made up its mind it was going to win it with those three points. They were punting on third down, taking no chances, and Jake Gibbs was getting off some beautiful punts.

We had a rule that you were not supposed to catch a punt behind the 15-yard line. But Jake got off a low kick, and I got the perfect bounce and caught it on the 11 and started to go to the outside. I faked Larry Grantham and came back into the short side of the field and got some great blocks. Emile Fournet took a guy right off my hip with a block. I went down on my hand once, but kept going and kept getting blocks, and the last tackle I broke was against Gibbs.

Then Johnny Vaught did something I had never seen him do. He sat Jake Gibbs, his All-American, and he put in Doug Elmore. Doug took them the length of the field. They got down to our goal line, and we got into the old gap-eight defense. They went over the top three times with their fullback Charlie Flowers, and we made the stop all three times. On fourth down, Elmore rolled out, and Warren Rabb came up and made first contact. I got there right after that and stopped him on the 1- or 2-yard line.

It was a classic SEC football game. In 1958, the year before, we beat them 14–0 on two bootleg plays. I remember Warren Rabb running—they had us stopped at the 1-yard line—and the defensive tackle hit Rabb right in the ass and knocked him into the end zone for a touchdown.

Back in that era, when you beat Johnny Vaught's teams, you beat the best, most physical team you could find anywhere. And you also beat one of the best coaches. If you beat them, you played a fantastic ballgame. In the 1950s and 1960s their records were unmatched. He had bookend quarterbacks, Charlie Connerly and Archie Manning.

The one thing about us is we had great high school football back then. My high school was Istrouma; I'm from the north side. We played teams from Memphis; we played Little Rock Central; and after I left we played Nederland, Texas, whose head coach was Bum Phillips.

We played a high-level brand of high school football. We put in weightlifting at Istrouma High, which was before many high schools. Paul Dietzel put it in here at LSU after he saw what I and a couple of other kids could do with extra strength. Coach Dietzel would work out all summer, and he had a weight room put in under the stadium here.

In Coach Dietzel's first couple of years, the teams were mediocre. They were going to fire him after the 1956 season, but he had a president, General Troy Middleton, who stood by him.

In 1957, my sophomore year, we had the great Jimmy Taylor. Tough as a boot. He took a beating all year. He played linebacker and was as good a linebacker as he was a fullback. What an All-American.

We went out and opened the season. They were going to stop the senior, Jimmy Taylor, so they left me alone, and I was having a ball. I faked a punt against Alabama and ran 60 yards, ran a kick back 100 yards against Texas Tech, caught a pass, hurdled a guy, and scored a touchdown. Pretty soon, I was thinking, *This Southeastern Conference football isn't so bad.*

Every Sunday morning, there was Jimmy Taylor in the whirlpool for treatment because they were beating him to death. We couldn't help him because we didn't have the ballplayers to help him.

We went to Florida to play the Gators and, all of a sudden, they switched their attentions from Jimmy Taylor to Billy Cannon, and now the games were not so much fun. Now I was getting killed, and Jimmy was starting to get some more openings. All Jimmy needed was a fair shake, and there he went.

We were playing up at Ole Miss, and Jimmy was playing with a hip pointer. He missed two extra-point kicks and finally couldn't take it any more and went out. We put our second-team linebacker in, who was just 160 pounds, and he was lining up on the inside over Gene Hickerson. He had hooked our safety and was looking at me to block me. Hickerson played in the NFL a long time....I just wanted Jimmy back out there.

In 1958 we were better and ready to go. There was a game against Tulane where we were way ahead, and with the substitution rules, the starters were out of the game and couldn't go back in. Scooter Purvis, who was on the Go Team, made a fantastic run down the sideline and got hurt. I had to go back in because, if we tried to put another kid in, he would lose his redshirt.

Dietzel told me to go and tell Durel Matherne, the quarterback, to run the ball into the ground and kill the clock. I went in there and said, "Coach Dietzel said to run the toss play to me right now." Durel did his job and tossed it to me, and I went 45 yards for the touchdown.

The Tulane coach, Andy Pilney, was out there in the middle of the field screaming at Dietzel and calling him a rotten SOB. Dietzel said whenever he goes to banquets, there is a guy there who curses him, and he thinks it is Pilney, 50 years later. He swears Dietzel told me to run the toss sweep.

The game where everyone took us seriously in 1958 was in Miami when we won 41–0. All the eastern press was there. Scooter Purvis had this long run where he must have broken six tackles. The next day the paper had my name as the guy who made that run.

My point is that I was able to do some things on that '58 team I couldn't have done on lesser teams. We had a lot of talent around me, a lot of blocking, and I took advantage of it. I reaped the benefits.

That 1958 season was perfect for the platoon system that Dietzel put in because we had the players. In 1957 it would not have worked because we had not stocked up on players yet. I can name three players from 1956 and 1957 who could have played with us in 1958 and 1959. Jim Taylor, the big right tackle, Alvin Aucoin, and Earl Leggett, another tackle. The rest were too slow.

I remember how Dietzel would not let anything split up that team in 1958. We had a 12:30 team meeting on Mondays, and you had better not be late because Dietzel was using that time to practice his remarks on us for the weekly television show. Well, just before the team meeting one Monday, there was some pushing and shoving in the lunch line, and it got taken outside with a fight between Durel Matherne and Merle Schexnaildre.

We went into the meeting, and one of them was bleeding and the other had a knot on the side of his head. Dietzel looked at them and didn't say a word—didn't faze him. He went on and gave his speech and walked out without saying a word.

That night he ordered that they be made roommates for the rest of the year. It was a great move. If they had stayed mad, become bitter enemies, it could have divided that team, and Dietzel wasn't going to let that happen.

We could have had another national championship in 1959, except for that call in Tennessee. I have a 16-millimeter film of it, shot from down on the goal line. I ran off right tackle, was in the end zone, and then got pushed back. We lost that game 14–13 and a chance to win the national title. I will go to my grave knowing I was in that end zone.

This school is full of opportunities. They will put things there for you to take. They won't give it to you, but they will put it there to take, and if you take it and run with it, you can succeed. We had guys on our team go on to become doctors, and then we had one dummy, me, who was a dentist.

Guys in sales tell me it is an instant door-opener having played football at LSU. You go someplace and tell them you played at LSU and give them the years. Well, there is somebody in that building who saw you, or the team you were on, play. It's an entrée, and you are proud of the association.

21

Billy Cannon is still considered the greatest player in the history of LSU football. He is the only Tiger to win the Heisman Trophy, which he took home in 1959. He was an All-American in 1958 as a junior when he led the Tigers to their first national championship, which has helped spur 50 years of winning in the program. Cannon was also a valuable player on defense. A Baton Rouge native, Cannon is a dentist in Louisiana.

MAX FUGLER

CENTER/LINEBACKER

1957–1959

WE NOTICED SOMETHING ABOUT our team and our program about the fourth or fifth game of the 1958 season. We started the season and thought we might have something, and when we got to the midway part of the season, we definitely knew we had something. The fans saw we had something, too, because they started to fill up that stadium.

I was a center and played middle linebacker, that was my strong suit. We were a good team, but we were so lucky because we never had a major injury on that '58 team that won the national championship.

Marty Broussard, the trainer, took care of us. He put up with no bull. If you had a hangnail, he would tell you to spit on it and go out and play. If you were hurt, he would stand up to Paul Dietzel or any of the coaches and tell them you were not playing.

He did that for me one year. I had a strained knee, and he told Dietzel I was not playing, that I could be crippled for life with the wrong hit. That was my sophomore year. Broussard was wonderful for this program, a legend.

When we lost that first game of the 1957 season, my sophomore season, to Rice [20–14], it was the first game I had lost in a long time. We had played three games as freshmen and won those, and my little school in Ferriday, Louisiana, had won 54 games in a row. I didn't know what losing was.

That was Jim Taylor's senior season. No offense to him, but that boy did more with less ability than anyone. He had the heart of a lion.

Max Fugler was an All-America center in 1959, but was even more valuable as a middle linebacker. He was part of a defense that allowed just 29 points in the regular season in 1959.

We thought we would be better than 5–5. We were actually dumbfounded because we had Taylor and a good class of guys. We had Billy Cannon as a sophomore and other good players.

We were playing in front of 20,000 people in 1957, and then by 1958 it just took off and went nuts. People were wearing the coolie hats and wearing gold shirts for the Gold Team, which was shortened to "Go Team."

There was a lot of camaraderie with the whole city and with the whole state. None of us were much bigger than the other, no one could outrun the other, except for Billy [Cannon]. No one could catch him. But we all had great speed. We played some big people, but speed will beat anything, except for big speed.

The one different guy was Bob Lilly of TCU. They also had Don Floyd, and he and Lilly played on either side of me in a 1959 game. The next day you couldn't touch me with a powder puff, it hurt so bad.

That team we had in 1958 brought us to the top. Our recruiting was great, and Dietzel brought in some great assistant coaches. Charlie McClendon, Abner Wimberly, Carl Maddox, George Terry, and Bill Peterson. They let you do things and ad lib. You could tell them, "I can do it this way if you let me," and they would let me try it and see.

Coach McClendon did the defense, and he might have waved my defense off five or six times all season. I was the middle linebacker and gave the defensive signals, and he let me call a lot of the game. We had stunts out there he would let me call.

Red [Billy] Hendrix and I had one called "Music and Lightning." If I said, "Music," we would play normally. If I said, "Lightning," I was crashing in and he was dropping back to play linebacker. It was a blitz. He was defensive end.

When the quarterback started his cadence and after he said, "One," I would start moving. Teams never went on one back then. I would roll in behind him, and he would drop.

We ran out of a 5-3 on defense, but we could disguise it as a seven-man front. We could change back into pass coverage. Teams thought we had a seven-man front to come after them.

We allowed 53 points that 1958 season, and that was in 11 games because we were 11–0. In 1959 I think we were even better on defense—and a better team overall—but we didn't win the title.

A key game in that 1958 season was Florida where Tommy Davis kicked a winning field goal midway through the fourth quarter, and we won 10–7. Dietzel came by Tommy and told him to "warm up his toe." Tommy looked at him and said, "How do you warm up your toe?" I died laughing. Tommy made the kick, and we won and kept the perfect season alive. A tie would have hurt us because there were teams undefeated right there at the top of the rankings with us. There was no overtime back then.

Tommy was the best. He was my roommate when I went to San Francisco, and he had a great career. Back then, they did not put anybody over the center on a punt. I would snap the ball and then be gone to cover. Tommy would tell me, "I'm going to nose it over, and it is going to hit and come back. I am going to lay it on its back."

That 1958 season we beat Tulane 62–0. At halftime it was 6–0 and Tommy was averaging 63 yards a punt to save us. We couldn't make a first down, they couldn't make a first down, and we kept kicking it back and forth.

We put them away in the second half behind Johnny Robinson, our other halfback and the best athlete I ever saw. He could do anything. He was drafted by the Cincinnati Reds as a catcher and was the best tennis player in the state of Louisiana. His daddy was the tennis coach, and if one of his players got sick, he would take Johnny off the practice field with Coach Dietzel's permission and play tennis. Johnny beat the No. 1 seed from another school in a match one time. He was a super athlete and a heck of a guy.

Another key game in 1958 was against Ole Miss when we beat them [14–0]. They got to our 1-yard line and we were offside, but they refused the penalty. It was the dumbest thing I had ever seen. They were that confident they were going to score with three downs.

They ended the possession on the 3. The last play of the series they lost two yards.

That was the best game I ever played. I made three unassisted tackles on that goal-line stand and assisted on another one. On one play, and Dietzel mentioned it one time, I made two tackles on the same play. I tackled the quarterback, flung him to the ground, and then tackled the flip man.

Tiger Stadium was rocking, and they were going into the south end zone. The south end zone has always been the loudest part of that stadium. They started on the 1-yard line. I promise you, to Tiger fans a goal-line stand is better than a 100-yard kick return or a long punt return.

I had 16 tackles that game. They were running the T formation, but they were running the option quite a bit and the sprint-out passes.

Ole Miss back then was like Florida and Alabama are now to LSU. Back then there wasn't a lot of recruiting from out of state. Of the 33 regulars, on the White, Go, and Bandits, there were probably five that weren't from the state of Louisiana. It was that way with Ole Miss—all their boys were from Mississippi. So it was state versus state; that's why it was such a big rivalry.

We won that game against Ole Miss, and a few weeks later we played at Mississippi State in the mud. I lost 26 pounds in that game. A lot of it was blood. I got hit in the mouth. My mother was sitting on the sideline and didn't even recognize me. I had blood covering my number, everything.

I got sewn up on the sideline by Dr. Noto. He was the sideline physician. He never used deadener. He said that deadener has to go somewhere, and it is going to swell when it goes somewhere. Then when the body absorbs that deadener, there is going to be a scar. In my career down there I probably got 40 stitches in my face, and you can't see but one, when I shave on my right cheekbone. He was a hell of a sewing man.

We won a close game at Mississippi State [7–6], shut out Tulane, then blanked Clemson in the Sugar Bowl, and we were national champions. The program took off, and right now if they went 5–5 they would still fill the stadium. We started something 50 years ago that carries on today.

The crowds were still horrible in 1957. In 1958 we took off, and the crowds came.

There were a lot of key games in that season, but that field goal by Tommy Davis against Florida was big. You could set him on fire before a field goal or a punt, and he wouldn't get upset. Tommy could kick with either two steps or just a rocker step. When I was snapping it to him, he would just say, "Max, put it on my right side." If we were against the back line of the end zone, he could just kick with rocker step.

The only person who could outrun me on the team was Billy [Cannon], so my speed was an asset. I also enjoyed it so much it made me better; I thoroughly enjoyed it.

I was 205 pounds and ran a 10 flat in the 100-yard dash. They tried to make me a fullback for my sophomore year, but the other boy playing center got kicked out of school, so I moved back to center. That was fine because the first-string fullback was Jimmy Taylor, and I wasn't going to get to play much. It would have been tough to beat him out.

I always felt I was pretty quick, if not heavy. Coach Robinson, our coach in high school, taught us a lot about footwork, he really did. He taught us to keep people away from our feet. As it turned out, I was drafted as a linebacker by San Francisco.

The next year [1958] we were ranked No. 1 and beat [No. 3] Ole Miss on Billy's run on Halloween. It set the Richter scale off in the geology building because the stadium was shaking so much.

Billy Cannon was hit nine times on that run and never veered three feet either way. It was the most determined run I have ever seen. There was no zigging and no zagging. I was not on the field; I got kicked in the groin the play before. Ole Miss came back down the field after Billy's touchdown, and we got an interception to stop them.

The truth is we should have had back-to-back championships. If it hadn't been for Tennessee, we would have. There is a film on it. When they scored their last touchdown, there is a man illegally in motion and another man with his hand on my belt holding me and keeping me from making the tackle.

People remember Billy scoring the two-point conversion, and it looked like he made it to everybody but the referee. We had a better football team in 1959 than we did in 1958 when we won the title. Tennessee kept us from proving it in the rankings.

It cost us not having Tommy Davis in 1959. He had eligibility left and decided to go to the NFL. It cost us a lot. But he made a great decision going to professional football. We could have used him. We could have come back and kicked the field goal against Tennessee to win.

We lost that game and ended up having to play Ole Miss in the Sugar Bowl, and that was a letdown. Nobody wanted to play that game again. If you beat Ole Miss once, you're lucky. When you beat somebody in the regular season, you don't ever want to play them again.

We had to take three votes before they got the vote they wanted from the players. I voted no every time. It was not unanimous. I don't know why there was more than one vote. All we got out of it was an 80-mile bus ride to New Orleans.

I try and make it back three or four times a year, and when the team goes on the field, I still get chills up and down my back. If you ever played in Tiger Stadium and don't get a chill, you're sick. I wish they would build that stadium to 200,000 because they would fill it. It's a great place to play, and that was a great four years of my life.

Max Fugler was an All-America center in 1959 but was considered a better middle linebacker. He called the signals for a defense that allowed just 29 points in the regular season in 1959. Fugler was drafted by the San Francisco 49ers in the 1960 draft. He lives in the Houston area.

JOHNNY ROBINSON

HALFBACK

1957–1959

THERE WERE CROWDS OF 35,000 or so in the stadium prior to 1958. It was good football at LSU, but they didn't sell out. People didn't all show up to the game and pack the place.

Then we won the national championship, and it all changed.

We had 65,000 people, sometimes more, showing up for our games. For the first time, we had sellouts at Tiger Stadium, four or five of them packing the place. You could hardly get a ticket, which is what it is like these days with 90,000 people in there.

I think that 1958 season, while we were going undefeated, was the last time you could safely get a ticket to a game. When we won that national championship, the interest level took off for LSU football.

It meant a lot to be a Tiger on that 1958 team because there was a closeness, and Paul Dietzel was responsible for a lot of that. We had gone to a platoon system with the White Team, the Go Team, and the Chinese Bandits. There was not a lack of trust on our team; everybody knew we had more than 11 good players. We had more than 33, so no one got mad when he came out at the start of a quarter.

That was our identity, our chemistry. Dietzel used everybody, and I think he is the guy who got platoon football going in college football. He invented it because he wasn't afraid to use his whole squad.

We had three teams, and Dietzel tried to make sure there was publicity and praise for all three. He wasn't making it up; there was a nice collection of players on all three of those teams. It was Dietzel who came up with the name "Chinese Bandits."

Billy Cannon had something to do with that chemistry because he was a star, and if he had been mad about getting taken out of game, maybe others would have been mad, too. But he was a team guy, a very generous fellow who helped me a lot after football.

Billy was the star. He was a 9.3 sprinter who weighed 205 pounds. Red Brodnax was the fullback and was one of the best blockers in the Southeastern Conference. I think he got an award saying so. [Brodnax won the Jacobs Award in 1958, which is given annually to the best blocker in the SEC.]

Billy, like I said, was more than a great football player. He was part of the team and a leader. He was an unselfish guy. I don't think he had a selfish bone in his body, and we were proud to be on his team. He was the 100-yard-dash champion in the SEC and also won the shot put in the SEC. He is the strongest fast man that I ever played with or against.

Like I said, that was our identity. We didn't have jealousy out there. The Go Team could also move the ball when Billy would come out and Scooter Purvis would take his place. It worked out to be a miracle season, and that closeness helped us in tight games.

I think we knew we had a chance to win the national championship when we beat Ole Miss 14–0. They were undefeated, and we were undefeated. It was the seventh game of the season, I think, and we won at home and were pretty much on our way.

We almost let it get away from us two weeks later when we played at Mississippi State and won just 7–6. We couldn't do much because it was so muddy. It rained and took away our advantage of speed. They had an All-America quarterback who was tough to handle, but we managed to win, just barely.

I played the right halfback in a three-back set, two backs in the backfield behind the quarterback and a wingback in a wing-T. We had a fullback and then either Billy or I would line up as a wingback. It was pretty easy to understand who was going to get the ball in a particular formation, but you still had to stop it, and then we would give you some misdirection to keep you honest.

Johnny Robinson was a starting right halfback for LSU's national championship team in 1958 and the team that finished 9–2 in 1959. He started the Johnny Robinson's Boys Home in Monroe for children ages 11 to 16, which still operates today.

30

The main thing about the wing-T was that everybody was at the line of scrimmage, and it was all bunched together. You didn't have flankers and split ends and spread formations. It was a run offense, and that meant the defense was in close on you, too.

One of the best plays we had to keep the defense honest was when Warren Rabb, our quarterback, would turn and hand to one of one us who was set up behind him, and then we would hand to the wingback cutting in front. That was a real effective play for us. It was a reverse, or counter play, and it was a magical play for us.

The time I remember where it worked the best was against Tulane, the last game of the regular season in '58. They were a really good team with Richie Petitbon, who was among a lot of good players they had.

We were ahead only 6–0 at the half. Early in the third quarter, we ran our counter, and I had a long run with some blocking. I don't think I scored on it, but things exploded after that, and we went on to win 62–0. That clinched the national championship for us because, in those days, the national champion was announced before the bowl game.

Before that Tulane game was over, Billy had scored three touchdowns, and I had scored four. We had been really worried about that game because they had an awesome team, but we just took off in that game. I think I scored on two runs, a pass, and an interception return.

We played Clemson in the Sugar Bowl in New Orleans and were not expecting them to be as good as they were. They were a lot better than we thought. We could not run the ball to one side because of the tackle they had on defense, I think it was Jim Padgett.

We finally scored in the third quarter when Billy passed to Mickey Mangham for the touchdown. It was slippery on the field. Warren Rabb got hurt, I remember, and their defense was very good, but we still pulled it out with that one score.

The next year we almost won another title. We lost by a point to Tennessee [14–13] on a controversial play when Billy was stopped at the goal line. I was blocking and didn't see it, but there are some who say that he was in, no question, and the Tennessee people, of course, said he didn't make it. It was the only game we lost in the regular season, and if we had won it, we would have won another championship.

It makes you awfully proud to be a Tiger and part of this school, not just the football program. I have a granddaughter who has a tennis scholarship at LSU, which means a lot because my father was the tennis coach at LSU for 29 years. They call the stadium Doug Robinson Stadium, so our family is very much a part of the tradition at LSU.

Playing football at LSU has given me the ability to give back to the community with the boys' home we started. It has been a blessing to pass along the traditions, and the school has been a major influence in my life. Being a Tiger has always been very special to me.

Johnny Robinson was a starting right halfback for LSU's national championship team in 1958 and the team that finished 9–2 in 1959. After a career as a professional football player, he coached in the World Football League and coached the tennis team at Northeast Louisiana and was an assistant coach on the football team. He started the Johnny Robinson's Boys Home in Monroe for children ages 11 to 16, which still operates today.

WARREN RABB

QUARTERBACK/DEFENSIVE BACK

1957–1959

I WAS BORN AND RAISED IN BATON ROUGE. I went to Bernard Terrace, Baton Rouge Junior High School, and Baton Rouge High School, and from there to LSU. When I was a young kid, I went to the LSU football games and sold Coca-Colas and programs in the stands. I said to myself even then, *Wouldn't it be great if I ever got to play in something like this?*

A guy who stands out more in my mind more than anybody, not because he was a great player but because of his name, was Leroy Labat from LaPlace, and they called him the "Black Stallion." He wasn't real fast, but he had great feet and was a real shifty runner.

I went to see Georgia Tech in Tiger Stadium, and Georgia Tech came in here with a guy named Leon Hardeman, an All-America back, and the excitement of that ballgame was kind of like now when they play Florida and Ole Miss. That sticks out in my mind.

Dietzel recruited me. I was in his first recruiting class. I graduated in '56 from high school. At Baton Rouge High School—we were one of the few schools doing this—I was a tailback in the single wing. UCLA ran the single wing at that time and so did Tenneseee, and I did have interest in that. I was going to visit Tennessee, but Dietzel said, "You don't really want to go up there, do you?" So I said no, I would stay right here.

We really had a good class. Dietzel got probably every top-notch player in the state that year. I can't remember one he lost that he really wanted.

Warren Rabb was the quarterback of the 1958 national championship team, and a starting defensive back. He helped the Tigers to an 11–0 record and was first-team All-SEC in 1958 as a junior.

Max Fugler from Ferriday was an outstanding high school player. He came here as a center. Outstanding nose for the ball. He played linebacker on defense. He just knew where the football was at all times. Tremendous hitter.

I knew my good buddy, Johnny Robinson, from University High School. Johnny didn't get nearly the publicity that Billy Cannon got, but he was only a half-step behind when it came to football ability, like when it came to blocking, running with the football, being a good receiver. Somebody you could count on any time you called his number.

I heard Boots Garland say the other night he thought Billy Cannon was the finest football player he'd ever seen. Billy had such great ability. He could run half-speed and outrun all of us, probably. I will never forget how Carl Maddox would get on him all the time: "C'mon, Cannon, give us a hundred percent." And he didn't really have to do that. Like I say, he was a lot quicker than the rest of us. Great ability, strong, tough runner who could run inside, run outside.

I think about Lynn LeBlanc. He came in as a sophomore and started three years for LSU. Not a big guy, but a big heart. You might say there were other guys with more athletic ability, but not any better, because of his enthusiasm to play. He just got the job done.

Bo Strange was a guy with a lot of athletic ability. Compared to today's standards, a lot of the guys were pretty small, but they hit just as hard. For two years in a row we were one of the top two teams in the nation on defense. When we were seniors we went something like six games before we had a rushing touchdown scored against us.

My favorite game was probably in '58, the Ole Miss ballgame. I think by that time we were ranked way up, probably No. 1, and they were No. 2 or 3. Ole Miss back then had the best-looking athletes you'd ever seen. When they walked on the field, they looked like racehorses. Even their linemen. I knew we were pretty good at that time.

It was a Halloween week game, but that wasn't the night of Billy's run. That was the next year. This was a tough ballgame. It was just very physical, and we wound up winning 14–0. They had a good offense, but we had a good defense. Shutting them out 14–0, we felt pretty good about that.

We just played one game at a time. We never thought about winning a national championship, even when we were moving up in the polls. To be honest, I can never remember the first time anything about that ever came up, not from the players or the coaches. We just got ready to play, and that was it.

We were No. 1 going into the bowl. We were national champions. The bowl had nothing to do with it.

There was nothing LSU did, but a few of us—Johnny Robinson, Billy, myself, Fugler—celebrated a little bit.

One time we had a party. My mom and dad had a camp down in Port Vincent on the Amite River. So, one time after a ballgame, a whole lot of us—maybe 25, 30 of us, something like that—went down there to take it easy and celebrate. Sunday rolled around, Monday rolled around, and some of the guys were still down there. I came back, but I had told them to stay as long as they wanted.

That week I was coming through the lunch line at Broussard Hall, and Dietzel came to me and said, "Come here, I need to ask you something."

I said, "What's that, Coach?"

"Will you do me a favor?" he asked.

I said, "Sure. What is it?"

"Will you go down to your camp and close it down?"

I asked, "Why?"

"So those guys will come back to school," he said.

In '59 we were better. It was a tough year. Every time we stepped on the field, everybody wanted to knock us off. Everybody was trying to kill us. It wasn't a whole lot of fun for me, I'll tell you. Dietzel called me in his office one day. He said, "Look, I need to talk to you. Listen, you're not playing that well right now. You're not playing as well as you can." And he said, "You need to pick it up, or I'm going to have to put you on the bench." He kind of got my attention. And I don't know if it was that I wasn't trying that hard, but the pressure was really tough.

But we got it done pretty much.

Going to LSU was the greatest thing that really ever happened to me. I loved playing football there and liked the people I was involved with. But football only lasts four years, so more than that, it's helped me in what I do now in dealing with high schools and teachers and principals in my business.

Over the years I've had the opportunity to talk to kids who were going to play football in college, and they were looking at different schools. I've always told them, "Look, you're a Louisiana boy. If you're gonna live in Louisiana and make your home here and make a name for yourself at LSU, even if you just play them, it's gonna help you. It can help you tremendously. Now, if you're gonna move away, go wherever you want. But if you're gonna live here, you ought to think about staying here."

It amazes me how people have not forgotten about the '58 team. I travel all over south Louisiana up to Alexandria to the north and to Bogalusa to the east and Lake Charles to the west, and the people, when I'm introduced, say, "Are you the guy who played for LSU?" It just amazes me after 50 years. A lot of these people weren't even born at the time, but for some reason they know about the '58 team.

I don't know if it was because it was the beginning of LSU's success in football or that 24 of the kids who played were from Louisiana and most of them were from within a hundred miles of Baton Rouge. I don't know. But it does amaze me. I'm still asked to speak at Rotary Clubs or at high school banquets. I spoke at an LSU alumni gathering and had a great time, and believe it or not they wanted autographs. I was flabbergasted!

The reunion was great and showed that, even though most of us don't see each other as much as we would like to, we have really stuck together. We really have, and let me tell you, the older you get, you realize how important that is.

Warren Rabb was the quarterback of the 1958 national championship team, as well as defensive back. He completed 45-of-90 passes for 591 yards and eight touchdowns for the 11–0 Tigers, who defeated Clemson in the Sugar Bowl. Rabb was first-team All-SEC in 1958 as a junior. He lives in Baton Rouge.

ROY "MOONIE" WINSTON
GUARD
1959–1961

IN 1958 I WAS A FRESHMAN and would watch the Chinese Bandits, which was the third team, and there were some studs on that team, some real good football players who could have been starting for other schools. If there was a point where LSU really started to become a national power in college football, that was it because we had talent to where some good players were on the Bandits. The program was moving forward with depth and quality of players.

I have looked back and considered why the players were better in our era of LSU than the players right before us. The biggest reason is we came along right after the war, and they started putting in athletic systems in school for us. I started playing football in the fifth grade in 1950, 1951. They didn't do that before; I don't even know if the players right in front of us in the late 1940s had junior varsity football in high school.

For us, it was competition, competition, and competition. They had basketball for us, then baseball. They had track and they had football. It was more available to us; that training system came along for us in Baton Rouge where I was growing up, and we took advantage of it by playing one sport after another.

Billy Cannon, Warren Rabb, Wendell Harris, some really good athletes, came out of that system. I went to Istrouma High, which is where Cannon went, and we started going over to Little Rock, Arkansas, to play them. That

Roy Winston was an All-American in 1961 and elected by his teammates as the Tigers' team captain. Winston was drafted in the fourth round of the NFL draft by the Minnesota Vikings and played in four Super Bowls.

started when Billy was there. We went to Texas to play, too. You could see LSU football benefiting from this because we were pulling in a lot of younger players who had the advantage of playing in the system. The high schools got more competitive, and the feeder system filled in right behind it.

One of the things that really helped us at Istrouma was that we lifted weights. Alvin Roy, the Olympic trainer, worked with us and was a pioneer in weight training. I don't know what the arrangement was with him, but he worked with us, and we would have some weights around the locker room. We had that extra edge in strength, and it meant a lot.

My first game was in 1959, and I was on the Bandits. We were playing Rice, and I went down on our first punt and made a tackle. I felt a part of it out there. It shook off the butterflies, but I always had butterflies in games, even in the NFL for all those years.

The game I remember most is the first game of the 1961 season when Rice beat us. We went 9–0 for the rest of the regular season, then beat Colorado pretty good in the Orange Bowl. I mean, we were good enough to be national champions that season, except for that first game. It still bothers me. It was like we didn't wake up until the end of that Rice game, and it cost us. You have to hand it to Rice, though, they played us well.

We knew that 1961 team had a chance to be pretty good because the year before we gave up just 50 points in 10 games and we had a lot of guys coming back from that 1960 team. We finished strong that season. We had the defense, but we just didn't have the offense. We lost 6–2, 3–0, and we had a much better team than the 5–4–1 record.

We lost our quarterback, Warren Rabb, going into the 1960 season and were trying to get a new quarterback broken in. In 1961 we had some offense to go with the defense and had a fine season. What was funny about that season was that we didn't play Alabama, and they were 10–0 and won the national championship. We tied them for the SEC Championship. It would have been nice to have played them that season.

That was Paul Dietzel's last season, 1961. He told us at the Orange Bowl he was leaving. First, he told some of us he wasn't going, but he left. You have to do what you have to do. It had always been his dream to go back to Army.

The thing that got me ready to play Colorado in the 1962 Orange Bowl is that I met some of the Colorado guys at the All-America banquets in December. I thought, *These guys are good, we have to beat them.* I didn't know how good they were, we never saw any TV of other teams, but we knew we had to beat them.

What was interesting about the Colorado game was they had black players, and we didn't play against black players in the SEC; they weren't on any of the teams we played. My junior year I went out for baseball. We won the SEC but couldn't go on to play in the regionals because we would have played against black athletes.

So in January 1962 we played against black players. Six months earlier, we couldn't play them in baseball. It didn't make sense. Nobody said anything. In June 1961 we couldn't play blacks in baseball.

We ended up beating Colorado pretty good [25–7]. They didn't get much going all day. We pressured the quarterback a lot. Of course, they got behind and had to try and pass, and we kept up the pressure then.

After the game we went to a party, and Wendell Harris and I flew out the next day from Miami to Chicago, then to Los Angeles, and then to Hawaii to play in the Hula Bowl. When I got out there, I was so messed up with the time change, I was worn out. I missed the banquet they had for us because I was sleeping. I fell asleep in my room.

We played a different style of football than other people when it came to punting the ball away. We were defense, defense, defense. If we were inside our 30-yard line and had third-and-long, even over three yards for a first down, Coach Dietzel was punting the ball. It was defense and field position.

Cholly Mac recruited me in high school, and he and I got to be real good friends because my dad and mom liked him. When the day came to sign with LSU, it was Dietzel who came to my house. I said, "Where's Coach Mac?" Guys used to get on me for being Coach Mac's favorite, his pet.

He was a technique guy and would show you the best way to do it. He took care of the front eight—we played a 5–3 back then—and he coached the linemen and linebackers. Coach Mac worked with us and could get us ready to play mentally, but he also knew the fundamentals.

Coach Mac worked with the defense, and then we had George Terry, who was our scouting expert. Those coaches had it together. Dietzel was the organizer. He had his whistle and his pad. You did it right to the note on the pad.

Terry would watch the film, but he would try and get to games of upcoming opponents. If we played at night, George Terry would try and go see somebody in the afternoon and fly back. If we were playing Ole Miss in two weeks, he would try and get there to see them. Dietzel would say, "The Mastermind has a plan."

You found out later that, when he wasn't the head coach, Dietzel was a great guy underneath. We just didn't see it because he was making things go and organizing and establishing a program. So while Dietzel distanced himself away from the guys—the man up on the pedestal because he was the head coach—Mac had that way of warmth and being down on the field. He wasn't afraid, when you made a play, to come up and hug you.

I played left guard on offense and right tackle on defense for those teams. I remember him grabbing me on the sideline to send me into a game my senior year against Ole Miss and telling me to do something, make a play. He and I were close. He liked to fish, and he and my dad, Jack, were close.

When you are playing a 5-3 defense in college, and you are on the line, you are there for one reason, and that is to make them block you with two people. You shade the outside of the tackle, and the end he is right there. So any play going off tackle, they are going to double-team you. For you to just hold your ground, and maybe be able to slide inside once in a while, was a success.

I got pretty good at that. My left forearm was pretty good; I developed it. Use up two blockers so the linebacker can come up and make a play. I used to tell Mac, "Damnit, all you all want me here for is a blocking dummy."

Then you get to where you can feel that end coming down, so instead of hitting the tackle you can shock the end a little bit. The ends aren't expecting you to charge into them, and every now and then you can roll them a little bit. Sometimes I was able to slide back in and catch the running back. My best thing, I think, was quickness. I probably weighed 205. I wouldn't be big enough to be a strong safety in today's NFL.

In the NFL, I was probably one of the shortest linebackers. I'm 5′11″. Of course, they used to try and list me at 6′1″. The Vikings tried to play me at offensive guard when I first got there, and that was a disaster. Then they put me at middle linebacker, and Norm Van Brocklin got on me one day and said I couldn't play guard or linebacker.

I finally told him, "You haven't played me where you said you were going to play me, which was outside linebacker." The next year when I came back I was starting outside linebacker. I had a guy who played next to me, Carl Eller, which is the reason I played 15 years.

One of my favorite teammates at LSU was Fred Miller. You couldn't hardly move him back then. He was 215 pounds, which was good size for us, and he was raw-boned strong. I still remember the day Fred drove up in a Volkswagen, one of those little bugs. He came to the athletic dorm in this thing, and I remember him getting out of that thing, and he was proud of himself because it got 30 miles to the gallon. When Fred was in that car, that was it, no one else could fit in it.

When I was in the pros I always had a sense of pride coming from the SEC and LSU. After I played, they were always near to getting in a bowl or were in a bowl game. They didn't win a national championship, but they were good. We really have a lot of professional players, they are all over the NFL, so you take some pride in that.

Cholly Mac use to tell us that we were from Louisiana and we represented the state and always be proud of it. It was not the school we were playing for, it was the state.

In 1958 it started to get packed in Tiger Stadium for games. I benefited from that in 1959 when I was a freshman. I got two tickets to the Ole Miss game, and Billy Cannon sold them for me for $100, and I was able to buy a shotgun. Somebody might have paid a little extra for the tickets to help a player along, but when you could get that kind of money for tickets, you knew Tiger football was becoming popular.

A 1961 All-America selection at guard, Roy Winston was elected by his teammates as the Tigers' team captain in 1961. Winston also earned first-team All-SEC honors from the AP and UPI. He played on LSU's SEC champion baseball team in the early 1960s. Winston was drafted in the fourth round of the NFL draft by the Minnesota Vikings and in the sixth round of the AFL draft by the San Diego Chargers. He signed with the Vikings and played in four Super Bowls.

PAUL DIETZEL

COACH

1955–1961

IWAS ALL SET TO GO TO MEDICAL SCHOOL at Columbia Medical School in New York in the late 1940s. Sid Gillman, who was an assistant at West Point, hired me as Plebe coach, the freshman coach at West Point. Then Sid went to Cincinnati, and I went with him. I was the defensive coach, and that is when I first started the Chinese Bandits. I got the idea from the *Terry and the Pirates* comic strip.

In 1953 and 1954 I went back to West Point. I was offensive line, and Vince Lombardi was the backfield coach. He was the most intense coach I was ever around. He was intense about cooking a steak.

Gaynell Tinsley was the head coach at LSU, and he was a legend. He was a great athlete. But the people here at Louisiana can be unrelenting with a coach who is not winning.

There was a time when Huey Long, the governor, came down to the dressing room when Biff Jones was the coach. He went up to the chute door with two bodyguards with their guns in their holsters and told Herman Lang, the trainer, "Tell Jones that the governor wants to speak to the team."

Biff told Herman to tell the governor, "Nobody speaks to this team but me."

Jones then wrote on a matchbook cover, "I resign right after this game," and had Herman take it out to the president of the university. So after Huey stormed out of there, really hacked off that Jones wouldn't let him speak to the team, he walked over to the president and said, "I want that coach fired."

The president said, "I can't fire him. He quit." Biff went to Nebraska and was successful. Biff had been a good friend of Colonel Blaik at Army, my boss, so I got on the phone with Biff Jones, who had come back to LSU as athletic director.

"Biff, someone has asked me to put my oar in for the LSU job." He told me it was a great job if "you could keep the politics out of it. Unfortunately at LSU, you will not get the politics out of it."

The reason Jones was so famous is he bucked Huey Long. He was an icon. When you mentioned Biff Jones, they recognized his name. He had one real strong connection back to LSU, and that was with General Troy Middleton, who was the president of LSU.

Biff recommended me, and I got the job. I was 30 years old, and I think I was the youngest coach at a major institution.

Before I came to LSU, though, there was an opening at Kentucky. Bear Bryant had left and gone to Arkansas. Bernie Shively, who was the athletic director, was a good friend of mine and called and said get down here as fast as you can, we just lost our coach. I knew I had the Kentucky job.

I was coming from West Point, where I was an assistant coach. So I got on the airplane and flew down there. I got to the hotel, but I couldn't sleep, so early in the morning I woke up and went to the president's office. Bernie met me on the steps and said, "I'm sorry, we hired a coach."

I was disappointed until he said it was Blanton Collier, who was an assistant with the Cleveland Browns and a very good football coach and friend of mine. They made a good hire. A month later I went to LSU and got that job.

Well, my first game as head coach was against Kentucky. I was so fired up, and we beat the stew out of them. We didn't win that many games after that and finished 3–5–2.

One thing you never want to do is follow a legend, and Tinsley was a legend on the field. But the team under him as a coach had not done well before me, and he had fallen out of favor. That's a good time to come in as a coach, but of course your material is going to be pretty thin, too.

Charlie McClendon was one of my assistant coaches, and we worked closely for seven years. He became a real close friend.

After we got settled in, I found out several players were getting unofficial financial help, so I stopped that immediately.

In our first spring practice, we started off with 73 players, and by fall we had 37. Our practices were really tough. We were trying to teach football,

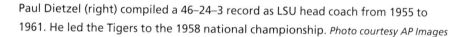

Paul Dietzel (right) compiled a 46–24–3 record as LSU head coach from 1955 to 1961. He led the Tigers to the 1958 national championship. *Photo courtesy AP Images*

and they were not doing well, so players had to buy into the system. Many did not, some did.

We made some rules. No facial hair, and sideburns could not come down below your ear. We had a curfew in the dormitory because I had heard about guys getting in trouble during the season and driving their cars across the river to some pretty tough dives. When football season started, we took the cars away from them.

It didn't do much good. We didn't win right away. We had some nice players, but not enough of them. We had Jimmy Taylor, who was a great football player, but we had one team, 11 good players, that was it.

That year we played a very good Ole Miss team and led at the half, but we were so tired at halftime, I had to squeegee the players off the floor in the dressing room. They ended up beating us [14–12]. We finished 5–5.

The next spring, in 1958, we decided we needed to have more players contribute. And the natives were getting restless because we hadn't done very well. They can get restless fast here. I might have been fired, except for our president, Troy Middleton, who was a strong person.

I got a letter after the 1957 season. It said, "Dear Paul, I hear there are rumblings down on 3rd Street"—that was where the armchair quarterbacks met on Monday to say what I should have done on Saturday. He went on to say, "I like the way you are running the football program, and I am running this university." That put some spunk in me.

We had been recruiting well and had some good athletes. We took our best 11 athletes and we put them on the White Team. We had the white jerseys and gold pants. We took the next 11 offensive players and called them the Gold Team, and the press shortened that down, and they became the "Go Team."

Then we took the best players we had left for defense and called them the "Chinese Bandits."

Back then, you could enter the game in each quarter, but when you came out in that quarter, you could not go back in, you were not eligible. So we worked out a system of running out of bounds, throwing out of bounds, stopping the clock, and using the few timeouts so we could platoon. We would play the White Team for the first half of each quarter, about eight minutes, and then we would platoon the Go Team on offense and the Bandits on defense.

They always went in as a team. The White Team played both ways, but the Go Team would practice just offense, and the Bandits would go in as defense.

In first three quarters, we would play teams even, but then the platoon system would start to help us. I had players from other teams telling me after the season how tired they were, and we would be coming at them fresh and flying at them. They were intimidated in the fourth quarter. We figured if we could stay with them for three quarters, we would win the fourth.

We allowed 53 points in the 1958 regular season. We played great defense. And our priority was the kicking game. You have to be so good at it that no one notices it. We played field-position football. It helped that we had Tommy Davis as our punter, and he was the best I ever had.

In 1958, the season we won the national championship, we opened with Rice and beat them and then had to play my old coach, Bear Bryant, and

Alabama in Mobile. That was the game where the bleachers fell down at half-time, but it was also the game where the Chinese Bandits were made.

Billy Cannon was snorting and fighting for yards on a play and fumbled—the ball popped up in the air, and they returned it to our 3-yard line. Well, the White Team had been playing, and I thought Alabama would score anyway, so I sent the Bandits in.

Alabama did not score a touchdown and had to kick a field goal. The Bandits were jubilant. They had come into their own. They started eating by themselves in the dormitory. They wanted different-colored socks, so we got them red socks. From that time on, they played like madmen.

A disc jockey from Memphis wrote a Chinese Bandits chant and sent it to me. I took it to the band director, and he set the music. So when the Chinese Bandits went in, we would play the "Bandit Chant." They still play the "Bandit Chant" at games.

So when we were playing a home game against Florida, the public address announcer for the first time announced, "Here come the Chinese Bandits," and people were wondering what the heck he was talking about.

Florida ran an off-tackle play. We met the runner right in the hole, the ball popped up, and Gus Kinchen, a defensive end for the Bandits, caught the ball in midair and downed the ball. The Bandits were jumping up and down.

Life magazine came out and took this picture of the Bandits with the Chinese masks on, and that ran in the magazine. They were not big, they were small. Our middle guard, Tommy Lott, was 180 pounds.

I remember we had to move Tommy up to the White Team from the Bandits because of an injury. He could play more. One day, I heard this knock on my door, and it was Tommy Lott. He said to me, "Is this permanent?" I told him no, and he said, "Good, I want to play on the Bandits." Freshmen would come by and wanted to play for the Bandits when they became eligible.

Back then we graded them on defense, and if they were not within a yard of the play on the tackle they got a zero. We had ferocious gang-tackling. It helped that offensive back get down on the ground faster because he didn't want to get pummeled by 11 guys. There was a game where we had nine or 10 players around the ball on every play with the Bandits out there. They were wild. I don't think they were that good, but they thought they were.

The first time I thought we had a pretty good football team is when we beat Miami 41–0 in '58. They were a pretty good football program then. The

47

Go Team had a splendid night. That was the night we ran a double-reverse with Scooter Purvis, and he must have run 300 yards.

The same people who wanted me fired wanted me to run for governor.

We should have won two national titles; we should have won in 1959 with that team, if not for that Tennessee game. That was disappointing. We were 7–0 and really good.

We dominated that team. People thought they [Tennessee] were ragtag, but they were a good team. They gained less than 100 yards, and we gained more than 500 yards.

We scored a touchdown and were down 14–13. The smart thing would have been to kick the extra point and then come back down and win it later in the game. I figured, wrongly so, that if you are the national champion you cannot possibly go for the tie, you have to go for the win.

So we ran our best play, Billy Cannon off tackle. He insists to this day he was in the end zone up to his waist. The head linesman said no.

We came back and missed a field goal. Tommy Davis was kicking for the 49ers, not for us anymore, and we missed the kick, and that was it. We lost. I still don't like Tennessee.

General Neyland, who made Tennessee's program famous when he was the coach, came to our bus after the game. He was the athletic director, and he wanted to talk to our team. He said, "Men, I just wanted to tell you, you are the finest football team I have ever seen on this field." Then he turned around and left.

We flew back to Baton Rouge, but we couldn't land because there were 10,000 people waiting for us on the airfield. I am rather sentimental, and that has always gotten to me.

Winning does a lot of good things, and LSU football came of age with those teams in 1958 and 1959.

Paul Dietzel compiled a 46–24–3 record as LSU head coach from 1955 to 1961. He led the Tigers to the 1958 national championship and is credited with getting the program rolling after a downswing in the mid-1950s. Dietzel went on to be the head coach at Army and South Carolina. He lives in Baton Rouge.

The

SIXTIES

FRED MILLER

TACKLE

1960–1962

I WAS ON THE MATTRESS SQUAD for two years, my freshman season in 1958 and my redshirt season in 1959. We ran the defenses for the opposing team and wore big overalls, big mattresses that they strapped around your legs and around your bodies. We got beat on all the time. They had two teams running at us all the time. You had three teams, and two of them were always running offensive plays. They alternated, so we needed some pads.

We didn't get to alternate, we got beat on. That's pretty much how we spent the practice the whole time. Then the whistle would blow, and the team on the other field, the defense, would come over and hit on us. We always had two teams coming at us.

If you did good and hustled on the Mattress Squad, Coach Dietzel would give you a couple of tickets to the ballgame and that kept me hustling. I could sell those tickets for $15 or $20 apiece, and that's how I got my spending money.

Now, I remember how it was one time with Billy Cannon versus me, a guy on the Mattress Squad. I like Billy Cannon, he was a great ball player, but we had to have an understanding one day. He came around end and popped me with a forearm. Well, they ran the next play, and I popped Billy with a forearm.

That made a statement. You hit me, I'm going to hit you. Billy and I have had a great understanding since then. I think the world of Billy Cannon.

Fred Miller was named All-America tackle in 1962 and was named to LSU's Modern Day Team of the Century. He was named first-team All-SEC in 1962 and was considered one of the strongest players in all of college football.

Coming up through school, I never had a dream of playing football. I just played what was handy, high school ball, get a high school education, and that was it. My parents couldn't afford to send me to school anywhere. So when I got a scholarship, that was a big thing.

My first choice was Tulane, but I didn't have a fourth English credit, and I needed that fourth English credit to go there. So after I signed with them, I couldn't go. Then I decided I was going to go to Texas A&M, where my buddy Ray Wilkins went.

Coach Dietzel put the whammy on my mom, and I ended up going to LSU, which was the best thing I could have done. My buddy Ray stayed at Texas A&M and then got out of there and became my roommate.

By 1960 I was ready to play. Twenty of the 33 guys, Cannon, Warren Rabb, that bunch, had moved on, and we were rebuilding. We got off to a tough start, 1–4 or something.

Then in 1961 we lost that first game to Rice, and I know I was pissed off about the game. I couldn't believe Rice was killing the clock and just hanging on. I remember cursing at some folks across the way.

The season ended up well; we went 10–1. We didn't know, never thought of it really, that we were co-champions of the Southeastern Conference. I didn't know it until a reunion 25 years later, and they gave us rings or something. There wasn't all this hoopla back then about football.

Cholly Mac—Coach McClendon—was my coach my senior year in 1962 after Coach Dietzel went to Army. Mac was one of my favorite people of all time. Next to my dad, he was the man I respected most.

Coach Mac was the kind of guy who, if he sent you into the ballgame and told you to do something, he meant go in there and stop somebody. And you did. I did it a couple of times for him, and I saw him do it with Moonie Winston the year before.

It was just that way. Coach Mac inspired people that way.

I was disappointed at first that Coach Dietzel left for Army. He was never my favorite coach, and I almost left there on account of Coach Dietzel a couple of times back when I was redshirting. Coach Mac took me aside a few times and said, "Don't worry about anything, you come to me."

I guess the thing that disappointed me was we were at the Orange Bowl and there were rumors of Dietzel going to Army. I asked him point blank in the dressing room, "Coach Dietzel, are you going to Army?" and he looked me straight in the face and said no. I never have forgiven him for that, though I understood the situation.

I was tickled to death when it came down to Cholly Mac. We had a meeting in the dormitory after Coach Dietzel left, and Mr. Corbett, the athletic director, was there. He was talking to us and said, "I am going to introduce you to the coach," and he looked over to the door like somebody was going to come in, and then introduced Cholly Mac, who was already in the room.

We were tickled because we didn't get a new guy, we got somebody we knew we could play for. His friends were there in Baton Rouge, his relatives were there, and he wanted to stay.

There are a couple of games that stick out. One was the Orange Bowl against Colorado. It was the first time we played against black guys.

We had a ball that game, not because they had black guys, but because we were just keyed up and happy and saying these guys can't beat us. We had just a beautiful time. We were almost laughing and giggling before it was all over.

I don't think they expected us to come out like a bunch of crazy guys. I remember Sammy Joe Odom going down on the kickoff and just screaming and waving his arms like a wild man. He was not running. He was flailing. The only way to stop Sammy Joe was to kill him. He didn't care if you busted his mouth open.

The Colorado guy, I think his name was Harris, he saw Sammy Joe coming, and his eyes got as big as saucers. He had never seen anything like this. They were not going to come out and beat us; we knew they were going to be a good football team, and we had to fight them.

The other game was when we played the Cotton Bowl and beat Texas 13–0. Our first play on defense, I caught them in the backfield, and that pretty much set the tone. The first play they tried didn't go anywhere. Guys said, "They can't run against us." Our guys responded; we had some tough people.

That was for bragging rights. We heard a lot about Texas this and Texas that. We're right next door to them, so we heard a lot about Texas.

Ray Wilkins, my buddy, was a favorite teammate, along with Moonie Winston. He was a heck of a fisherman. Give Moonie a fishing pole, and he's happy. He won two Bass Masters Tournaments down there in Louisiana.

Another favorite of mine was Bill Arnsparger, who came in to coach LSU in the mid-1980s for three years. He was a defensive line coach with the Baltimore Colts, and when I heard he was going to LSU, I knew the Tigers would be good.

He started to rebuild the program and had some good teams. He put things back together and had it going in the right direction. I was sick when he left LSU after three years. When the Florida athletic director vacated the post and the job was open, I knew Bill was gone. He knew how to coach and how to run a program. When he left, it set back the LSU program.

Here's how much we love LSU in our family. I have four sons, and they didn't go to LSU, but they love LSU football. They would have loved to have gone down there to college, but it was too far from Maryland, and their mother didn't want them that far away from home. My No. 3 son, Jake, has the basement of his home filled with LSU stuff. I gave him the ring they gave us for a Southeastern Conference championship, and you would have thought I gave him the world. He lives and dies it.

My oldest son is a big LSU fan; my No. 4 son lives and dies it. My No. 2 son doesn't care as much about football, but he is a fan of LSU. When they are on TV, I will get a phone call if they think I'm not paying attention and don't know LSU is on TV.

54

My No. 3 son and I went down to the induction of Cholly Mac into the Hall of Fame, and we got a tour of the football complex. There are pro teams that can't even touch what LSU has for a football facility. The Baltimore Ravens have a nice one up here, but it doesn't outshine LSU in any area.

The LSU guys must be disappointed when they get to the NFL. What a place. My son, Jake, went to the national championship against Ohio State. He came home with $500 worth of LSU stuff.

I get a thrill out of it, too, now that I am retired and can halfway keep up with them.

I got a big LSU flag and took it down only to put up the American flag. We will put up the LSU flag in June to get ready for the football season.

I still remember one year playing TCU and their quarterback Sonny Gibbs. The dressing room for the visitors was down in the southeast corner, and that's where they had the big opening to bring in the equipment and where they would bring in Mike the Tiger.

They would keep it covered until right before the game. Well, Sonny thought he was going to get a peek at Mike. He thought Mike was going to be this little old Tomcat. He picked up that cover, and Mike threw himself at

Sonny, all 400 pounds. Sonny didn't stop running until he got back to the locker room. We shut them out that day.

There were a lot of guys I played with who took advantage of the education and became doctors and accountants. I'm sure it helped we had some guys who were pretty smart on our football team. Guys like my roommate, Ray Wilkins, who was like me and finished in forestry. I came up here to Baltimore to play ball, and Ray stayed there and has done extremely well. He was in natural resources and the timber industry and is a sharp guy, and I'm sure a millionaire several times over.

I enjoyed every year and I enjoyed every ballgame, except the ones we lost. I took a loss pretty hard. I can't say I had a favorite year; we ended up going to a bowl somewhere in four of the five years I was in the program. In 1961 we took on Colorado in the Orange Bowl, and in 1962 we took on Texas in the Cotton. My freshman year and redshirt year we ended up in the Sugar Bowl.

It was always full in Tiger Stadium when we played. When you went out that chute and under the goal posts and ran out there, you were no longer walking on the ground, you were walking on air. You were looking for somebody to hit. It was a good thing you didn't run across somebody with the color of the other team as you were running out because you wanted to hit somebody.

It was always great playing in Tiger Stadium.

55

Fred Miller was named All-America tackle in 1962 and was named to LSU's Modern Day Team of the Century. Miller was named first-team All-SEC in 1962. He was drafted by the Baltimore Colts and was named All-Pro. He lives in Maryland.

JERRY STOVALL

HALFBACK

1960–1962

I WAS A SENIOR IN HIGH SCHOOL when one of LSU's recruits decided not to go, and they ended up with a scholarship left over. Coach Deitzel decided that they might as well give it to the old boy, Stovall; he's been down here a bunch, might as well hand it out to him. That's how I ended up at LSU.

There was a wonderful gentleman, Red Swanson, who was the director of LTI, which was a detention facility. In my high school days we played them in football. He was on the LSU board of supervisors. He must have taken me down to four or five games my senior year in high school, and I think one day he just told them, "I'm going to leave him. If you want him, great, if not send him back on the bus to West Monroe."

Mr. Swanson was as much responsible for my scholarship as anyone because I was the runt of the litter in that recruiting class. You know what helped in recruiting when I was a head coach, hearing dads say, "My son is not big enough for your program." I would say to them, "Well, let your son decide that."

Dalton Hilliard was 5′9″, 176 pounds coming out of high school, and people told me, "Jerry, he's not very big and not very fast." I told them, "He just doesn't know it yet." When he left, he owned just about every rushing record LSU had and played eight years in the NFL. He didn't grow to 6′4″, but he grew to 220 pounds and had a big heart.

What does it mean to get recruited by a place like LSU? You walk into a select few schools, and all you have to do is look up in their arena or their stadium, and all you see are banners. This is one of the select places.

You can walk down a hallway here and see an artist's rendering of every All-American. You can see on the opposite wall every helmet of the National Football League where one of our players played, and there is a nameplate there of an LSU guy. There are other schools where it might look like they are on permanent probation, no bowl games, no postseason, no banners, none of the NFL connections. Here, it is all about bowl games, postseason, the NFL.

It is the people who are on that wall or have worn that jersey who can say they are part of the full stadium on Saturday, and they helped build this program. People will ask, "Jerry can you imagine playing in a packed house, a full stadium?" And I can tell them, "Yeah, I've done that. At LSU."

Just take a pad and write down the top 25 football programs in the country today. Look who is there today. Look back in five-year increments, and I will promise you that 25 years ago there are 20 schools from today still on that list. The tradition keeps going, and LSU is there. Oklahoma is there. Florida is there. Auburn is there. Georgia is there. USC is there.

57

They made a commitment. Everything we have been talking about—how LSU got to where it is today—comes down to one word: commitment. If you have a brilliant coach, why would he go somewhere without the commitment?

If you haven't seen LSU's new weight room, you need to see it. Tell me where you will find one like it, including the 32 in the NFL. Look at the practice facility. We don't have snow here, or freezing weather, but we have a tremendous indoor facility. Why? Commitment.

LSU went out and found the brightest young coach it could find in the mid-1950s, Paul Dietzel. When you start looking at a coach, look at his mentors. For Coach Dietzel, that was Red Blaik at Army and the great Sid Gillman. Miami of Ohio was the "Cradle of Coaches," and that's where Paul Dietzel came from, too. Look at Kentucky and Bear Bryant's staff.

The administration said, "We're going to hire a young man from Army who has never been a head coach." It took a big commitment from them to hire Paul Dietzel. LSU had not had great winning tradition in football.

So Coach Dietzel was hired, and before he started recruiting great players to get this going, he recruited a great staff. It is often overlooked, but the

Jerry Stovall was the runner-up in the Heisman Trophy balloting in 1962. He won the Walter Camp Memorial Trophy in 1962 and later was named National Coach of the Year in 1982 by the Walter Camp Foundation.

ability to recruit a staff is critical. He got Charlie McClendon, George Terry, Bill Peterson, Abner Wimberly, and others.

We had no weight room, nothing. We had this man, though, Paul Dietzel, who had a military background, and they did not take anyone who was not a fine student. So when I was recruited, we had young men who came here to play football and had the intent of going to medical school. We had two guys who went on to be surgeons.

The things that were important to us under Coach Dietzel were behaving ourselves and having good academics. Military men walk with a different purpose, and Coach Dietzel had that step and that confidence, and we followed that lead. It wasn't a swagger; it was just a confidence. So they would give us a blazer to travel in. You belonged to something special.

There is a big difference in the game today. Back then you could not report until September 1, and you did not play until the third week of September. Freshmen were not eligible. It is not hard to understand why students today are not making their grades. They were playing before 5,000; now they are playing before 80,000.

You can't equate that with coming from West Monroe in my day. There were 30 in a classroom; now there are 400 in a class. Freshmen being eligible is a bad rule.

What is not different between today's game and the one back in the early 1960s is that one word: commitment. We are committed to excellence. We are committed to having the best staff that money can buy. We have athletic directors who put their legacy on the line when they hire a football coach at one of these top 25 schools, and they are committed to getting the right coach.

In 1958 LSU came out of nowhere to win the national championship, and something started. In 1959, my freshman year, they lost one game in the regular season to Tennessee. In 1960 came my sophomore class. We were 5–4–1 because we were young and had lost Billy Cannon and all those great players.

Our freshman team in 1959 was undefeated, 3–0. And we also played the infamous Dust Bowl every Monday, which was a ballgame between the freshmen team and all the men on the varsity who did not play. For the first couple of times we played that group, we beat up on them pretty good.

One day we looked up, and here came Coach Dietzel and the staff. They sat down in the stands to watch us. It turned up the heat a little bit, and we did well. It served notice that we were a good group of guys, and we bonded pretty well. It got us ready for the three years we were going to play—1960, 1961, and 1962.

You could see things going in the right direction for the LSU football program. We proved we could play. Going into the 1960 spring practice, we thought we could play, and guys started moving up the depth chart. We bought into the system and were ready to prove that 1958 and 1959 were not a fluke, with just the controversial loss to Tennessee in the regular season and then a loss to Ole Miss in the Sugar Bowl, which was a rematch game. In 21 regular-season games, we were 20–1, which was pretty good, and we were a power.

So we came into the 1960 season, people were really looking at us, and we were awful, 5–4–1. If you look at the scores, none were runaways. We lost a close one to Georgia Tech and we lost a close one to Tulane.

That season we played Ole Miss in Oxford, and they kicked a long field goal to tie us 6–6. We had lost four in a row, then we tied them. No one was putting us away. We ended up winning the last four games, so we were getting better.

In our junior year, we were pretty good. We went to the Orange Bowl. We lost just one game, the opener at Rice, which we never should have lost. We won 10 straight and beat Colorado in the bowl game.

You talk about a tragedy, that loss to Rice was it. We won the next nine regular-season games because of that loss. We thought we were good and we went over there and found out we weren't as good as we thought. We had to work harder; we had gone out with the wrong attitude.

We came back from the bowl game, and Coach Dietzel told us he was going to Army. It hit us hard because we thought we were set up to be national champions. I was at home when he called the meeting. The media started calling, and I said, "I don't believe it." It was a huge disappointment.

What was happening was that not only was Coach Dietzel leaving for Army, but Coach McClendon, we thought, was leaving for Kentucky. Jim Corbett called in Coach Mac and said, "You're not going anywhere, we need you here." Coach McClendon was the architect of the defense, and we needed him to stay.

In our senior year, a memorable game for me was the 10–7 win over Georgia Tech in Atlanta. I ran the second half kick back for a touchdown. That was a big thrill, but winning was the biggest thrill. It was 90-something yards. If you look at the film, Tech players were gaining real fast at the end of that run. Most everybody got blocked, so I didn't have to make many moves. Coach Dietzel had a little play with the kickoff where another player would come down and face you and you would either hand it off to him or keep it and take off. It is designed to slow down the kicking team on the kickoff return. I faked it to him, and he faked it to two backs crossing, and I went the other way with the ball. It was 0–0 at the half, and that put us up.

When you walk onto that campus, you are confronted by the excellence and commitment to excellence that Coach Dietzel brought to LSU. It is something foreign to most people. You have a lot of schools that could win games, but there is something extra here, some integrity.

We had guys on our team, like me and my roommate who had just jeans and T-shirts and tennis shoes before they were fashionable, and then we had other teammates who wore blazers and fine clothes. How many coaches have the capacity to take students from varying backgrounds and have them put those different characteristics away?

One of the things that I remember was the dress-out team would all go to a movie. At a certain point in time we would gather at the athletic dorm, and

Coach Dietzel would lead us to film room at the stadium. A lot of times we would watch *Gunsmoke*. Then, when we would get back to the dorm, he would have a case of apples for us, and we would say good night to our coach.

I was part of LSU in its golden era. Several times in the last couple of years, people would come up to me and say, "Jerry, do you think this is golden era of LSU football?" I would say you would have to define "golden era" first. If you are talking about athletes being bigger, stronger, faster, quicker, yes. The equipment, yes, much better. If you talk about the integrity and commitment of the athlete, I don't think it is close to the golden era. We had a lot of young men that did not stay at LSU because excellence was so hard to live up to here.

My daddy told me, "If you go to LSU and you play, you'll know you can play for anybody, anywhere." He told me that after I decided I was going to go somewhere else. If you go to LSU and can't play, he said maybe that school will take you back.

So that's what it means to be a Tiger. If you can go to LSU and succeed, you can succeed anywhere. You can compete academically, athletically, and you can compete as a citizen.

Jerry Stovall was the last player signed in his recruiting class and became an All-America halfback in 1962. He was the runner-up in the Heisman Trophy balloting and won the Walter Camp Memorial Trophy in 1962. Stovall was inducted in the Louisiana Hall of Fame in 1981. He played nine seasons in the NFL for the St. Louis Cardinals and was the LSU head coach from 1980 to 1983 and compiled a 22–21–2 record. He was named National Coach of the Year in 1982 by the Walter Camp Foundation. Stovall is the president and CEO of the Baton Rouge Area Sports Foundation.

BILLY TRUAX

END

1961–1963

I TOOK SOME RECRUITING TRIPS to Florida, Alabama, Tulane, and both Army and Navy. So I could have gone to some good schools besides LSU. I thought about Navy and playing with Roger Staubach, but I was just 16 when I graduated from high school, so I would have had to go to prep school for a year before the Naval Academy.

Paul Dietzel recruited me for LSU when LSU was coming on in the late 1950s. I'm from Mississippi but went to an all-boys boarding school in New Orleans, Holy Cross.

To a young, naïve, teenage kid, the most exciting thing you could encounter in your life was LSU football. It was really getting big, and I had a chance to play there. You went from crowds of 4,000 to playing before 60,000, and people around the state watched your games.

You ask how you are going to play before that many against guys from all over the state. You were hooking up with the best guys from Louisiana. Then you started hearing about this guy, Billy Cannon.

My first two years I was just offense, and my senior year I played both ways. I played tight end, but I was a blocking tight end. I didn't catch many passes; we were a running team. I caught about six passes in three years. I had good hands, we just didn't throw it. You just did what they told you to do and hoped you didn't make a mistake. It was good fundamentals, and as it turned out, it helped me in the pros with the Rams.

We only had a half dozen plays at LSU when I was there. It was up the middle, over the guard, over the tackle, around the end, and, boom, that was it. You just had to beat the guy who was in front of you. The ball was snapped, there was a collision, and that was it. You hoped to get three or four yards on every down. It was simple, basic, fundamental football.

I started on the Go Team my sophomore and junior year, which was the offensive specialists, and my senior year I made the White Team and could play both ways. They would put us in at the end of the quarter.

That 1961 team, my sophomore year, was a damn good football team, and we could have played with anybody in the country. We were 10–1. We lost the first game to Rice and then ran the table. I don't think we realized at the time how good we were.

Rice back then was good. I think the year before they played in the Sugar Bowl [and lost to Ole Miss 14–6], so that was a strong football team. The next game for them after losing to Ole Miss was to play us, and they beat us 16–3 in Houston.

That was my very first college game, and we didn't lose again that season. We went another 15 or 16 games before we lost again [to Ole Miss in the seventh game of the 1962 season].

Everybody came back from Houston and that loss, and it was dead silent on the trip. We were favorites, and nobody expected us to lose. Dietzel told us not to give up and that we would have a good football team, and we did end up with a good team.

I had broken my leg in 1960 as a freshman in Starkville and only played in one of the three freshman games. I was ready to go in 1961, my sophomore year.

That 1961 team had Jerry Stovall, Moonie Winston, and Fred Miller, some NFL guys. There were still some guys around from the 1959 season when they were good [9–2], so it was nice squad.

That era I was there was when LSU really got going in football. There was a lot of momentum from the Billy Cannon era of 1958 and 1959. The '59 team, of course, should have won a national title. The recruiting push we got from those two seasons was tremendous, and there was a lot of notoriety for the program.

You had to go to class; you had to take real courses. We had study hall, and they did not create a major for you. You had to make a C average. If you had a B+ average you could skip study hall, but I was a study hall guy all the way.

Coach McClendon was a disciplinarian, and Dietzel had a military background and was an organizer, so we were under good leadership.

In those years there was an awakening for the program. The foundation for the modern day surfaced from 1958 to 1962. Ever since, there have been high hopes for LSU football. We beat Texas in the Cotton Bowl, and that was Darrell Royal, and they were the best. We won the Orange Bowl, too. Expectations took off.

I equate it to Tom Landry and the Cowboys. People didn't believe he could win the big game until he did, and then Dallas took off. It was a phoenix rising for the Tigers. We joined Alabama and Tennessee and Georgia Tech as a power in southern football.

I'm 65 years old, and we still talk about that era of LSU football with the guys who I call the Bayou Boys—Granier, Schwab, Trosclair, Gene Sykes, and Ruffin Rodrigue, the crawfish guys.

It was a different lifestyle over there in Louisiana than when I was growing up early in Mississippi. We had a two-bedroom, one-bath house, and I had four sisters and a brother. I went to an all-boys boarding school when I was 12, so that was the first big change. It exposed me to some different things and to New Orleans. I had probably been in every joint on Bourbon Street by the time I was 16 years old. I grew up fast.

LSU recruited me strong. We had some great guys on our freshman team, the best players from around the state. The ones who did survive made it a good program. I was really young and physically immature when I got to college; I was just 16 years old. The two-a-day practices were hard on me, and I didn't know if I was going to make it or not. I guess they didn't have anybody better to put out there, so I made the team.

They kept me around my sophomore year, and I made a big catch for them, so they liked me for another year. It was against Ole Miss, and we called a pass play on fourth down. It was a play we had run a couple of times in practice, and Dietzel called the play on fourth down.

It was in Tiger Stadium [1961]. It was the only play I was in for the whole game. It was an emergency situation. I was the only one who ran it in practice, so they called for me on the sideline.

It was a fourth-and-six. I caught it just before it hit the ground. Some of the Ole Miss guys said if they hadn't bumped me at the line I wouldn't have made the catch. We got a first down, kept a drive going, and won the game [10–7].

Billy Truax was an All-America end at LSU in 1963 and the team captain, but he had a more productive career as a pass catcher for the Los Angeles Rams in the NFL.

Johnny Reb still swears the ball hit the ground first. They never forget. Lynn Amedee jumped up and threw the ball under pressure. It had a downward arc, and I grabbed it just in time. Then I got tackled. I was lying on my back and heard the crowd. The referee was standing over me, motioned with his hand, and said, "First down." That was a big deal. I ran off the field, I couldn't believe it.

Wendell Harris, another great running back on that team, did a halfback sweep and ran in for a touchdown on the next play. We were down 7–3 when I made that catch. If they had stopped us there, they would have had the game won.

Back then Ole Miss was serious football. Johnny Vaught, the Ole Miss coach, used to go at it with LSU. He was from Texas and had all these Mississippi guys. These two half-assed schools from down south had really good football teams and highly ranked teams. We were all local guys, but it was a big rivalry. The winner of our game would get the big bowl game.

Ole Miss had Jake Gibbs and Bobby Franklin, a stable of quarterbacks who were all Mississippi guys. They had a finesse offense, more than we did, and threw the ball. They recruited me, but my dad pretty much said I had to go to LSU. He worked in New Orleans, so I had no choice.

I was 6'3", 200 pounds. That catch I made against Ole Miss as a sophomore was strictly a fluke in the passing game as far as they were concerned. It was just a last gasp thing. I had relatives from all over in the stands. The relatives were down from Jackson, and people were excited about that game.

My junior season we had another good team and were 9–1–1. So we won 19 games in two seasons. The big thing my senior season was I caught a touchdown pass against Texas in the Cotton Bowl, but they called it back. We still won the game [13–0]. That was tremendous for our program because that was the University of Texas, which was a great program. All that Texas BS we had to deal with, and we hit them hard in the Fairgrounds and upset them.

They expected to beat us, but Fred Miller made a big play early in the game, a tackle for a loss, that set the tone. He nailed somebody, and we handled them that day. Texas had sold out the house, and we beat them.

In 1963 we played in the Bluebonnet Bowl and lost to Baylor [14–7]. We were all tired and worn out that season. We were 7–4 and a regular, basic old football team. We should have finished that season with a win, but we were drained.

We had a team meeting before accepting that bowl bid, and Mac asked us if we wanted to go, and most of us said no. We were tired. Ole Miss had beat the hell out of us [37–3], which was embarrassing.

It was a long, hard year. We did beat Georgia Tech that year. That was probably my best game because I intercepted a pass. Billy Lothridge had dropped back, and I batted the ball up in the air and turned around and caught it. That was late in the game.

We had a winning streak, and then Ole Miss crushed us. We had a good record [5–1], but then it fell apart on us in that game with the Rebs, and we never recovered.

Being a Tiger is part of my fabric and fiber and being. You go in that stadium today, and there is some familiarity the other 80,000 people don't have, so you feel you were part of something special. There are just a couple of hundred players on a game day who can feel the same way you do. It can get in your blood, that's the best way to describe it. It is mostly Louisiana people that make up this heritage. I don't know many guys from the Midwest who played there. It is bred into you. The first time you see those guys come out of the tunnel, you think someday you can do that and you dream about it.

When it happens, and you get that chance to run out—oh, boy, then you have to perform and prove you belong.

Billy Truax was an All-America end at LSU in 1963 and the team captain. He played in three bowl games for squads that won 26 games over three seasons and was first-team All-SEC in 1963. Truax was selected in the second round of the 1964 NFL Draft by Cleveland, but played most of his career with the Los Angeles Rams. Truax is in commercial real estate in Gulfport, Mississippi.

DOUG MOREAU

SPLIT END

1963–1965

I GET INVITED TO TALK TO THE TEAM before every season about law enforce-ment issues, and I tell them how much recruiting has changed. I went to University High School and made my "official visit" in the fall of 1961. I had always sold Cokes and peanuts in Tiger Stadium or at basketball games when I was growing up. My dad was track coach, as well as horticulturalist, at LSU.

Anyway, on my official visit I was invited to sit on the bench at the Ole Miss–LSU game. So I went out to the stadium at 1:00 in the afternoon to get the programs to sell, sold those until 5:00, and then went to Broussard Hall, which was the athletic dorm where recruits went to eat. Then I went back to the stadium at 6:15, finished selling the programs, turned the money in, and then went out and sat on the bench.

I watched LSU beat Ole Miss 10–7 in a great game, with the winning touchdown scored right in front of me. I could not have been more thrilled. The kids I talk to these days have it much different—they are flown every-where, given what they need, recruited heavily, and get treated like royalty.

When you come here you realize there are a lot of players just like you, and you are no longer the big fish in the little pond. LSU has been recruit-ing high-quality athletes in the last nine, 10, 11 years. Recruiting established LSU in what I call this, the third phase of excellence. They had good teams in 1908 or so, then when Coach Dietzel came in the late 1950s, and today.

When I played, we looked back at those days of Coach Dietzel and Billy Cannon to set the expectations for us.

So I tell these players they are expected to reach that level if they are going to play for LSU. The coaches have that expectation for them. Coach Saban has done that, and Coach Miles has done that. Players reach for that level.

They have so much better weight rooms and facilities than we had. Then again, LSU won the 2003 national championship without that stuff—we didn't have that indoor facility. It gets down to the people, and coaches will tell you the players are more important than the plays.

Coach Mac was one of Coach Bryant's players at Kentucky, and Coach Bryant was his reference point for excellence. Coach Dietzel first hired him, and Coach Mac was as good a position coach as I ever ran across. Coach Dietzel was very organized and very polished and a maestro. Coach Mac was more hands-on, but both of them were really good on-field coaches. Coach Mac was never able to get to that final rung of a national championship.

I felt I was highly recruited because LSU was the school that recruited me. I was 17 years old when I finished high school, weighed 165 pounds, and was lucky to get a scholarship. I learned how to place-kick and loved to catch passes. If I had any skills, those were the two.

We ran the wing-T, which was a tight formation, and the ends, well, we blocked. Occasionally, we would throw a pass. But I got to kick, which was fun. Coach Mac decided to go to the I formation going into the 1964 season, my junior season. We went to the I formation with a flanker, similar to what Southern Cal was doing.

There were a few things I could do well. I got to try a lot of field goals my junior year because we had a hard time scoring touchdowns. We were 8–2–1—I thought we were better than that—and won a bowl game.

We had a quarterback, Pat Screen, who chose LSU over Notre Dame. Pat separated his shoulder in the third game of the season in 1963, and I think that was one of the reasons we put in an offense like the I formation. Defenses were getting some big players, and you didn't want your quarterback getting hit that hard anymore in the wing-T. You realized if you damaged the quarterback, you were in trouble.

In 1964 Screen was back and Billy Ezell was the backup. Pat hurt his knee halfway through the season, and Billy came back. Our senior year we had Nelson Stokley, who was this scrawny, skinny guy who had skills you couldn't

Doug Moreau was named the MVP of the 1965 Sugar Bowl win over Syracuse (13–10) when he caught a 57-yard touchdown pass from Billy Ezell and kicked the winning field goal. He is a commentator for LSU football radio broadcasts.

believe. He was quick, he was fast, he had an arm. He was accurate and had leadership abilities. You would look at him and wonder what he was doing playing football, and then you saw it. When he stepped into the huddle, he had a commanding presence.

In 1965 we had the potential to be a really great team. We beat up Florida in one game, but made all these turnovers and lost, and then Nelson got hurt. He had become our team. We had come to rely on him so much, so when he got hurt early in the Ole Miss game, we fell apart and lost [23–0]. We followed that up by getting the hell beat out of us by Alabama [31–7] in Tiger Stadium. They ended up as national champions, but we didn't play well.

We had a great finish and beat No. 2 Arkansas in the Cotton Bowl. We made a commitment to overcome what we had done, or not done. Arkansas had won 22 in a row, and if they'd beat us, they would have been national champions.

Well, our scout team all wore No. 22, which was the number of victories in a row for Arkansas. Every jersey was No. 22, in red. It was a constant reminder. Coach Mac came up with that. We thought we could win, but they had a great team with Coach Frank Broyles.

Physically, we beat them and won 14–7. It wasn't lucky. That loss allowed Alabama to get past Arkansas and win the title. I remember I made two extra points and missed a short field goal, which would have iced the game. I tell people I missed it to keep it close and keep the fans there. It was a lack of concentration. But overall, a positive game for me.

I had a very fortuitous junior season when I kicked 14 field goals, which was a lot at that time. I had 22 chances, 46 yards was my longest. The kicking game is more than a third of the game, so it was important. Offensively, we would get inside the 20-yard line a lot, but we had trouble scoring touchdowns. My senior year I didn't get a chance to kick as many, which was fine with me because we learned how to score touchdowns.

As far as receiving, it was not near as complicated as it is today where you have three and four receivers. We might have two receivers. I liked double-move patterns. Raymond Berry of the Colts was my hero. If you wanted to be a receiver, you tried to copy him.

We had one game my sophomore year where we played Ole Miss. It was the game where Pat Screen got hurt and Billy Ezell came in at quarterback. We were down 10–3, and coach sent in the play. But Billy and I, being the geniuses we were, we decided to change the pass pattern.

The play he called was "I-right angle at two circle," which was a turn route. We changed it to an out route. What we forgot to do was change the other patterns and there was a fullback in the flat, which was why there was another defender over there.

Fortunately it worked, and we won 11–10. The ball got tipped, and I caught it on the sideline. Coach Mac never said anything about it, even though we had not run the play he called. We ran the protection, but not the play. It was a great thrill at Tiger Stadium. It was the north end in the northeast corner. Tommy Luke of Ole Miss tipped it. He dove at it, and we were lucky. God protects you sometimes.

My dad was the captain of the 1933 LSU track team, which was made up of five people, and they won the national championship. His coach was Bernie Moore, who was the commissioner of the SEC later on. Daddy had held the world record in the high hurdles. He never ran in the Olympics, but he held the world record one year. He had graduated in horticulture and was living in Thibodaux when Coach Moore was leaving in 1949. Moore recommended my dad for the job. My dad and Coach Moore were very good friends. Daddy took the job, and we moved to Baton Rouge, as along as he could work in horticulture in ag extension. We lived a block off campus.

So I grew up with LSU being the most important thing in our life. My dad worked there; my mother worked there doing administrative things. I sold peanuts and Cokes at all the sporting events, and when you ask, "What does it mean to be a Tiger?" it's my life, that's what it means. It has always been a central part of everything that I did.

I went and played pro ball for four years with the Dolphins and then came back and went to law school. My second year in law school, Pat Screen, the quarterback, who had graduated from the law school, had gotten a job working on the LSU broadcasts as the sideline reporter. LSU's radio network was the first to have a sideline reporter.

Pat did that for a couple of years, and then they were looking for a freshman team announcer. Pat and I also did a postgame show from a local restaurant. When Pat left to work for the New Orleans Jazz, John Ferguson offered me the job as the sideline guy. So I started working on the broadcasts in 1972 on freshmen broadcasts, then the sideline for varsity games in 1974, and then I moved upstairs. That was probably 1978.

My roommate in law school was James Carville. My parents knew his parents. I ran into him the night before our first year in law school. James had just gotten out of the Marines, and we worked the freshman football team together.

It was funny because I am very conservative philosophically, and James and Pat Screen, two of my closest friends, were liberals.

There are things because of where you are situated in life that have become essential to your life. It is just like your children, they are essential to your life. LSU is essential to my life. I don't consider it one of those things that you turn off and on, it's always there. You hope that you can make LSU better for it.

Doug Moreau was named the MVP of the 1965 Sugar Bowl win over Syracuse (13–10) when he caught a 57-yard touchdown pass from Billy Ezell and kicked the winning field goal. Moreau retired in 2008 as the district attorney in Baton Rouge. He continues as a commentator for LSU football radio broadcasts.

GEORGE RICE

TACKLE

1963–1965

My BEST GAME WAS PROBABLY the Sugar Bowl against Syracuse, which was one of the first times LSU played an integrated team in football. We beat them 13–10. They had a very good back named Floyd Little, and I tackled him in the end zone for a safety.

It was hilarious to look back and think about some of the stuff we were told before the game. I don't know if *hilarious* is the right word, but it was just some of the things they tried to tell us about how to act around black players. I was young and I remember the banquet that night after the game we were sitting there at the banquet wondering if the black players would sit next to us. I guess we were nervous because we weren't sure how to act. People had told us so many things.

Floyd Little and Jim Nance came and sat next to us, and they were the best guys I have ever met. The one white guy in the group was the worst. I thought, *This is not a bad deal after all.* We weren't around black folks like that when I was younger and a teenager and in my early twenties. It was a different time. It was a pretty cool banquet and a great awakening for me. People had told us stories about black people, and they weren't true. But that is how people were raised. There were always the stories that if you played against blacks, this and this was going to happen. Well, it didn't happen, none of those bad things happened.

The one thing that was true is that they had fast running backs, and Little was an excellent back. It was mostly running, so we could base our defense to stop the run. The passing game had not come along enough to help the running game.

In 1972 I went back to finish my degree after my NFL career. I was a student assistant coach, and that's when they decided they were going to offer scholarships to black athletes for the first time. There was a two-hour conversation in that meeting about what to do about facial hair. LSU had a rule: no facial hair. We had to be clean-shaven, but most of the black athletes had little mustaches or goatees. That was a big discussion, the dress code. They decided they were going to let everybody have a mustache, white or black.

My junior year I played both ways, and my senior year we went to platoon football. The platoon system let you blossom into what you could become. When I went to the NFL, they tried me as an offensive tackle, then they put me on defense. I knew that I liked to hit somebody rather than them hit me. We played a 4-3 on defense, but we would shift to the strong side or weak side.

The other game I remember the most besides the Syracuse game was probably the 14–7 win over Arkansas in the 1966 Cotton Bowl, which would have been after the 1965 season. They had a back named Jon Brittenum who had not fumbled in his career. I hit him once, and he fumbled. Overall, it was a pretty good game. The big thing about that was stopping their 22-game winning streak.

If it had not been for Jim Corbett, the athletic director, we would not have been in either the Sugar Bowl or Cotton Bowl. In 1964 we had a couple of losses [8–2–1], and he got us in the Sugar Bowl, anyway. He was a politician and convinced those people we could sell the tickets down in New Orleans and that they should take us. He was right. People followed the Tigers, and his politicking got us in there. We were the second choice until he got us in there.

That 1964 season, when we went to the Sugar Bowl, we'd had that hurricane game. We were supposed to play Florida, but the game got postponed because this hurricane came right up the Mississippi River, and we played the game in December. We lost that game to the Gators [20–6], and the newspapers had headlines that said, "Sugar Is Spoiled" or something like that. We'd had to wait two weeks to play the game, and when we lost, we thought there was no chance to go to the Sugar Bowl. People did not think we could play with the big boys in a major bowl game, but we got a chance and beat Syracuse, which was a top program from the East.

We had a good team in that 1964 season. We beat Ole Miss 11–10, and thought we had a chance to get to any bowl. Back in those days if you beat Johnny Vaught and Ole Miss, it was a good season. We were ranked pretty highly [No. 9], and I remember three plays in that game where I came from the backside and tackled one of their runners on the other side of the field.

Here's a trivia question: who was the first man Cholly Mac signed when he became the head coach? It was me. He had two scholarships left after Paul Dietzel left to go to Army. I would not have gone to LSU with Paul Dietzel. I had waited, and LSU was almost finished with its recruiting class. I signed my scholarship after signing day because I was waiting to see what LSU was going to do as far as hiring a coach, and just taking a good look.

I could have gone any place I wanted. I talked to Bear Bryant; Notre Dame was after me; and Ole Miss was really after me. I was born in Mississippi, but was raised in Baton Rouge, and went to Istrouma High School where Billy Cannon went. But I still thought about leaving.

I just liked Coach Mac. He was a down-to-earth guy, and you could believe what he told you. I would have had to figure things out if he didn't get the job.

I didn't play as a freshman, of course, but I played as a sophomore, and we were 7–4. Then we had some better teams, record-wise, when I was a junior [8–2–1] and senior [8–3]. Defense was our big thing, of course. The Chinese Bandits were still around.

75

The year before I signed, they signed a big class of players. They signed 80-some people, and my freshman class was very small because they maxed out on scholarships. We had something like two tackles in my class. They redshirted a lot of those guys, and that was the nucleus of those 1964 and 1965 teams. Those guys in that big class were seniors with me because I did not redshirt.

We thought we were going to have a pretty good team in the 1965 season. We won eight games, but we lost two games in the middle of the season [to Alabama and Ole Miss].

People didn't think we had a snowball's chance when we got to that Arkansas game in the Cotton Bowl. They had the big winning streak and a lot of talent. Jim Corbett's politicking got us in the game, and his neck was on the line.

We ran the same play over and over in that game with Dave McCormick our left tackle, a big guy, and Joe Labruzzo, who was our halfback. We ran it and ran it and ran it. They didn't stop it. Joe scored two touchdowns. They had an All-America end, and Dave had his number. Joe was this little scatback. We would make a hole, and he was through it.

We had a thing at LSU about using two quarterbacks. Back then you had more of a running quarterback, and when we signed Pat Screen, he stayed nicked up. You had to have somebody else ready, and we had Billy Ezell ready.

That 1965 team was better than 8–3, so it wasn't a surprise to us we beat Arkansas. We were ranked highly at one time in that season [No. 5] and then had a very low point with the loss to Ole Miss [23–0] in Jackson. We had some issues that season with quarterbacks getting hurt.

One of the hardest things to describe to people is that feeling of running out through those goal posts at Tiger Stadium. You have to be on the team and run out and hear those people cheering, and that feeling is what it means to be a Tiger.

Back in my days it was 67,000 people, and I can hardly describe that feeling. I remember every time I ran out of the tunnel. That was the thing, an experience I will never forget.

George Rice was an All-America tackle in 1965, named by *Time* magazine and *The Sporting News*. He is a Baton Rouge native who also threw the shot put for the track team and played basketball for the Tigers. Rice was also first-team All-SEC before going on to a successful career in pro football. Rice earned a degree in industrial arts education. He lives in Sealy, Texas, and has worked for a drilling contractor in the Houston area for the last 30 years.

GEORGE BEVAN

LINEBACKER
1966–1967, 1969

WE LOST ONE GAME IN THE 1969 SEASON. It was to Ole Miss, and it was a bitter loss. I tell Archie Manning, who was the Ole Miss quarterback, that I'm still chasing him in my dreams and trying to jump on his back. We were ahead 23–12 at the half and had a conservative coach, a good man, Cholly Mac, and we didn't throw the ball again in that game until we got behind, 26–23.

That was a particularly disappointing game to me because I had played just two years at LSU because of an injury, a ruptured Achilles tendon. I missed most of 1967 and all of 1968, and that 1969 season I was looking forward to a bowl game. It also kept us from playing for the national championship.

That one loss should not have kept us out of a bowl game. At first, it didn't. We had beaten Mississippi State [61–6] pretty good and thought after that game we had accepted a bid to the Cotton Bowl to play Texas. We were one of the leading defensive teams in the country, and they were one of the leading offenses running that veer, or wishbone.

What happened was that Notre Dame renounced a longtime policy of never participating in a bowl game and went to the Cotton Bowl ahead of us. All of the other bowl spots had been taken, and there wasn't a place for us. The Cotton Bowl people decided to take Notre Dame. We were ranked No. 7, but it didn't matter.

George Bevan weighed just 180 pounds but still played middle linebacker for one of the best defenses in college football. He was named All-SEC in 1969.

We had a very good team with players like Tommy Casanova, Ronnie Estay, and Eddie Ray, who played with the Falcons. We had a two-quarterback system as Coach Mac always did and a good offense, and we were really good on defense.

So it turned out that Ole Miss loss cost us. I remember we got down to their 23-yard line, faced fourth down, and called time out. Coach Mac kind of got the seniors together and said it was our team, did we want to kick the field goal or go for the win? We had a good field-goal kicker, Mark Lumpkin, but we decided to go for the win. He acted like it was in our hands, and we wanted to go for the win. We called a pass, and their safety broke it up.

So that's how we were in position not to go to the Cotton Bowl. We had all cheered when we got the bid and we went back to our dorm that night. The next morning a proctor came, knocked on everybody's door, and told us we had a meeting in the squad room. We went down there, and Coach McClendon informed us about Notre Dame's decision. We're thinking, *There is another bowl that will take us*. He said, "Guys, the worst thing about it is all the other bowls have teams. There is no place for us."

We were devastated. We stayed home New Year's Eve. It was one of the best teams we had in some time in that era of the late '60s and early '70s. It was a chance to get on a national stage with a team that gave up 36 yards per game rushing. It was a shock to us.

I played middle linebacker and was able to make some plays in a 4-3 scheme because our linemen kept their offensive linemen off me and the other linebackers. They just sacrificed themselves so we could make plays. We also had Mike Anderson and Bill Thompson at linebacker. We had incredible intensity on defense and just ran to the ball all the time and played hard.

The play that scared me the most was the dive where I had to take on the center. I was about 180 pounds, which was a little light for a middle linebacker, but not too bad. A big offensive lineman back then was 240 pounds.

I remember talking to one of our coaches from back then, and he was scared in the spring that we wouldn't have a team because the offense couldn't score on the defense. We always felt going into a game with that defense we were going to win every game.

That 1969 season was the season we started with wins over Texas A&M, Rice, and Baylor. We used to laugh that we could have been the champs of the Southwest Conference the way we started by beating the Texas teams.

Miami had beaten us pretty good in 1968, and then we went back down there in 1969 and beat them in the middle of the season with a shutout. We knew we could be pretty good.

Back then Coach Mac put his best players on defense. I had gone there thinking I was going to play running back, so I was a little disappointed at first to get stuck on defense as a sophomore.

My first game was in 1966 against South Carolina and Paul Dietzel, the former LSU coach who coached the South Carolina team. We beat them in a game Coach McClendon remembered well because he was the guy who had to replace Coach Dieztel, who had won a national championship at LSU. The monkey would have been on Coach Mac's back if he we had lost that game. We were still in the 50 defense in 1966, and I played inside linebacker.

We were 5–4–1 that season, and we had a very good defense, but we just couldn't score. We had a quarterback get hurt and we just couldn't get going on offense.

Then, in 1967, the first play of the second quarter of the first game of the season against Rice, I got hurt. I was backpedaling and ruptured my Achilles tendon. I had four surgeries and was in a full leg cast for a year.

It did not heal with the first three surgeries, so they took a piece of tendon from my thigh, and that is how it finally connected. I feel very fortunate that it finally healed after 12 months in a cast.

We played in the first Peach Bowl in Atlanta against Florida State at the end of the 1968 season. So the next time I was able to play was more than a year after the injury as a member of the scout team in December 1968.

The one game I played in 1967 cost me a year of eligibility and 1968 I sat out, so I played just two seasons. When the 1969 season started, I was ready to go. I remember from the old scrapbooks a story that I was running a fever before the start of the first game of the 1969 season against Texas A&M. A professor asked me if I was going to be able to play, and I said, "I've been waiting two years; a little fever is not going to keep me out of this game."

How many times do you get a second chance and end up being a hero? We beat Auburn 21–20 when they missed an extra point. The play before the extra point was a touchdown pass from Auburn's Pat Sullivan to a halfback named Mickey Zofko. It was 29 yards. As a middle linebacker, I had man-to-man coverage and was step-for-step with him, but he made a leaping catch in the southwest corner of north end zone.

I was on the verge of being the goat, but I blocked the extra point from the left defensive side. It was actually a planned rush that we had practiced during the week and had resulted in two other blocked field goals from the other side by Bill Thompson earlier in game.

Under Mac's system, the first team would go two series, and the second team would go one series, and that was for both offense and defense. The thing about our second team was they were really good, it wasn't much of a difference between us and them.

Coach Mac stayed for about 18 years and won a lot of games. They always said he couldn't win the big one, but he was a great coach.

LSU has rekindled the tradition with Les Miles and Nick Saban over the last eight years. We had some golden years in the late '60s and into the '70s and then had a downturn. We were not in the same breath as the Alabamas, Tennessees, Georgias, and Floridas for a while there, but now we have it back.

Everyone has a downturn, but the program has been brought back. I grew up with LSU football; I sold Coca-Colas in the stands so I could get into the game.

Once people know you played football at LSU, they open up to you. I'm still active in the program, as well as the company I work for. We are probably their largest donor. It means a lot to me.

We went for the longest time without any major reunions or anything like that, but now the athletic department or athletic foundation organizes a reunion. So I know most of the guys from the late '50s. The older you get, the more it means to you.

My favorite tradition is coming out of the tunnel under the goal posts. The band was on either side, and we lined up and ran out. It was a great thrill. It was like putting your head inside a bell and having the bell rung. If you talk to players at LSU, I bet most of them will say that is their favorite tradition.

George Bevan was an All-America linebacker in 1969 and is considered one of the best linebackers in the history of the program despite weighing just 180 pounds. He was named All-SEC in 1969. Bevan is the president of the Shaw Environmental & Infrastructure Group in Baton Rouge. He received an undergraduate degree in Finance from LSU, attended law school, and worked in the oil and gas industry in Louisiana.

MIKE ANDERSON

LINEBACKER

1968–1970

Our thing at LSU was to run through the goal posts, no matter where we were. It was our tradition to run through the goal posts. One year we were playing Kentucky, and they had the band jammed up under the goal posts because they knew we were going to run through the goal posts.

Cholly Mac said, "Run 'em over." We had a tuba player, maybe two, on the ground. We ran 'em over, just like Coach McClendon said. No matter what, we were running through the goal posts, and the Kentucky band was in the way.

There was a lot of camaraderie with the defenses I played on, everybody just wanted to play football, too. We had a lot of leadership from the seniors, and the chemistry was unbelievable.

We played a 4-3 defense, and I was strongside linebacker taking on the tight end and tackle, too. We were fast, and I still believe I was the biggest guy on our defensive team at 220. We had defensive ends weighing 175. George Bevan, they said, was 190, but he was probably playing 165. And that was middle linebacker.

When we got into games with Nebraska and Notre Dame, we found out what big really was. All SEC teams back then were small. I don't know why, but that was the way it was. They still didn't crush us.

Notre Dame beat us, barely, on some bad calls in 1970 [3–0]. Nebraska beat us in the Orange Bowl by just five points [17–12] when our No. 1

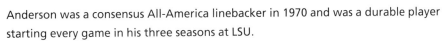

Anderson was a consensus All-America linebacker in 1970 and was a durable player starting every game in his three seasons at LSU.

quarterback was hurt. We had to put in Bert Jones, who was just a sopho-more and had not played much.

Nebraska was tough. My first move of the game is to always let the guy in front of me know whom he is playing against. It was this huge old guy, and I thought, *Well, I'm going to let this big old slob know somethin'*.

The ball snapped, and he hit me before I knew what was happening. I thought, *Uh-oh, long day today*. We hung in there with them. If Buddy Lee had not been hurt, we could have won the game. I'm not taking anything away from Bert Jones, but he was a raw kid who had not played, and he got put into a big game like that against a team that was named national champi-ons. They were just good.

I think that 1970 team was the last all-white team at LSU.

The secret of that team was, if you are on one hash mark and the ball went to the other hash mark away from you, 11 guys got to that hash mark where the play was being run. It's not like three or four guys were there, all 11 guys were there. Ronnie Estay was a captain, and he rallied us. We swarmed to the ball.

Charlie McClendon was a very good defensive coach. We had a good line-backer coach in Doug Hamley, and we just believed in defense.

There were a couple of games that stick out for me. One was against Ken-tucky. I played middle linebacker in goal-line defense, and Dicky Lyons kept wanting to dive over the pile into the end zone, but I would catch him in a cradle and throw him back. It wasn't any killing blows. He kept doing it, and I kept tackling him. That was a close game. We won [14–7].

There was a game against Auburn where they lined up to run a play close to our goal line, and they came out and seemed to be split a little too wide in their splits. So I got John Sage, a tackle, and put him in the gap. When the ball was snapped, Sage went at an angle and took two men out, leaving this gigantic hole.

Here came their Mickey Zofko with the ball. The fullback. I thought, *Oh my God, what do I do now?* He was a big one. Luckily, I was able to tackle him. It was in the fourth quarter, and we won the game 17–9. They totally called the wrong play.

Those Auburn teams were very good back then. They were in the top 10 with Pat Sullivan and Terry Beasley. They were among the best, but not the best. Archie Manning was the best.

Archie beat us by himself our sophomore and junior seasons. We got to be good friends after the fact, but we didn't like him then. Two years in a row it was unbelievable what he did to us—27–24 in one game, then he brought them back in 1969 for another win.

The last year, 1970, he had a broken hand, which was in a cast. The first series he took them down there and scored. A little later on in the game, after I sacked him, I said, "You SOB, you're not going to beat us one-handed."

About that time, Tommy Casanova and Craig Burns started running back punts, and we beat them 61–17. If Archie had not been hurt, I think we could have won, but it would have been closer. He is still the best college quarterback I've seen.

We lost that one game 26–23 to Ole Miss where we might have gotten a little conservative with the offense, but the reason we lost was because of Archie. He was the main culprit.

I grew up in Baton Rouge and went to Lee High, and I was going to LSU all the way. I got a bunch of letters from other schools. Bear Bryant called one day from Alabama, and I'll never forget it.

"Mike, this is Paul 'Bear' Bryant, and I want you to come play for us at Alabama."

I stuttered and stammered, I didn't know what to say. Here was Bear Bryant calling me. I just said real fast to get it over with, "Coach I'm going to LSU, I'm going to LSU, sorry, bye." I was in shock.

I was real good friends with Paul Dietzel's son, Steve. Paul had left LSU for Army, and I think he was still at West Point in 1966 when I was a high school senior. He knew I was going to LSU, but he still made a try at it.

I watched Billy Cannon run his punt back against Ole Miss on Halloween Night. I was right there. My father had tickets to the game in the south end zone of the stadium.

I never did play in the NFL because of the surgeries on my knee, four of them, but I told them I only had two. There was big talk that I was going to be the No. 1 pick of the Giants in the [1971] draft, but I showed up for an All-America awards show hosted by Bob Hope, and he introduced me by saying, "This is Mike Anderson, he has had so many knee operations, he had one during the commercial," or something like that.

Well, the NFL started investigating, and I went from the No. 1 pick of the Giants to the ninth-round pick of the Steelers. I couldn't play. My knees were screwed up so much by that point. Now they are artificial. I would have surgery after each season.

That era I played in was a golden era of LSU football, and it was made by the defense. Nobody threw the ball back then. It was really conservative. Teams always ran, and you let the defense control the game. There were a lot of low-scoring games. Not many games got out of hand. You relied on defense.

It was a great honor to play for LSU. Just to run through those goal posts in Tiger Stadium is something else. To run onto the field is unbelievable there.

I've got a bunch of stuff, a bunch of memorabilia in the bar at the restaurant. I still have a lot of pride in the program. There are pictures of the coaches and pictures of big plays. It means a lot to be a Tiger.

Mike Anderson was a consensus All-America linebacker in 1970. He started every game in his three seasons. Anderson was also named All-SEC in 1970. He owns several restaurants in Baton Rouge and the vicinity.

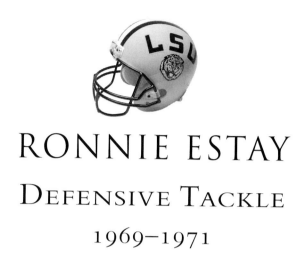

RONNIE ESTAY

DEFENSIVE TACKLE

1969–1971

I WAS 6′1″, 215 POUNDS AND PLAYED defensive tackle. They wanted me to lose weight at LSU because I weighed 230 in high school. We had a defensive end, Arthur Davis, who weighed 175. So here we were playing against Notre Dame, who were big guys, but we did good things, and we did them fast.

They wanted the speed and quickness, and that was how we played. Alabama was big, too, with the wishbone. We were so in tune to what we were doing and aggressive. I was playing nose over the center, and I would read the center so well, Bear Bryant made his center put his head the other way and try and turn around and block me with his butt to the side where they were running.

It was all about speed and quickness, and they wanted you light. It was a 4-3 scheme, but not the 4-3 of today's defenses. We had four down guys and three linebackers, but the two outside linebackers could be on the line. It was almost like a 6-1.

That was on passing downs, but on running downs we would go to a 50 and move left and right, so I could be over the center, over the guard, or over the right tackle, depending where the strength of the formation was.

We were so precise in practicing those things we had to do to win on defense. If they played the wishbone, then I had the fullback, and the next

Ronnie Estay was an All-America defensive tackle in 1971 and was known for his relentless effort on every snap. He was also first-team All-SEC in 1971.

guy, the defensive end, had the quarterback. The defensive back had the pitch man. We played that man-for-man every play, every down.

So there we were in 1969 with the No. 1–ranked defense in the nation, ranked fifth overall, and Coach Mac called us in to vote for the bowl game we wanted to go to, and we said Cotton Bowl. We turned down every other bowl game, and there weren't that many bowl games.

We thought we were going to play Texas for the national championship. We had beaten Alabama and its wishbone, which was the dominant offense, so we thought we would get invited to match up against Texas.

That team of ours held opponents to 37 yards per game [actually 38.9, second fewest per game ever in the SEC] and in 1970 we held teams to 52 yards per game [fifth lowest average].

Then, all of a sudden, Notre Dame decided it wanted to go to a bowl game. They had been turning down bowls and not going, but that year they decided to go. When they decided to go, the Cotton Bowl forgot about us and jumped at Notre Dame. It was awful. I have still have a plaque that the bowl association sent us with a regular screw on it to signify that we got screwed. Every player and every coach got one.

We could have gone to the Orange Bowl and played against Nebraska. We could've gone to any bowl we wanted. But we didn't go anywhere. We knew that we could beat Texas. They were scared of us, and I think that is why they picked Notre Dame.

The next year, Notre Dame went back to the Cotton Bowl and beat Texas, and we went to the Orange Bowl and lost a close game to Nebraska, 17–12.

In 1970 we lost to Notre Dame 3–0. The SEC official threw a flag on Johnnie Nagle for pass interference at our 30-yard line. When you see the film, Nagle never touched the guy. The official was behind the play and couldn't see. They got a chance to kick the game-winning field goal and beat us.

Notre Dame came down to us in Baton Rouge in 1971, ranked No. 7 in the country, and we beat them 28–8. We held them scoreless until the fourth quarter in both of those games. They were going to go to New Orleans and celebrate, but Ara Parseghian put them on the plane and took them home. There was no celebration for Notre Dame.

These were big guys on the offensive line for Notre Dame, 260, 270 pounds. I got a chance to sack Joe Theismann, their quarterback. We shot through there and had three or four goal-line stands. I waited a whole year to play Notre Dame again after losing 3–0 to them. Funny thing, I got a chance to sack Theismann when he played in the Canadian Football League.

There was no way Notre Dame was going to come into Tiger Stadium and do anything against us. I think I had 17 tackles, 13 solo. We finally got even for them keeping us out of the Cotton Bowl in '69 and beating us 3–0.

In 1970 we played Nebraska in the Orange Bowl and lost. I finally saw the film of that game last year, and I saw where they double-teamed me the whole time. That week of the Orange Bowl, we had a lot of strict practices and a curfew while the Nebraska guys got to go out at night. We lost 17–12 and didn't play as well.

The SEC was a good league back then. In 1969 we were 9–1, and in 1970 we were SEC champions. In 1970 we had to beat Ole Miss and Archie Manning, and we beat them because he had a cast on his arm. His mom wrote a letter to Coach Mac thanking me for not sacking him too hard in the end zone when we were ahead. I kind of threw him on my body, laid him back on me.

He was hurt in that game, but we kicked off in that game, and they went down and scored right away. He had a cast on, and I said, "That's enough guys, he can't beat us with a cast on, let's go." At the end of the game it was 61–17. In that game they filled up these holes where the benches sit on the LSU sideline with oranges. They were throwing the oranges on the field because we were going to the Orange Bowl.

I was light for a defensive tackle, but I had strong legs from hunting in the swamp and bayou. My nickname in Louisiana was "Crocket," and at LSU it was "Big Ron." Here in the CFL it was "Swamp Dog" from the swamps of Louisiana to the prairie dogs of Alberta. I used to walk into the water up to my waist going hunting every day. It would build up my legs. I never really lifted weights; I didn't get into it like some guys did. The thing that built my legs up was walking in the swamp with hip boots. And sometimes you would have to run away from the alligators.

I might have been 12, 13, 14 years old. The last gator I killed was 13 feet long. I had him almost in my lap. He weighed 800 pounds. My cousin shot him.

In Louisiana when your son goes to LSU, your dad is proud of you, like when the president said he was proud of his son following him. It's the same thing. My brother, Maxie, went there in 1963 and then he got killed in a car accident in 1964.

When we picked up my dad off the plane after my brother died, my dad said, "What do I have to live for now?" I was 15 years old and in the ninth grade. Deep down inside, I said, *Here I am, live for me. I am going to be the best football player I can be so my dad can have something to live for.* Two weeks after I signed with LSU, my dad died of bone cancer. His name was Mack Estay.

So I had a good career at LSU and then came up here and played in nine [CFL] championships with Edmonton and won six of them. We won five in a row from 1978 to 1982. I just got another award from the Sun Bowl. They had 75 years of games and picked 75 players to honor, and I was one of the players. That was from the 1971 Sun Bowl when we beat Iowa State.

People up here in Canada know what LSU is about. There are some American football players coming up here to play, and they know what Tiger football is all about. You bleed purple and gold even this far away from LSU, up here in the North.

Ronnie Estay was an All-America defensive tackle in 1971. He was also a first-team All-SEC defensive tackle in 1971. Estay went on to play in the Canadian Football League, where his teams were CFL champions six times in Edmonton. He is currently an assistant coach in the CFL.

TOMMY CASANOVA

CORNERBACK

1969–1971

THE LEGACY OF THAT ERA OF LSU FOOTBALL was a bunch of kids who were too small and did what they were not expected to do. We had reunion in Baton Rouge recently, and you look now at us, and we were just smaller. We were outgunned in virtually every game. Coach Mac had convinced us—I don't know how he did it—that we were expected to win.

It wasn't until later when I got into the NFL when I heard the NFL folks saying how they follow LSU closely because of the tradition and history, but that we didn't have have any star players. I took offense to that and said we had a lot of players. They said that's what they're talking about. How many kids from LSU are in the NFL? There was Bert Jones and myself.

The NFL guy told me that the Notre Dame and Colorado teams we played had four guys just in the first round. LSU hardly put anybody in the NFL. When I started to think about it that way, he was right. Coach Mac had us convinced we could beat those people, and that's what made LSU football so special to me. It wasn't a bunch of good athletes just running over people. It was a bunch of kids, small athletes, who worked as a team.

It was Paul Brown who brought that to my attention. He said Charlie McClendon was an enigma to the NFL because no one knows what he does to get those kids to play the way they play.

We did not have big kids in Louisiana; we were smaller than kids up in the Midwest. There was a tradition established, and Coach Mac had us convinced

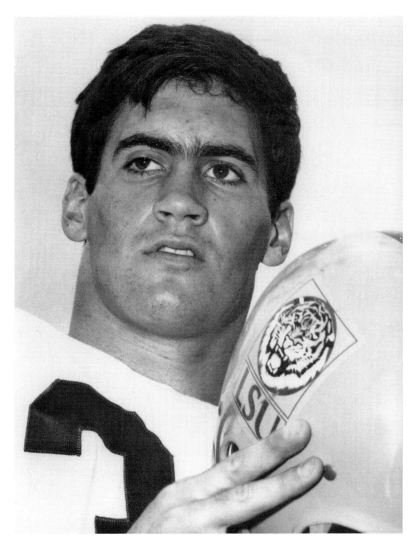

Tommy Casanova, a defensive back and kick returner, who also played some offense, is the only three-time All-American in LSU history.

we were supposed to win. That carried over to our lives after we left school. No matter the size of the challenge, you got after it.

I remember when we played Notre Dame, they had four first-round draft choices, and they beat us by three points. The next year we beat them by three touchdowns in Baton Rouge.

My junior year we played Nebraska in the Orange Bowl, and it was the worst game I ever played in my life. I was so sick of being in Miami, I didn't even care if we played the ballgame anymore. I just wanted to go home. They had first-round draft picks, and we should have beaten them, anyway.

When you have a bunch of kids cooped up together on Miami Beach and have to do everything together and are there 10 days, you go stir crazy. I just wanted to go home. We did not play our "A" game, and they won the game and the national championship. They outgunned us and were a good team, but if we had played to our standards we would have won that game.

We would come in at 9:30 at night for curfew, and the Nebraska kids were just going out. They were letting them have a ball down there. They were out running around. Maybe it was good they did pen some of us up. I wasn't in it that game. I was completely unfulfilled. I was out there, but nothing stands out.

When I graduated I was 6'2", 190 pounds. When I got there I was 6'2", 180 pounds. We didn't have a weight-lifting program. I was big as a defensive back today, but we had a lot of smaller guys. I would play some offense, too, but every time I went in the game, they all knew I was getting the ball, which kind of defeated the purpose. I loved running the football. I was pretty good outside the ends, but running inside wasn't my cup of tea.

I returned punts and some kickoffs. I got two letters in track, so I could run some. I wouldn't go to practice, but I would run in the track meet when they needed sprinters or guys for the relay team. I did a lot of quarter miles and the 100-yard dash.

The game I remember most was the Auburn game my sophomore year [1969]. We always played at nighttime, but that was the first game I played during the day, and it was on national television. We were ranked in the top 10, and they were nationally ranked.

Pat Sullivan and Terry Beasley were just coming into their own as a quarterback and receiver. We had to block a field goal and extra point to win that game [21–20], and we did it. They were better than we were, so I got more gratification from that game than any other. We rose to the occasion.

We scored on the first play of the game on a halfback pass from Jim Gilbert to Andy Hamilton. Their safety was really aggressive, and all week in practice we talked about how he would just fly up and hit people on the sweep. The more we looked at it, we thought we could throw on this guy.

The whole LSU team was waiting for that first play of the game. That safety wanted to set the pace of the game and make a big tackle and let us know that Auburn was a physical bunch. He got a little more finesse than he expected. Jimmy Gilbert had played quarterback in high school and a little at LSU. He was a senior; it wasn't like we were putting a special person in. He had a good arm, and Andy Hamilton was one of the best college receivers I've ever seen.

Andy was 6′3″ and could get open running beautiful patterns. Bert Jones' dad taught Andy how to run patterns. Andy turned them every which way but loose. He had the best hands God ever made.

In that Auburn game, Andy was split out and acted like he was going to crack back with a block, and the safety was coming up for support. Who would start off a game with a halfback pass? Well, Les Miles, I guess he might do anything. But anyway, it was some call.

The only major-college offers I had were Tulane and LSU, along with some of the smaller schools. A lot of schools tried to convince me that I was going to go to LSU, redshirt my first year, play a little bit my second year, a little bit the third, and that was all. They said LSU was too big for me, and I took that as a challenge.

Nelson Stokley was an LSU quarterback from Crowley, and he came over to my house one day. He asked me where I was thinking of going to college. I told him Tulane. He said I was crazy. It made me sit down and think about it, and I never regretted it.

If I had told Nelson I was going to Texas or Alabama, he might have said, "Well, that's a good choice." But he made me stop and give it some thought, and I realized he was right.

We won 27 games in my three seasons, and we should have won more. The thing people need to look at with that defense for three years is how few rushing yards we gave up. It is ridiculous. We always led the nation in rushing defense.

In the secondary, we played predominantly zone, then played some man. We had a lineman, Freddie Michaelson, who might have weighed 170 pounds, and he was in the backfield all the time. Ronnie Estay was 220 pounds, and he was also in the backfield a lot causing problems for teams.

I have never seen anybody pursue the football like Ronnie Estay. There have been faster players, better players, and bigger players. He was just unbelievable. As long as the ball was in play, he was chasing it. He was strong enough and quick enough that he could get leverage on anybody.

We were so well-prepared. Freddie told me he knew where the ball was going before the ball was snapped. We basically stayed in a 4-3.

Terry Beasley of Auburn was a very good receiver and was good at running patterns. The best way to cover Beasley was to get up and bump and run with him. I had enough speed I could do that. He was a sprinter, too, and he was a real strong kid. If you bump and run with a guy, you don't have to worry about the quick moves.

His big thing was he would run go patterns, and Pat Sullivan, the quarterback, would throw it over his outside shoulder. You couldn't get to the ball. Beasley would run looking for the ball over his inside shoulder and then catch it over his outside shoulder. You couldn't break it up without interfering with him. We had some battles.

I go to LSU for games, and people come up and still want to talk to me and tell me how much they enjoyed watching me. I have never been that much of a fan, but I appreciate people. I loved playing the games more than all the other stuff around it.

I don't mind seeing LSU lose, but nothing aggravates me more than to see them play poorly. It drives me insane when people don't tackle, when they don't block, when they don't do things correctly. That bothers me more than losing. I don't get caught up in the hysteria as much. When you have been down on the field playing the game, you look at it differently.

The band is the best part of the game for me. The pregame performance by the band is one of the greatest things about LSU football. I remember after I stopped playing and went back for a game, I got there early and saw this pregame performance for the first time. It was unbelievable. They told me, "Tom, they do that every week." I didn't know. LSU's band is the best, and they will get the crowd so wound up.

If you look back at my career, what we experienced with Coach Mac, those small teams, those overachievers—don't look at the size of the mountain, just start climbing. That was us.

When I finished LSU and was drafted by Cincinnati, they said I couldn't go to medical school. They said it was too tough. I said I wanted to do both, and they said I couldn't. Finally, they said they would allow me to do it. They said, "We don't think you can, but go ahead and try." All I wanted was a chance. It took me six years to get through, instead of four. I played in the NFL six years.

A few years back when I ran for state senate, people said that I couldn't do that and maintain a practice. I said, "Give me a chance."

Telling me I can't do something probably fires me up to prove that I can. I think where that comes from are those three LSU teams I played on. A lot comes from my mother; she was the same way. A lot of it comes from being a Tiger.

Tommy Casanova was a three-time All-American at LSU (1969–1971) and one of just six LSU players to be named first-team All-SEC three times. Casanova was a cornerback, but he was so skilled he returned kicks and lined up as a wide receiver in some games for the Tigers. LSU won 27 games in Casanova's three seasons in a golden era of SEC football, which featured powerhouse programs at Alabama, Auburn, and Tennessee, as well as the Archie Manning–led teams at Ole Miss. Casanova is a member of the College Football Hall of Fame. He was a second-round pick of the Cincinnati Bengals. He is an ophthamologist in his hometown of Crowley, Louisiana.

CHARLIE McCLENDON
COACH
1962–1979

*T*HIS NARRATIVE WAS WRITTEN *by Ray Glier based on interviews with McClendon's family and former players.*

★ ★ ★

IT WAS EARLY JANUARY 1962, and Paul Dietzel had resigned as LSU coach to become the head coach at Army. Inside Athletic Director Jim Corbett's house, Charlie McClendon, Dietzel's top assistant, waited for Corbett to say the job was McClendon's.

Corbett wavered.

"Mac, we think we can give it to you, we just have to wait a while," Corbett said.

McClendon did not want to wait. In his back pocket, he had an offer from Kentucky, his alma mater, to be its next coach.

"We had two jobs to pick from," Dorothy McClendon, the coach's wife said. "LSU was dragging its feet."

Charles said, "That's fine. If you are going to wait, I'm going to call Kentucky right now."

Corbett blinked. He called whomever he needed to call in the administration to tell them McClendon should be the next coach.

"Charles had the Kentucky job, and again, he was fighting for his life," Dorothy McClendon said. "He asked me what I wanted to do, and I told him I thought it was best to stay here rather than uproot the families of all those assistant coaches and go to Kentucky. He said the same thing; let's keep everybody intact."

For most of the next 18 years, McClendon kept LSU intact near the top of the heap in college football. He was 137–59–7, more wins than any other coach in LSU history.

What Dietzel had started with the national championship team of 1958, McClendon kept pouring into with a zeal for defense and emotional fight. The Tigers forged an identity as a feisty defensive team where ball carriers went down on the first tackle rather than get swarmed by 11 bandits.

McClendon did his job so well he was inducted into the Louisiana Sports Hall of Fame in 1982 and College Football Hall of Fame in 1986. In 18 seasons, McClendon suffered just one losing season.

There was a magic to his words, his former players said. His passion was verifiable every week as he stirred them toward a win, or at least a performance that was competitive. Rarely were McClendon teams thrashed.

Tommy Casanova, the three-time All-American, said he could never quite explain how McClendon commanded his team to run through the proverbial wall.

Dorothy Faye McClendon understood, though. "He would tell the players, 'You are letting down the whole state of Louisiana,'" Mrs. McClendon said. "It was tough love. Charles loved them so, and he would tell them that."

There were many high points in McClendon's reign. There were 13 bowl appearances in 18 seasons and seven bowl wins.

His first game as head coach was a 21–0 shutout of Texas A&M in 1962, and the shutout was appropriate given McClendon's leanings as a defensive line coach. That season was capped by a 13–0 victory over Texas in the Cotton Bowl, finishing off a 9–1–1 season and certifying McClendon as the right coach for the job.

The Tigers kept churning wins as players spun through the dorm doors. Perhaps McClendon's biggest win was the victory over No. 2 Arkansas, his home-state team, in the 1966 Cotton Bowl. The 14–7 victory prevented the Razorbacks from winning a national championship, broke their 22-game winning streak, and finished off an 8–3 season for LSU.

There were some disappointments. The 1969 team finished 9–1 and thought it had a chance to play Texas for a crack at the national championship in the Cotton Bowl. George Bevan, a linebacker for the team, said the Tigers had already been invited to the Dallas game, but when Notre Dame officials decided to lift the ban on the Irish playing in a bowl game, LSU was dropped.

"It nearly killed all of us, it was awful," Dorothy Faye McClendon said.

The Tigers got even with the Catholics in 1971 when Bert Jones and Andy Hamilton led a 28–8 victory over the No. 7 Irish in Tiger Stadium.

The disappointments for McClendon started to roll into one starting with the 1974 team, which finished 5–5–1. It was his first non-winning season in his tenure. Then, in 1975, the Tigers slipped to 5–6, McClendon's first losing season in 14 years. Things got better with an 8–4 record in 1978 and a 7–5 record in 1979, but there were higher expectations, which McClendon had created, and he was fired.

McClendon's last game was in the Tangerine Bowl on December 22, 1979. The Tigers beat Wake Forest 34–10. He gushed over the bowl and its Orlando setting, and the caretakers of the game asked him to become executive director. In 1982 McClendon became the executive director of the American Football Coaches Association. He moved back to Baton Rouge in 2000.

There is a glow to Dorothy Faye McClendon, as if she were still living in the day of "Cholly Mac," the coach, when he was adored by Tiger fans. She is walking around her home, the same house she shared with the coach, and points out the memorabilia and the names on the walls and the pictures of her husband.

Her face is brightest, however, when the subject is not the 137 wins by her husband's team, which still makes him the winningnest coach in LSU football history. It is what her husband did off the field.

He cradled the families of assistant coaches with his work as the executive director of the American Football Coaches Association. He pushed for their contracts to extend until June, in case any got fired in December.

McClendon rallied support for a foundation to help defray the costs of the education of his former players' children. The Charlie McClendon Scholarship Fund was launched during the ill-fated four seasons of the Curley Hallman regime (1991–1994).

"That's one thing he wanted to do, was have a foundation to help with the education of his former players," Dorothy Faye said. "They spilled their guts out on the field, and he wanted to do something for them in return."

Charlie McClendon has more wins than any coach in LSU history, compiling a 137–59–7 record. He was inducted into the Louisiana Sports Hall of Fame in 1982 and College Football Hall of Fame in 1986.

There were trademarks to McClendon's style. One was the defense and the five-man fronts. Another was that hat, which was cocked at a crooked angle on his head. "I think it was an attitude thing," said Dee Alberty, his daughter.

There was also a competitiveness that drove him and, in turn, drove his players. "He was one of seven boys, and he was the youngest of seven, that's what drove him and made him competitive," Dorothy Faye said. "His older brothers would sign him up to box. One of them he had to box was the ice man's son, who lifted blocks of ice and was very strong, and Charles said the boy nearly killed him.

"They would fish competitively, and one brother put weights in a fish that was already caught and made it weigh a pound more. Things like that made him very competitive."

Dee Alberty said her father was competitive from the time he was born. "His mother lay dying from the childbirth, so they put Daddy on the side of the bed and tended to her because the caregivers said the older boys needed a mother more than they needed another brother. Daddy had to breathe on his own," Dee Alberty said.

McClendon didn't play football until he went to college at Magnolia A&M Junior College. He was there on a basketball scholarship and then decided he wanted to play football. He was so unfamiliar with the game, McClendon didn't know how to put the pads on. Two years later, Bear Bryant, the coach at Kentucky, gave McClendon a scholarship.

Even as a pupil to Bryant, regarded as the greatest college coach of all time, McClendon tried to find his own path. "You never could copy anybody, be yourself, do not try and imitate somebody else, that's what he believed," Dorothy Faye said. "He was as close to Coach Bryant as anybody could be to Coach Bryant, but Charles wanted to do things his own way."

McClendon won just two games against Alabama while he was at LSU, and that was part of McClendon's downfall. There was not that big game win—a national championship—that could help swim through turbulent waters toward the end of his reign.

During McClendon's last six seasons as LSU's head coach (1974–1979), LSU had no appearances in the final AP poll. During this time, LSU's record was 40–27–2 (.594 winning percentage), and he was ousted.

His playfulness endured even with the bitterness of being fired. The bumper stickers—"Help Mac Pack"— displayed the ruthlessness of the profession. But he fired back at the dissension the day he was packing up his office by quipping, "Well, ol' Mac is packing, and there is nobody here to help me."

Mac finally packed for good on December 6, 2001, when he died at his home in Baton Rouge.

The
SEVENTIES

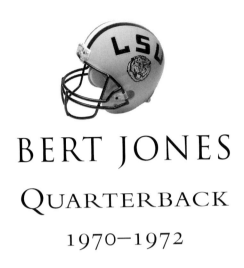

BERT JONES

QUARTERBACK

1970–1972

MY SITUATION WAS RATHER UNIQUE coming out of high school. When I was playing ball in high school, my father was the offensive coordinator of the Cleveland Browns. I didn't think about playing ball in college. Every summer, myself, my four brothers, and my two sisters would go up to training camp. That was a condition of training camp, that the family be there.

So every summer I would go to training camp, and everything I related to with football was related to pro football. I was the ball boy with the Cleveland Browns, and I would hide in the locker from Jim Brown and jump out when he would come in, and he would act like he was scared.

I was washing jocks and socks and cleaning up after practice. I warmed up Frank Ryan and Jim Ninowski on the sideline. That was my thought process. I really didn't think about college.

Finally, when I was a senior, I started to realize I was going to have to play. That was also the year a dear friend of mine then, and now, was coming out of high school and was heavily recruited, and that was Joe Ferguson. He was all-world. He was the quarterback to beat all quarterbacks.

Every college in the South was hard pressed recruiting him. They were apprehensive recruiting me because I wasn't as good, and they were worried that we wanted to go to the same place. We were good enough friends back

Bert Jones was the first consensus All-America quarterback in LSU history, even though he was not a full-time player under LSU's platoon system. The "Ruston Rifle" finished fourth in the Heisman Trophy balloting in 1972.

then that we both realized it would have been a waste of time to go to the same place.

I didn't have that many grand opportunities coming out of high school. My father was a graduate of Tulane. Louisiana Tech, a great school, was right here in my hometown where Terry Bradshaw had played.

I kind of wanted to go to a bigger arena, so to speak. My father's good friend, Ara Parseghian, was coaching at a school in northern Indiana [Notre Dame]. I considered going there. Daddy was with Ara at a reunion of the 1948 Browns team, and he said, "Dub, one of my greatest regrets in college was not making you tell your son to play for me at Notre Dame."

Joe Ferguson ended up signing with Arkansas. LSU ended up putting on a full-court press, and I considered Tulane because both my father and grandfather were All-Americans at Tulane.

My first cousin, Andy Hamilton, had signed with LSU, and my running back from my high school, Allen Shorey, was on the LSU squad. It wasn't regarded as a quarterbacks' school, but it was still a wonderful place to choose.

We ended up playing Coach Parseghian. The first time was when I was a sophomore, which was one of those embarrassing moments of your lifetime. We lost 3–0.

The Notre Dame game was unique because my father was friends with a lot of people in the industry, and they all wanted to go to that game [1970]. My cousin, Andy Hamilton, was going to play, and friends and all sorts of people wanted to go. It was Notre Dame.

I couldn't get them tickets, but guess who got them tickets? Ara Parseghian. I looked over at the Notre Dame bench before the game, and guess who is over there—my father. He was sitting right behind the bench. I said, "Dad, you can't be on the field."

I played a good bit in that game. It was an inauspicious performance, to say the least, we didn't score.

Andy Hamilton grew up down the street. He was one of my receivers, and my older brother was another one of my receivers, in high school. My younger brother, Ben Jones, came to LSU as a wide receiver when I was there.

Andy was a talent. He had good hands, great moves, good, not great speed, and was a vacuum cleaner when it came to catching the football. He was very precise. Andy was probably 6'3", 190 pounds, good size.

He caught a lot of deep balls. Everything to the inside was our favorite route because we didn't have an out route. They didn't think that was a good pass pattern to throw.

One of the memorable games was certainly against Notre Dame [28–8 win in 1971] against the All-America defensive back Clarence Ellis. Andy took him to school that day and caught two touchdowns against him. That was a big game in Tiger Stadium.

They tried to single cover Andy with Clarence Ellis, and that was a mistake. We had no qualms going after him. I don't know if they underestimated him, but they weren't able to cover Andy. That's not taking anything away from Clarence, because he is a wonderful player, but Andy just did a superb job that day.

Somebody just sent me a DVD of that Notre Dame game, which is the first time I have ever seen it. Most of it came back to me, some of it didn't. I was impressed by my first cousin, Andy, and his ability to get open. We only threw the ball 11 times and completed nine. He caught three touchdown passes.

The other game I remember was the last-second win against Ole Miss [17–16 in 1972]. We ran three plays in eight seconds, and Brad Davis caught a touchdown pass with time having expired.

We started the possession on our own 20. We had no timeouts. We finished the drive with one of the biggest plays ever in Tiger Stadium. They show that play along with the Billy Cannon [Halloween Night] runback against Ole Miss.

How do you run three plays in eight seconds? I guess it's running the clock with close kinfolk in Tiger Stadium. Everybody on the Ole Miss side said it was my brother. It was really my cousin running the clock. I'm just kidding.

"OK" Buddy Davis gave me the name the "Ruston Rifle," and he is still a sportswriter here. He is a wonderful writer and a good friend. I was a baseball pitcher in high school, and he tagged me with that. When I was a little leaguer, he came up to me and said, "You realize you pitched for two years without anybody getting a hit." He was one of the stat kind of guys. I hit a few with the ball, but nobody got a hit.

I certainly refined all my skill with my arm, but there were some good genes that were responsible. My father was an All-American who was the first flanker in the NFL and still holds the NFL record for touchdowns in one game [six]. My mother's father was an All-American at Tulane in both football and baseball. What made him unique was that he was ambidextrous.

The person who had the most profound influence on me at LSU was the legendary trainer, Dr. Marty Broussard. He was a renowned trainer. There were times when things were a little difficult for me, and he was there to counsel me.

I'm not complaining or casting blame or fault to anyone, and I'm not disgruntled, but there was a time when, actually to the bitter end, when I would play only half the time. That didn't seem very good to me. But they had great success at LSU doing it, so who am I to argue?

I felt like I was the player and wanted to be on the field. There was a point that I told myself that, even though I love LSU, my playing ability could be utilized better somewhere else. Marty was without question the man who was instrumental in squelching those thoughts.

He told me, "Bert, there is no question you could go anywhere else to school, wait a year, be a starter, and be successful. I know you too well, I know your family, I know you are going to live in Louisiana after football."

He encouraged me to grin and bear it and that I would be a better man even though I didn't play all the time.

So I stayed. He literally was the one person who kept me there. He shepherded me through to see a bigger picture. He said people might have understood eventually if I left LSU, but he was right. I was going to live in Louisiana and have a business and a life, and I needed to stay.

I had great success at LSU, even though I didn't play all the time. I cherish my time there, and if I could go back I wouldn't do anything differently. I would do it again tomorrow.

Marty could be mean as a snake, but he was truly a mentor for me. I did have knee surgery while I was there between my sophomore and junior year. He nurtured me back to good health. Marty did that for everyone there. He was truly a care-giving person. Underneath his being mean as a snake was the biggest heart you can imagine.

I am extremely proud to be part of a great school with people like Marty Broussard. It was a great athletic program and one with tremendous tradition, and I was part of it.

Bert Jones finished fourth in the balloting for the Heisman Trophy in 1972 as a senior and was named All-American and All-SEC, despite not being the full-time quarterback. He was the quarterback for the Tigers as a sophomore in 1970 when they won their first SEC championship since 1962. Jones was the first pick of the 1973 NFL Draft by the Baltimore Colts. Jones is third all-time in pass completions and passing yards in Colts history behind only Peyton Manning and the legendary Johnny Unitas. Jones currently owns a wood processing company outside his hometown of Ruston, Louisiana.

TYLER LaFAUCI

OFFENSIVE GUARD/
DEFENSIVE TACKLE

1971–1973

As a high school player coming up, I had never played football before. At all. Coming from Kenner and going to New Orleans and going to De la Salle, I had to sit out a year as a freshman. And then I found myself as a sophomore, for the first time in my life, playing a game I had been watching on TV all my life and wishing I was playing for the Green Bay Packers.

I didn't know what to think. I was overwhelmed. But what happened to me was instantly I realized that God had given me some talent, and I was really blessed with some natural ability to react and have some quickness in the line. I actually started as a defensive tackle on my high school football team the first time I played. I was excited, I mean, I was just really, really excited. I was so excited when the stuff came out in the paper. I got honorable mention for all-district, and that made my day. It just seemed to accelerate my junior year.

I started as an offensive guard and defensive tackle, and that's when my skills increased. I would have to stay I was very teachable because I realized all the guys who were coaching me knew a lot more than I did, and I grasped everything they were saying.

Then it just started happening on the field. By the time I was a senior, I was all-state and All-America, and I just amazed myself. I was the first person in

Tyler LaFauci played defense as a sophomore but moved over to offense as a junior and senior and was named All-America as an offensive guard in 1973 by the Associated Press, National Editorial Alliance, and Walter Camp.

my family to do anything athletically. I was the first one to go through college, and it was all through athletics, all through football.

Looking back, it was an exciting time in my life, but even though those things were happening to me in high school, I knew I could get better. I knew there was still stuff in me to progress, so I was excited to be able to sign with LSU.

I think the most influential guy to coach me in high school was a guy named Jimmy Stubbs. He was a lineman who played at McNeese. He was the first person in my life, football-wise, who taught me technique. It gave me a solid foundation and propelled me to doing the right thing.

I was even shorter in high school. Right now I'd say I'm 5′ 10″ at the most. My arms, I had that. I was just a squatty body. I had sprained my ankle in high school, and Coach Stubbs was doing the training, and he said, "Tyler, you know you don't really have an ankle. You just have a leg that's attached to your foot."

I was so close to going to Alabama. I actually wanted to go to Alabama, but my parents wanted me to go to LSU. The recruiting night, the night before signing day, Tulane, Alabama, and LSU came to our house, our little 900-square-foot house in Kenner. I knew I wasn't going to go to Tulane, but I felt that, living in New Orleans, I needed to listen. Then the Alabama guy came, and I was really excited about that. And then LSU came in. It was Coach McClendon, Barry Wilson (who was actually recruiting me), and Donald Ray Kennard, the academic advisor.

They sat down, and instead of getting a half hour, they got two and a half hours. I felt like I was in a Vietnamese prison camp. Everybody wanted me to go to LSU but me. He would say, "Son, we really want you to sign tomorrow." And I had a trip planned. I had never been out of town and had never been anywhere. I had a recruiting trip planned to Baylor.

It was unbelievable. Finally, two and a half hours later, my momma says, "Tyler, why don't you just sign tomorrow with LSU?" Okay, I'll sign.

It wasn't five minutes after they left that Coach Bryant called. I had visited Alabama, and they had offered me a scholarship in his office. I felt I had to come home and talk to my parents. But he called me five minutes after LSU left and told me he knew who had been there, but he really wanted me to sign with them, that I would be playing for them and the whole deal.

I was just sick about it, but I told him I just committed to LSU. He said, "Son, look, you're gonna be successful anywhere you go. I'm going to wish you the best of luck." And then he said, "I'll see you on Saturday night."

I hated to tell him no, but that's how I got to LSU. When I got to LSU, I was still in the developmental stages of football. I was still humble enough to realize that I was not up to par with the guys in college. I was just in awe of the opportunity to do this.

I thought you went to LSU to win and that these guys were going to be the best of the best. I was just in awe of getting on the field and getting to play. I was not a very confident guy going to LSU. But freshmen couldn't play. We practiced against the varsity, and they were pretty good. The previous year they held the rushing defense record. They allowed about 39 yards per game the previous year.

So I was practicing against guys like Mike Anderson, [Ronnie] Estay, and those guys, and it was a great experience.

I rolled that over into the spring, and it was the first time I was able to accelerate playing. I was second-team behind Mike Demarie. Then, during

111

the summer, they moved me to defensive tackle with [defensive line coach] Craig Randall, who was kind of crazy.

So here I was, second-team on the offensive line, and I knew I was going to play some. But they moved me because some guys quit and some got hurt, and it was like starting over. And college defense is a lot tougher than high school defense. Particularly on a defense of LSU's caliber. Plus Randall didn't really like me because I was too short. I wasn't the prototypical defensive lineman.

He was an ex-Marine and had some great ones. I'm over there, a midget. He called me "the midget." He told me to bring a box when I rushed the passer so I could stand on it to try to knock the ball down.

I wound up starting as right defensive tackle next to Ronnie Estay my sophomore year [1971]. I played through the experience, and it was something. I make the All-SEC sophomore team as a defensive tackle. My junior year they moved me back to offensive guard, and I was much more suited for that. I really could not see where the ball was as a defensive lineman. It was all instinct, because I couldn't see it. These guys were so big.

If I had stayed at defensive line, I would have played but I would not have excelled like I did on offense. My body structure, my center of gravity, just my ability as far as quickness goes—I was created to be an offensive lineman, an offensive guard. There was no question that I recognized that God gave me the ability to play offensive lineman, and so I tried to do everything in my power to respect that and to honor Him the way I played. That gave me motivation to be better. I didn't want to waste the talent and abilities He blessed me with.

I came to LSU with really no direction. I was the first one to come to college. My dad was a streetcar driver, and my momma was a bank teller. I had enrolled in business, then moved to education and was going on that coaching-teaching route. By sophomore year, though, I didn't think I would be as happy as I possibly could be going that route.

The thought went through my head that I had to make something of my life. So I went to visit Dr. [Marty] Broussard for some input, and he said there were two things I should consider: dental school and physical therapy. I visited with Francis Guglielmo, who was a physical therapy major and a student trainer with him, and got some input. Then I went to visit the people in Carville who were therapists. After that, I knew that was the direction I wanted to go in.

I went to Donald Ray Kennard and told him I wanted to change my schedule. And Donald Ray Kennard looked at me and said, "Son, I don't know if this is a very good route for you." I hadn't been a very good student up to that point. But I told him I really wanted to do it.

I walked out of his office and said to myself, *This is something I really want to do, and I'm going to do everything I need to do every inch of the way. And if I don't get in [to PT school] it won't be because I didn't try.* So I scheduled myself and took all these hard courses. I came back my junior year, and my life was basically go to school, practice, eat, and go to study hall. That was my life. The only time I didn't study was the Friday and Saturday before a game.

Everybody thought I was crazy. But I ended up making a 4.0 average with all those hard classes. And the next semester as well. My senior year, same thing, did great. I applied to physical therapy school in December, got in, in March, and started that June of 1974. Been doing it ever since, almost 35 years.

My sophomore year, we went to the Sun Bowl with Bert Jones, played Iowa State, and won. We beat Notre Dame that year, which was a great game. We had three goal-line stands against them. It was great. My junior year we were 6–0 and beat Ole Miss on the last play. We were 7–0 and played Alabama for the SEC championship [and lost 35–21]. The winner had the opportunity to play for the national championship.

113

My senior year, here we were again both 9–0, playing Alabama for the right to play for a national championship, and we lost that game, as well. Those were two tough games. But we had a great team.

I never talked to the Bear. I'd go on the field and make sure I'd see him, but I never did get a chance to talk to him.

My career was very satisfying. I hope today these guys understand what they have. It's hard to see it when you're going through it because you're so consumed with the football, with studies. It's consuming. I enjoyed it, but I know if I had been more mature I would have enjoyed it more.

Tyler LaFauci was named All-America as an offensive guard in 1973 by the Associated Press, National Editorial Alliance, and Walter Camp. He was also named All-SEC. LaFauci was part of an offensive line that led the Tigers to bowl games in 1972 and 1973. He played defense as a sophomore and was named to the SEC's All-Sophomore team. LaFauci is a physical therapist in Baton Rouge.

WARREN CAPONE

LINEBACKER

1971–1973

IT WAS AN UNBELIEVABLE TIME in my life. To dream about playing in Tiger Stadium and to have the opportunity to play with the guys I played with, it's just amazing how fortunate I feel. Some of the things that happened to me were so fortunate.

I really expected to be redshirted, but they moved somebody and made me a backup.

It was also such a unique time. We were there during desegregation. We had our first black player [Lora Hinton] join the team, which was pretty remarkable.

I remember when Alabama went to Southern Cal and got it handed to them. Bear Bryant was the leader and kind of dictated to the other SEC teams what would happen. When he brought in his first black player, it was just open for all the other schools.

It was probably the most unbelievable thing that could happen at that time. At least at LSU. Mike Williams came in right after that, and all those kids were well-received. All the things that people expected to happen never materialized. None of that happened. They were accepted and were good athletes and held up their own and did well. You have to believe that the coaches had a big part in that, but we never had meetings about it. I guess the way the coaches went about it was they didn't make a big deal about it, and neither did we.

Warren Capone was an All-America linebacker in 1972 and 1973 and was first-team All-SEC in 1972 and 1973.

In my sophomore year, 1972, we played Wisconsin. When we got there, we got chastised. Integration up there had been going on for a while. But it was new in the Deep South. But somehow or another, we found a way to win. That game opened our eyes a lot to what was going on in the country, and it was a very unique time to be at LSU.

At the same time, it proved to be a great time. We all enjoyed, black or white, the success we had during that period. From 1969 to 1973 without a doubt were Coach Mac's golden years.

The talent level was the highest for the time he was there. We had guys like Tommy Casanova, Bert Jones, and Mike Williams. We were roommates the entire time we were at LSU. He was a tremendous leader. We remain very close. And for both of us our senior year to make All-America, being roommates the entire time, must be pretty unique. They don't do it anymore, but with kids living in dorms I don't believe two guys living together four years and getting All-America honors, that couldn't have happened any other time.

Nineteen seventy-one was the year of Notre Dame. Everybody had that game highlighted. We played them in 1970, my freshman year, and lost to them up there. In 1971 those seniors, Casanova and that group, made this their game. The heart of the season was built around preparing for that game. We prepared for that game a couple of weeks prior to playing them. We started going over Notre Dame stuff. The coaches took a risk there.

It was a game that everyone was waiting for, and everyone knew what was at stake.

We were prepared like no other game. I never watched more film on a team than I watched on Notre Dame. We understood what they did. The buildup to that game was unbelievable. Someone even went to the dioceses here, the Catholic parish, to find out if it was okay to say, "Go to hell, Notre Dame!" And they gave us permission. That was what we said to Ole Miss— "Go to hell, Ole Miss!"

At that time it was probably the biggest win since they won the national championship [in 1958]. It was, without a doubt, my coming-out party. First of all, I had a veteran senior in front of me, Louis Cascio. He and I had split time. I got into the game, and on the first series I intercepted a pass. The coaches obviously thought I was the hot player, so I stayed in and had eight tackles, about five assists, and intercepted another pass. Without a doubt, it was the game for me to let everybody know there was another linebacker at LSU. You had George Bevan in '69, Mike Anderson in '70, and then in '72 and '73 I was first-team All-America. We were producing some pretty good linebackers during that era.

The Ole Miss game my junior year, that was Bert Jones' pass to Brad Davis. I had a phenomenal game as far as tackles and a couple on blitzes. It was a game of so many ups and downs. Late in that game we knew we had to stop Ole Miss to win the game. They had to go three and out. We knew Ole Miss would be pretty conservative.

We went out there and did exactly what we had to do. They ran the ball three times in a row. They had been moving the ball pretty well. We made some adjustments. It didn't slow them down that much but slowed them down enough.

But it was now or never. Three plays and out, and Bert moved the ball down the field. With one second left, Bert connected with Brad in the end zone.

My senior year was a great year. I led the team in tackling and had my share of interceptions and fumble recoveries and those types of things. We had some good football players around me. Freshman A.J. Duhe and Steve Cassidy, who turned out to be great football players, made the plays and made my job so much easier.

The biggest problem we had my senior year was we didn't rise to the occasion when we needed to, and that was mainly the Alabama game, which was moved to a Friday night game right after Thanksgiving. First time they had ever done that. It was a tremendous battle and a game that was much closer than the score. Give Alabama credit. We lost the game 21–7, but on two occasions we had a DB fall down, and they scored off of that. We didn't have that happen the entire season, and it happened twice. Give them credit, but it was a game we should have won and probably the most disappointing loss of my career.

We went to great bowls—the Sun Bowl my sophomore year to play Iowa State. Then we went to the Astrodome and played Tennessee. Our offense didn't come to play. We lost 24–17. We dominated them but could not make enough plays to win. The last year we played Penn State in the Orange Bowl. A great game. We lost 16–9 but should have won.

We won nine games every year when we only played 10 or 11 games and were nationally ranked every year. My senior year in '73 was probably the biggest fall. We were ranked about No. 4 in the country but lost our last three games and finished around 13th or 14th.

I can't put into words what it has meant to me to play at LSU. It was a dream come true and was a tremendous thing that my parents and brothers and family as a whole took a lot of pride in. And to have been able to do the things I was able to do was very humbling, because God blessed me.

Warren Capone was an All-America linebacker in 1972 and 1973. A Baton Rouge native, Capone played in three bowl games and was first-team All-SEC in 1972 and 1973. Capone played in the World Football League and in the NFL for the Dallas Cowboys. He is a high school football coach in Baton Rouge.

A.J. DUHE

DEFENSIVE TACKLE

1973–1976

I TELL PEOPLE I GOT RECRUITED by LSU by mistake. They were there looking at this great All-America offensive lineman. I happened to play against him the day they were there, and I took him to town. The next thing you know, they were forgetting about him and looking at the kid who just beat him up.

When you come from a school that is that bad—and my school was not good in football—you are on nobody's radar. Colleges are probably thinking, *If your school was 2–8 last year, 1–9 this year, who on that team can be any good?* It's like when they found Jerry Rice. You have to do homework to find good players, or find them by accident, like me.

I moved around in high school, from position to position on defense. If the other school had a strong center, I was nose tackle. If they had a strong outside linebacker, I was playing tight end. I mostly played offensive line and defensive line. We still lost.

I was getting recruited by some smaller schools in Louisana, what is now Louisiana-Lafayette, Louisiana Tech, Tulane. I didn't have any out-of-state schools looking at me. I was not a blue-chip prospect.

I am a couple of nickels short of 6′4″ and left high school weighing 225 to 228 pounds. I went to LSU and put on a few pounds and did some weight work.

When I played in the Louisiana all-star game early in the summer just after my senior year, I was the MVP on defense. Coach Mac came down to see me and said, "Son, I am going to give you a chance to play, go home and work hard." He inspired me and motivated me.

Coach Mac was kind of an intimidating guy to be around because you were this kid who grew up listening to LSU football on the radio and here you were now in the presence of a historical figure. My roots taught me to respect adults, and I respected him for that reason, but also because he was a big man and the LSU coach.

The best thing about committing before the end of my senior football season was I got to go to more games at LSU. I was the type of kid who sat in front of the radio on Saturday night and listened to the Tigers. Once LSU made a decision to offer me a scholarship, they were letting me come see them every weekend.

If you are from a high school 45 minutes away, and you can see the team every week, you jump at the chance. I was like a season-ticket holder when they asked me to come play for them my senior year in high school. I was tickled pink. Having a dad who was a big LSU fan and uncles who were fans, and my little town was a strong LSU town, purple and gold all over, I was into it.

I always followed the quarterback and wanted to be the quarterback. When I was a kid, before I got too big, I was the quarterback. Then I got so big and had to play the line. I liked to watch Bert Jones, and I admired Tommy Casanova.

In high school, I probably dominated every game I played in, and maybe I could have gone and got more publicity playing at one of the Catholic schools in the city. But that was a long drive away. Maybe I could have been one of those sought-after players, but was I out in the bayou, and my mom didn't want to send me 20 miles away.

When I got to LSU, I was No. 3 on the depth chart for a couple of days and then moved to No. 2. The guy ahead of me was the starter from the previous year. So I played in the first two games, Colorado and Texas A&M, as a part-timer. But in the third game I started against Rice and started every game after that.

I got a couple of sacks against Rice. That was a big thing for me because they had Tommy Kramer at quarterback, and he threw the ball all over the

A.J. Duhe was All-SEC in 1976 as a defensive tackle and became a first-round pick of the Miami Dolphins in the 1977 draft, the 13th pick overall.

place. I had a big edge because they were going back to pass with an offensive line that was not so good, so I could rush hard.

I was just 17 years old and made All-SEC Freshman team, so I was happy. I didn't turn 18 until after the last game of the regular season.

That was the year we started 9–0. There were all kinds of undefeated teams in 1973. We were 9–0 and just No. 7 in the country because of Penn State, Ohio State, Oklahoma. Then we lost to Alabama [21–7] in a big, nationally televised game. Then we lost to Tulane 14–0, and we hadn't done that in a long time.

We ended up losing the last three games of the season, including the Orange Bowl to Penn State. We held down John Cappelletti, their big running back, and still lost [16–9].

For a freshman, I was thinking I was blessed to be in that situation, part of a nine-win team. The seniors, I'm sure, were disappointed after going 9–0, and they felt like their hard work didn't result in the national championship they wanted. But for me, I thought this was great—*I get three more years at this place*. I was thanking God I had a chance to do what I wanted to do.

The next two years we were very average [5–5–1 in 1974 and 5–6 in 1975]. I think it could have had something to do with the fact that when I was at LSU there were very few African American players in our program. If you looked around the rest of the SEC, they had better players, more African Americans. More and more schools were receptive to African American players; that's being realistic.

121

Then we got a kid like Mike Williams, who was a stud, lock-down corner, an All-American. When you are 18, 19, 20 years old, you are not paying attention to that stuff, you know, who was black, who was white. Then you look back and you kind of see some differences in programs.

Look at Tennessee. We had maybe six African Americans on our team, and they have 17, guys like Condredge Holloway and Stanley Morgan. They were playing skill positions and had more speed. When they had much better athletes, it made it harder to compete. That's as honest as I can be.

My junior year in 1975 was disappointing because I dislocated my ankle and missed four or five games. It was against Rice, the third game of the season.

My senior year we opened the season with No. 1 Nebraska in Tiger Stadium, and it was a pretty intense night. We tied them 6–6.

My wife created a little room in our house where she put all my mounted trophies and framed pictures. One of my favorite pictures was of me running out of the tunnel in Tiger Stadium before the Nebraska game. I was jumping up three and a half feet in the air. I remember that game.

We thought about that game in spring practice. Being seniors, we probably started having those feelings about what we wanted to accomplish. We had been average, middle-of-the-pack for a couple of years. Nebraska was a way to open up some eyes and get some attention, and I think we did.

It was a pretty intense night in that stadium. When you went to the sideline you could hear it in there, and if you made a bad play, they sure as hell knew how to tell you.

We lost to nationally ranked teams that year, Alabama and Florida. And we lost to Kentucky, which had a great defensive end, Art Still, who played in the NFL a long time with the Chiefs. He was an All-American.

We played against a lot of wishbone teams, so I was not a guy who collected a lot of stats like sacks. I was a grinder and didn't stand out.

I made it as a first-round pick for the Dolphins because of the work I did in the all-star games and the work with Coach [Don] Shula and the staff at the Senior Bowl. There was not a lot of recognition for me then, but they saw something in these all-star-game workouts that they liked and picked me.

It made an impression on them how hard I worked. I was tabbed as a second-round pick. The guys who were named All-America had the statistics, the sacks, the tackles. We played against teams that ran the veer and we had to eat up blocks and keep the offensive linemen from getting to our linebackers, so I didn't have sacks.

There was no NFL combine back then. Coach Mac or our position coach would come into the lunch room on Monday in the spring and pull out five or six guys and say, "Thursday the Cowboys, Packers, and Rams will be here, and they want to see you work out."

I still stay connected after I left LSU. In fact, the school called me about Coach [Bill] Arnsparger and said they were considering him for the LSU head-coaching job [1984]. I was playing for the Dolphins, and he was my coach. That was a sad day for me—I didn't want to lose him. I had to make a great referral, he was a terrific coach. Here I was playing for the guy and my school wanted him.

They got a guy who knew football. He brought in a bunch of young, aggressive coaches, guys like Mike Archer, and Arnsy won a lot of games for

LSU. When he went to people's homes and met with parents, they felt like their kid was in good hands.

Arnsy is a brilliant football coach. I had to recommend him to the job to Bob Brodhead, who was the athletic director. Bob worked for the Dolphins and knew what Arnsy could do. The program had soured a little bit when he took over, but he got it back on track, and then it soured again. Archer did well for a while, and then when Hallman came in, it soured. Mike Archer is a solid football coach, so I don't know what happened with him there.

My daughter is going to school there next year, and I'm tickled about that. Both of my boys didn't have interest in LSU, but she was taken with it. My wife will be up there once a month, and I'll probably get up there and see a game a couple of times a year.

For so long, all people had to grab onto with sports was LSU football. The Saints did not come in until the 1960s, so for 60 to 70 years the fans poured themselves into it. You don't want to box in all people from Louisiana as being rabid Tiger fans—they have other interests—but there sure are a lot of them who love the football as much as their profession.

A.J. Duhe was All-SEC in 1976 as a defensive tackle and became a first-round pick of the Miami Dolphins in 1977, the 13th pick overall. He played in Miami for eight seasons. Duhe was AFC Rookie of the Year in 1977 and made the Pro Bowl in 1984. He works in south Florida for Harrah's Entertainment. Duhe has been in the casino business for 20 years.

CHARLES ALEXANDER

RUNNING BACK

1975–1978

I DON'T HAVE VERY MANY RECORDS LEFT, but there are a couple, most yards in a season [1,686] and most carries in one game [43]. There were great backs that came after me like Dalton Hilliard and Kevin Faulk, so the records were bound to fall.

We did not pass the ball much when I played. We ran it, and I got a lot of chances to run with the ball. We also had some very good offensive lines when I played, and I knew who was doing the hard work up front for me.

It was enjoyable, but I'm paying for it now. My junior year [1977] I carried the ball a lot and averaged 150 yards per game. That game where I had 43 carries [Wyoming, 1977], I only played three quarters. We were running the ball three out of every four downs.

Coach Mac really put himself on the line for me in that game because he wanted me to set a record. The other coach, I think it was Bill Lewis, was pretty angry that Coach Mac put me back in the game like that to set a record.

I was a four-year letterman, but I just started the last two years. I played behind Terry Robiskie my first two years. He was a big back, so he would wear them down, and then I would come in and get at them when they tired from trying to tackle him. My first start was against Indiana. I was very anxious and a little nervous. I had played a lot when Terry was there, but starting was different. I was anxious to start.

Charles Alexander holds the LSU record for most rushing yards in one season with 1,686, most carries in a season, 311, and most rushing attempts in a game with 43.

Back then I was considered a big back, 6'1", 220 pounds. That might be about normal now, but back in those days it was considered a big back. I was a slasher and relied on my speed a lot. I was not a dancer; it was one cut and go downhill.

It was man-on-man blocking. The play might be designed to go off tackle, but I had the freedom to pretty much bounce it wherever I saw daylight.

The reason I went to LSU was that I wanted to be an I formation tailback. I would watch Southern Cal on TV when I was a kid and saw Anthony Davis and O.J. Simpson running in the I formation as tailbacks, and that's what I wanted to do. LSU recruited me heavily, and that was one of the selling points, along with playing on grass and playing in front of a big crowd.

I had some good fullbacks blocking for me. My junior year I had Kelly Simmons, who was 5'10" and 185 pounds, which was small, except they didn't make a football player any tougher than that guy. He was tough.

My senior year I had the guy I know everybody has heard of—Hokie Gajan. What a player he was. A good fullback and a good runner. His name speaks for itself. He wasn't the biggest guy, but he would chop them down.

My favorite play was student body right and anything off tackle. You had three options off tackle. You could bounce it, you could go where the hole is supposed to be, or you could cut it back.

I had a lot of chances to play my sophomore year, even though I wasn't the starter. I had 800 yards rushing that second season at LSU so I knew what I was getting into. I was excited about carrying the ball a little more my junior year. I enjoyed getting the pigskin in my hands as often as I could.

When you are young you can bounce back eventually. The day after a game I could barely walk, but then I would get in the whirlpool and treatment, and my body would start to bounce back on that Sunday.

By Monday, I was good as new. *Let's do it again.* There was only that one day where I had the soreness, which was Sunday.

My first big game was my junior year at nighttime against Florida in Baton Rouge [170 yards, 31 attempts]. They were highly ranked [No. 9], but we beat them [36–14]. We ran the ball pretty well on them. You have to understand about that offensive line. One guy became a dentist. Two others are orthopedic surgeons. There is an architect and another is a successful salesman. They used to call those guys the Root Hogs, modeled after the Hogs that played for the Washington Redskins' Super Bowl teams. Our hogs were very smart guys and worked hard. A lot of my success I attribute to them.

I had a nickname. The guys called me "Sweet." We had a scrimmage when I was a freshman, and I broke off a run and somebody said, "Man, that was a sweet run," and the name "Sweet" just stuck with me for the rest of my career. The guys still call me that.

I was not that highly recruited out of high school because I played on a lot of average high school teams and played under three different head coaches. I had more success in track and field. I was a big kid who could run. There were just five or six schools that recruited me.

I didn't decide between LSU and the University of Houston until national signing day. Back then, the coaches could be at your home at signing day and get your signature.

In my mind, on national signing day, I was going to go to school and have the day to make up my mind. But when I walked outside my door that morning, there was coach Bill Yeoman of Houston and coach Jerry Stovall of LSU sitting in their cars waiting for me.

I had to make up my mind real quick. I had to fish or cut bait.

I walked to Coach Yeoman's car and thanked him for the opportunity to go to Houston and then jumped in the car with Coach Stovall. He drove me to school, and I signed. Coach Stovall was the running backs coach. If Coach Stovall had not been at LSU, I would have gone to Houston.

Houston ran the Houston Veer, which is geared toward backs that are 5′10″. I didn't think I could perform as well in that offense. They called them the Cotton Pickin' Cougars for going to the Cotton Bowl one year.

Playing in Tiger Stadium and on grass was a selling point, and I was comfortable with the academic atmosphere and with the players and coaches. I liked the weather and playing in front of 65,000 to 70,000 people.

I knew I was in the big time when we played at Nebraska [No. 6] my freshman season. I remember that as clear as any game. I made the traveling team as a true freshman and was scared to death. They had 75,000 people in red and white in their stadium. If I was on any kind of emotional high playing in my first game, that ended pretty quickly. The second quarter Coach McClendon told me I was going to be in the game. It brought me down to earth. Eight carries, −8 yards. I hardly made it back to the line of scrimmage. I wondered if I belonged.

I remember Coach McClendon telling me, "It's going to get better," and I looked up at him thinking, *You gotta be kidding*. My confidence was crushed. I didn't know what was going to happen in my career after that.

We had Rice on the schedule in Shreveport. I had some good carries in that game and 30 or 40 yards, so that made me feel better.

The last game of my freshman year we played Tulane. I got two touchdowns, and that boosted my confidence. My freshman year I just averaged 2.8 yards a carry, so it was a long year. After that year, with the help of the coaches and offensive line, I took off.

My sophomore year I averaged 5.7 yards a carry. My junior year was a dream season for me, and senior season I did okay. I made All-America my senior year, but my yards-per-carry average wasn't as high.

I wore No. 4 throughout my career, and there is a story to that. I chose No. 4 because in my senior year in high school I was the state champion in the 100-yard dash. I ran in lane 4 and won the state championship in lane 4, so I wanted to stick with that number.

This was after I was told I could not have my high school number, which was 20.

I went up to the equipment manager before the start of the season and said I would like No. 20. He just laughed at me and said, "You don't know your LSU history. No. 20 is Billy Cannon's number. You can't have No. 20."

Billy told me later, "Man, if I had known you were going to be that successful, I would have brought that number out of retirement."

I ran what would be a 4.3-second 40 in my day, and Baylor and Arkansas recruited me, as well as LSU and Houston. I also took a look at UCLA because my dad was living out in Los Angeles at the time. They said I would have to pay my own way, and that was not going to happen because my family did not have that kind of money.

My relatives are still amazed at how well all the Cajuns treated them and how much they loved to tailgate and party. That was some experience in the stands. My family was looked upon as celebrities—the red carpet was thrown out for them, and they were treated very well.

There was no hint of any racism, none we could see. We did not have as many black players as other teams in the SEC. We had eight to nine on the entire team, while others had 18 or 19 back in 1976 and 1977.

I remember Lora Hinton, the first black player, No. 24. He was a very good running back, but had a knee injury, and I don't know if he ever recuperated from that. It was serious, and he never got it back.

We all knew he was the first black player, but the subject did not come up when we would be alone and playing cards. I never heard anyone say anything about prejudice at LSU. Coach Mac would not have put up with it, and they knew not to go there. I can't think of any problems I had when I was there.

Coach Mac was a great coach who stuck his neck out for me a couple of times. He got criticized for some things he did for me. I love him to death. There was one game in particular—we were playing Wyoming—I had three touchdowns and had been sitting on the bench for over a quarter because we were winning by a lot. Coach Mac saw us get to the goal line and let me go in to score a touchdown to break a record.

I remember the Wyoming coach saying that he couldn't believe Coach McClendon put me back in the game. He said he wished I had broken my leg.

Coach Mac would still call on us periodically to make sure we were doing all right. When I was cut from the Cincinnati Bengals after playing there seven years, Coach Mac made several calls to see if I could get on another team. I found that out later; he didn't tell me he was doing it. There was nothing in it for him. He was genuinely concerned about his players.

He set up that Charles McClendon Scholarship Fund for the children of his former players. He would do all he could to help players.

Coach Mac had this look where you knew not to step out of line. I don't remember him as a big yeller or screamer. You got warned once, then paid the price.

LSU is a special place. I owe a lot of the little success I have had in life in going to LSU. I'm proud of what they have accomplished in the last few years with the national championships.

Charles Alexander, born and raised in Galveston, was the prototypical I formation back with power and speed. He holds the LSU record for most rushing yards in one season with 1,686, most carries in a season, 311, and most rushing attempts in a game with 43. He is third all-time in rushing yards for a career with 4,035 and averaged 4.7 yards per rush for his career. Alexander played for the Cincinnati Bengals in the NFL. He lives in Houston and works in the oilfield business.

ROBERT DUGAS

TACKLE

1976–1978

W<small>E WERE IN PRACTICE ONE DAY</small>, and we used to do a drill where we would come out of our stance and drive a big blocking dummy that was laid down on the ground. It was a goal-line drill, and whoever got low on the goal line won. We were taught to stay down low and push the dummy.

Well, one practice we had a wet day, and the defensive line coach, Lynn LeBlanc, was making fun of us, saying, "Look at those guys rooting around in the mud like a bunch of hogs." We adopted the name Root Hogs, and it stuck with us.

Fortunately, we had a running back who made everybody pay attention to us also. Charlie Alexander had a couple of great years [1977 and 1978].

The Hogs were: myself at right tackle, Chris Rich at left tackle, Craig Duhe at left guard, and Jay Whitley at center. Lou DeLaunay played some line, and the other guy was William Johnson.

We included a tight end in the Root Hogs because, back then with LSU, the tight end did not catch balls, and that was Cliff Lane. We made the fullback, Kelly Simmons, an Honorary Root Hog. He probably broke Charlie on those longer runs. Once you get outside, the fullback's block at the point of attack is the block that breaks you.

Charlie was not the little guy who could run the ball. He was the big guy who could run the football. He was 6′1″, 215 pounds, and fast. If he could run a 4.4 30 years ago, that was fast.

Charlie's toughness and size made him a great back, and people didn't expect a guy that big to be that fast. You didn't catch him. Once we got him broke through the line, he would run over a defensive back. If they tried to wave at him, he would run past them. They couldn't get close to putting a hand on him.

We saw a lot of eight-man lines. If we threw the ball 15 times a game, the quarterbacks were ecstatic. Third down was a draw play for us, our version of the pass. Every now and then we would try and surprise somebody with play-action. I don't even know if we had a drop-back pass in our playbook. If we had it, we didn't use it much.

I played around 265 pounds, 270, and I was 6'4". I only played against two people bigger than me my whole career. I was considered humongous. Today, at 265, they wouldn't have asked us to play. Chris was 255, Craig Duhe was 230, Jay Whitley 230-ish, and William Johnson 220.

My strength as a player was my preparation and using intelligence to know what was going to happen before the snap. We were restricted on blocking. We couldn't extend our arms to block. Today, it is a whole different ballgame. Now you can tackle them and throw them around.

We had our fists into the shoulder pads and chicken wings for arms, and we would try and shield people. That's why we did so much run blocking. It was difficult to pass block. If the referees saw you with your arms extended, it was a penalty.

The game that sticks out for me was the Florida game my junior season when we beat them [36–14]. They were ranked in the top 10, and we were playing at home. They had Wes Chandler, who was the version of Percy Harvin of today. We controlled the ball and had it two-thirds of the day. We would keep it eight or nine minutes, and they ran something like 35 plays the whole game.

That was the week when I was named National Lineman of the Week. That was unheard of back then. I was told it had never gone to an offensive lineman before. It brought light on the offensive line. Charlie was making us famous, and we were making him more famous.

It was power football. It was straight on, create holes for the back. I-right-24 was a favorite play, and Charlie was pretty much going to the 4 hole. If we went backside, it was 25. It stayed pretty much where it was called, and we tried to create the hole. When the veer came along, a lot of blocking changed. It was all zone, and they asked the running back to find the crease.

The run we gained more yards on was the pitch play, and that's when the fullback came in. The tight end, tackle, and guard sealed. It was the widest play we called. If we looked at the average gain per play, that one gave us the long runs, but we popped some up the middle, too.

There was one we got up the middle on Ole Miss [a 30–8 win]. My center friend, Jay Whitley, as we were putting them away, tapped one of the Ole Miss guys on the head and laughed and got an unsportsmanlike penalty.

We really enjoyed beating Ole Miss because we never could get it together to beat the Bear and Alabama. That was probably the one we wanted the most. We would play Ole Miss soon after the loss to Alabama, and we would take it out on them since we couldn't beat the Bear.

We always played them in Birmingham. My junior year we were about to get a lead on them, but Coach Bryant's presence started taking over the game. It was happening everywhere around us [with the officiating]. Alabama didn't lose that many games that decade.

Cholly Mac didn't struggle with many teams, but he struggled with Alabama.

I guess people look at the Ole Miss–LSU rivalry as having gone away a little bit. We had a downturn there for six or seven years, and so did they, but we have climbed back out of those doldrums.

The one rivalry that has disappeared is the in-state rivalry with Tulane. We looked forward to playing Tulane, but that is one of those sleepy games for them today. It's one of those we have to go play and make sure nothing bad happens.

There was not as much national recruiting back in the '50s and '60s. Kids stayed in state, so Tulane and LSU recruited against each other. We never had many out-of-state players.

When I was a senior in high school [1973] and LSU played Tulane in the old Sugar Bowl, I went to the game as a Tulane recruit knowing full well that I was just going to go to the game. I was going to play at LSU. I came from more of a Tulane family, but for whatever reason I would always go grab the radio and listen to the LSU games.

The night I was at the Tulane-LSU game was the first time in 25 years Tulane won. LSU had been 9–0, lost to Alabama, and then had to play Tulane. The Tigers were in the doldrums after losing to Alabama and lost 14–0. Tulane put it on them. LSU had lost a chance at the SEC championship and did not recover [LSU lost its last three games of the 1973 season].

It was a big celebration for them. The Tulane recruiters said to me, "What do you think? We've beaten the Tigers. Come play for us and help us do that some more." I had to go along with the recruiting scenario that night.

It became a contest between Tulane and LSU over the next few years. It was a local rivalry to watch. Fortunately, we were 5–0 when I was there. I was a redshirt.

In my senior year, the game I think about the most is the loss to Georgia [24–17] in Baton Rouge. We led 14–10 at halftime, and Lindsey Scott ran back the opening kickoff of the second half. He was 6'3" or 6'4" and he could run. It deflated us. We had been 4–0, then lost.

Erk Russell, the Georgia defensive coordinator, played a 4-4 defense and hid their linebackers. We could never get our running game going.

Those two seasons, 1977 and 1978, we lost bowl games. We lost to Guy Benjamin and Stanford in 1977. In 1978 we lost to Missouri. They had quarterback Phil Bradley, tight end Kellen Winslow, and James Wilder, a good running back who played Sundays.

We blame that Missouri game on LSU's bending to that passing game. We were ahead at halftime and suddenly started throwing it all over the place in the second half. We, as the offensive line, were upset about that. We got it turned around on us.

133

The fan story that comes to me is from Lincoln, Nebraska, where I lived for 16 years. I was one of the team physicians at the University of Nebraska from 1990 to 2006. The College World Series is in Nebraska, and LSU had great baseball teams, so Omaha would become LSU north for the two weeks.

The town took hold of the LSU fans and teams when they got there. The Huskers loved the LSU tailgating, and the city is disappointed when LSU doesn't make it to Omaha. They have a different bottom line for the restaurants and bars; they don't make as much money if the Tigers don't make it.

They take stuff off the walls and put up LSU stuff if the Tigers make it to Omaha. They don't sell as much food or alcohol if all the coon asses don't show up in Omaha. If it is Cal State playing Florida State, it is not nearly as much interest as when LSU is in the stadium. The LSU football mentality gets transferred to baseball.

The other thing I remember about the passion of fans is Big Red. He was this guy we never saw, but we heard. On Thursdays he would pull up in his camper while we were out practicing and start cheering behind the fence. "Here we go, Tigers, here we go!" He was one of the first tailgaters who began showing up and hanging around. The coaches knew him; they didn't mind.

For me, being a Tiger is people like Big Red, and it means having a huge family that would be there if you needed them. It includes coaches and players of your time, but other players who are now in the LSU fraternity. You could ask fans for anything you needed.

Robert Dugas was named All-America as an offensive tackle in 1978 by *The Football News*. He was also named to the CoSida Academic All-America team in 1977 and was All-SEC in 1977 and 1978. Dugas was part of an offensive line, the Root Hogs, that paved the way for running back Charles Alexander to become, at the time, LSU's all-time leading rusher. LSU led the SEC in rushing yards in 1977, averaging 304 yards per game, which is sixth best in the 60 years the SEC has kept the statistic. Dugas is an orthopedic surgeon in Baton Rouge.

The
EIGHTIES

LEONARD MARSHALL

DEFENSIVE TACKLE

1979–1982

W E WERE WALKING OFF THE FIELD at halftime of the Alabama game my senior season [1982], and I was walking with Pete Jenkins, the defensive line coach, who was a great defensive line coach. And Coach said to me, "Big Cheese"—he always called me Big Cheese—"listen to Bear Bryant giving Mal Moore a hard time."

We listened, and Bear was telling Moore, the offensive coordinator, "If you don't find a way to get that goddamned No. 97 blocked, I'm going to put you on their sideline."

I loved that Alabama game. We beat them 20–10. It was the game I remember most. Coach Jenkins told me I tackled their whole backfield in one play. I knocked out the quarterback. I think they had negative yardage in the first half.

It would have been a better season if we hadn't lost all those close games. We lost three games by seven points the last part of the season, three points to Mississippi State, three to Tulane, and one to Nebraska in the Orange Bowl, 21–20. They beat us and won the national championship.

I am from Franklin, Louisiana, and we had more NFL players come out of Franklin than any other small town in the state of Louisiana. Guys like Clinton Burrell, Ernie Ladd, Wallace Francis, Lyman White, Jim Files, and others. Must have been the water.

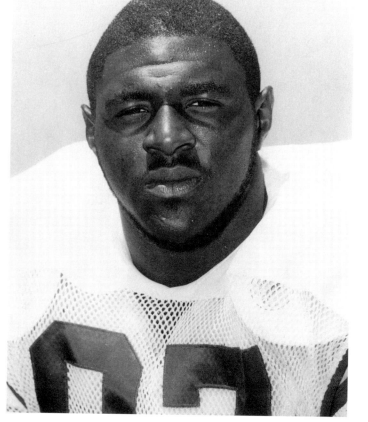

Leonard Marshall signed a Big 8 letter-of-intent to attend the University of Oklahoma, but Charlie McClendon turned him back toward LSU.

I got recruited by a lot of different schools and actually signed a Big 8 letter-of-intent to go to Oklahoma. Barry Switzer was at my parents' house, and I was so impressed by the Selmon brothers—Lee Roy, Lucious, and Dewey—that I thought I had to go there.

So I took the trip to OU, and my roommate on the visit was the running back, Eric Dickerson. On the trip I was saying to myself, *Leonard, you've got to do this*. A gentleman from Lafayette named Rick Roundtree, who was an oil and gas guy, and an OU guy, took us to Norman in a private jet.

I got a chance to meet Billy Sims and J.C. Watts, and they treated me with respect. I met Steve Owens, who was a Heisman Trophy winner. When I left, I signed a Big 8 letter-of-intent, and that was that…until this guy named Charlie McClendon came to see me. His hat was cocked to the side, there was a toothpick in his mouth. He said, "You got to stay here with me and come to school in Baton Rouge, boy. This is where you need to be, son." Cholly Mac won me over.

It killed me to see what happened to that man when he got older as the head coach. It killed me, and it was a tough time. That is the politics of big-time college sports. I was there just one season with him before he left as head coach.

But at least before he left I got to play for him in one of the most famous games on a Saturday night in Louisiana, and that was against Southern Cal. They were No. 1 in the country, and we gave them all they wanted. They beat us 17–12, but it was a moral victory because a much bigger program came into Baton Rouge. The SEC back then wasn't quite like it is today. We were smaller, and we battled them.

We got beat by Alabama 3–0 in the "Mud Bowl." We played in the Tangerine Bowl that year and beat Wake Forest 34–10. Those are the three games I remember. It was the senior year of some terrific LSU people like Hokie Gajan and Carlos Carson and Robert Dugas and Lyman White. David Woodley, John Ed Bradley, and Steve Emsinger were also on that team.

Alabama was No. 1 late in the season, and Southern Cal was No. 1 early in the season when we played them. I'll never forget the center at Alabama was Dwight Stephenson, the All-Pro who played for the Dolphins. Jim Bunch was the guard, and I just tried to level them on every play.

I was 6'3", 245 pounds, and they had me playing linebacker and defensive tackle. I was standing up in the inside and playing on the ground. I did both.

I knew I could play at that level and knew I wanted to make an impact at LSU. The best thing that could have happened to me was when they brought in Pete Jenkins, who was a really good defensive line coach. He is the bomb, brother. I never worked with a guy who knew defensive line play like he did, from a tactical and professional standpoint. He was a motivator, a creator, a teacher.

The only guy I worked with who was close to Pete was Lamar Leachman, who was a friend of Pete's and was a defensive line coach at the Giants.

We had a heck of a staff, a staff that came in with Bo Rein, who was killed in a plane crash just after he was named coach. Mack Brown of Texas ran the quarterbacks and the offense. George Belu was the offensive line coach. Pete got there with Bo Rein and stayed on the staff after Bo died.

The only season I really regretted was my junior season when we won just three games. That was 1981, and we were horrible. We didn't have kids who could play. We had some talent. We weren't strong enough. When Johnny Parker left LSU as the strength and conditioning coach, it hurt us. Guys worked out, they were ready for games.

When Jerry Stovall took over, we had a lot of guys who didn't want to go to class, they didn't want to train, they just wanted to party. These guys did not respect the system or the process to get better. He ran off a lot of players.

LSU had to find itself again, and it created a huge problem. Do what you are supposed to do when you are supposed to it. We didn't do those things, and Stovall ran off a lot of football players. He ran off the party boys.

The next season, 1982, things were much better. What did we lose? Three games, but by what, seven points? By three to Mississippi State, three to Tulane, and one to Nebraska. I was Defensive Player of the Year, and it was all because I put so much into that season. I was doing everything I could to lead by example, every ounce of energy I could muster. I took everything from Pete Jenkins and soaked it up. First guy to study hall, last guy to leave. First guy to practice, last guy to leave.

I loved that team. I wasn't the best student, but I tried hard. I might not have been the best teammate, but I tried hard. I wanted to lead by example. I tried to make work ethic a calling card.

Lawrence Williams was my roommate and a great kid. The turmoil of life got him. He went to prison. I think he is out now. You don't forget guys like Lawrence Williams. I get chillbones thinking about that team and guys like him. As close as my New York Giants teams were when we won our championships, that LSU team I played on was that close.

The games I remember that 1982 season? I tried to beat Alabama by myself in Tuscaloosa. They were in the top 10, and we beat them 20–10. They didn't know who the opponent really was; they were getting into a fight with somebody they didn't know.

There was another game against Ole Miss when we beat them 45–8—and we gave them those eight points. They had −22 yards of offense.

I look back at that whole year, and there was a lot of character on that team. It was a close-knit group. Alan Risher was the quarterback, and he wasn't going to lose the game for us. We had a pair of running backs who could run with anybody, Garry James and Dalton Hilliard. We had a kid named Eric Martin, who was a very good receiver.

I guess the one game that sticks out as a disappointment was the loss to Nebraska in the Orange Bowl. If we hadn't botched a punt, we would've won the game. We were winning 17–14, but they got a lot of pressure on our punter, stopped us, and went in for the winning score.

Nebraska had the best offense in the country that season, but we didn't go just to be in the Orange Bowl and have a good time. We went to play the game and get after Mike Rozier, their I-back who was really good. That Nebraska team was loaded, but we didn't go there to get our ass kicked, we went there to be the ass-kickers.

They had Dean Steinkuhler, who was a great offensive guard. They had Dave Rimington, who was another All-America lineman. But we had three guys up front who weren't going to be denied—myself, Billy Elko, and Ramsey Dardar. We fought Nebraska in that game.

It's sad Ramsey is in prison. I love that kid. He got a look with the Cardinals, and it worked for a while, but it didn't work as well as I wanted, as it turned out.

I guess the other game that was a disappointment was that Tulane game to close the 1982 regular season. That was a set-up. We got set up, and we did it to ourselves. Nobody embraced Tulane football in Louisiana. It was the red-headed stepchild—no love—while everyone was talking about how good we were. The fans were loving Jerry Stovall and our team, and we got beat.

Well, they got after us with a quick-hitting offense and big plays, and just took it to us. They won [31–28]. They had trick plays and did a lot of stuff we weren't ready for. It caused a big problem for us. We learned a lot from that beating. I'm glad we got our ass beat because it woke us up after the big win over Florida State and got us ready for Nebraska.

We were close to a national championship if you look back at that 1982 team. Seven points in three losses. We were really better than our record [8–3–1] and were a close team.

In 1970 LSU was the last school in the Southeastern Conference to sign a black athlete. They would run the clips on Sunday morning of LSU, and you never saw a black player in the 1960s.

I was little—eight, nine years old—and I would sit back and watch those reruns with my dad. There was never a black player in those clips. I grew up being a Grambling Tiger fan because of Eddie Robinson, the great coach, and my second cousin, Ernie Ladd.

So I told my dad one day he was going to see me on TV like those LSU guys. He would say, "Yeah, okay, sure." We lived in a small town on the bayou. What were my chances, really? Slim and none.

I always said to myself, *If I get my chance, what will I do?* So I became a Tiger fan, LSU and Grambling. I watched football. I rooted for Willie Wood and Willie Davis and all the Grambling guys. Coach Robinson recruited me, but I wasn't sane. I turned him down because I wanted to play on TV. My father worked three jobs, and I wanted him to see me play on TV. There were seven of us kids, and I wanted to make it work.

I had a chance to stay home, play for my state university, be close to my family, and play on TV, so I picked LSU. I finally understood while I was in school that if I didn't make it as a pro player that there would be relationships back in my home state that I could rely on in the business world. Those relationships I cherish today with the lawyers and businessmen and lobbyists and people like Coach Jerry Stovall.

I came to bleed purple and gold, and it will run through me the rest of my life. There are guys I didn't play football with, students, who had a big impact on me. Chris Roy, Alan LeGlue, Kyle Gauthier. That whole experience drives me today.

Leonard Marshall was a four-year starter on defense for LSU as a tackle and inside linebacker. He went on to the NFL and played 12 seasons, 10 with the New York Giants, where he was an All-Pro and won two Super Bowls. Marshall is a business executive in south Florida and provides services for current and retired athletes. The business (www.prosportstransition.com) is owned by Marshall Crowder and Neitlich Associates, LLC. He is the executive director of the Game Plan Foundation and manages a division at John Hancock Financial of Boca Raton.

LANCE SMITH

TACKLE

1982–1984

AFTER WE WENT 4–7 IN 1983, they ran off Jerry Stovall as the football coach. The athletic director, Bob Brodhead, started bringing in some coaches; he brought in the baseball coach, Skip Bertman, and he started winning championships. The guy he brought in for football is the guy I remember most, Bill Arnsparger. If he had stayed, LSU would have been set, and the program would not have stumbled like it did in the 1990s.

Arnsparger called me in when he got there and said, "Get your weight down." The previous year, they had told the offensive line that everybody had to weigh over 300 pounds. So we gained weight, nobody could move, and we were 4–7.

Arnsparger said from the first day he wanted me to be his leader and get my weight down and that we didn't have to weigh 300 pounds to play in the NFL. He told me to take charge. I went from 315 to 260 pounds from spring ball to the end of summer. I could run and do all that other stuff.

We had two backs behind us, Dalton Hilliard and Garry James, who could go. Hilliard was the best running back I ever played with. He had vision and could run between the tackles and still had speed to get outside. A lot of guys are one or the other. James was an outside guy; Hilliard could do both. He didn't practice during the week because he was so banged up, but he could play on Saturday.

Dalton was a freshman the year we went to the Orange Bowl [1982] and had a very good team under Coach Stovall. That Florida State game his freshman year, he ran for something like 180 yards against a highly ranked [No. 7] team.

Hilliard was 5'9", 187 pounds and had the biggest thighs I have ever seen. We had to play in Tuscaloosa against Alabama that season, and I remember this toss pitch to Hilliard, where the tackle kicked out the corner, and it was Dalton and the safety, Jeremiah Castille, who was a terrific football player. He was a big-time hitter, and Dalton never broke stride. *Boom.* Ran over him and he went 60 yards. We beat them 20–10. We were pretty good because 'Bama had guys like Mike Pitts and Cornelius Bennett and Jon Hand. They had some boys.

They ran behind me all the time, and I loved it. I was the ace guy. If it was fourth down or third down, they were coming behind me. And the defense knew it, too. Then it was playing football and having fun.

We had something called the Domination Block—I had the most in LSU history—where you take a guy and drive him five yards off the ball and put him on his back.

I was LSU Offensive Lineman of the Year for three years, so I was proud of that.

I started all four years, 1981 to 1984. I never missed a game. I was healthy and never got hurt. There were big things expected of me those four years because I was recruited by 150 major colleges out of my high school in Kannapolis, North Carolina. LSU, Miami, North Carolina, a bunch of them.

When I went down to LSU for my visit, it was raining outrageously. The fans never left the game, even in that storm. LSU was playing Tulane. The fans stayed and stayed and stayed. This was a 7–4 team, an okay team for LSU, but the fans stayed with this team as it rained. I said right then I was going to LSU, and it was because of the passion of the fans.

My pal Ethan Horton, who had committed to North Carolina, asked me where I was going when I got back home, and I told him LSU. I told him, "You should have seen these people. I'm not going anywhere else."

I had gone to football camps at North Carolina State since I was seven years old and knew everybody on their staff. I was still going to LSU.

The most memorable game for me at LSU was the game we played against Florida State at LSU for the right to go to the Orange Bowl. The Monday before the game these LSU fans bought all the oranges in the state of

Lance Smith turned down his home-state school, North Carolina, to attend LSU and became an All-America tackle in 1984. He was All-SEC as a sophomore in 1982 and as a senior in 1984.

Louisiana (and I think they bought all the ones in Alabama and maybe went to Houston and got those, too).

We went up 14–0 on Florida State, and the field turned into oranges. We beat them 55–21. We wore them out. The oranges were hitting the field in the first quarter, and the referees had to temporarily stop the game.

We were always ready because of the coaches. There were letdowns, you always had letdowns, but the coaches did not let down. Mack Brown ran a good offense.

But we also had a great defensive line in 1982. The whole front seven went to the NFL, and so did James Britt, the corner. We had Leonard Marshall. We had Ramsey Dardar at nose. Remember Dave Rimington at Nebraska, the big offensive lineman? Dardar whooped Rimington, the No. 1 offensive lineman, around. Dardar ate him up.

I didn't realize I could be in the NFL until I was actually drafted. You see guys who are supposed to get into the NFL and then don't get drafted, and you wonder, *If he can't make it, what chance do I have?* You see these guys who are 6′4″, 300 pounds, and you think they could get drafted, but then they don't go. We had a guy like that, Clint Berry, who did not get picked after 12 rounds, and he was good enough. How does that happen?

So I just didn't let myself think I was going to get drafted. You don't know. On draft day, the Steelers were at my house and said they were going to draft me in the second round. But then those jokers didn't draft me. They traded their pick.

The Cardinals got a steal in third round when they picked me. I was so excited to be drafted. I got 13 years in with the NFL. I played guard in the NFL, not tackle.

To have that LSU background and have played football there is great. You don't realize how great it is until you go back there. You go through the NFL, and the people at LSU are still pulling for you even after you have been gone 13 years. They treat you well back down there, and they don't forget you.

It's the same on and off the field with the LSU folks. If kids need jobs after football, they help them out. You never lose that pride and that sense of being a Tiger; I didn't, and I was in the NFL 13 years. There is not another place like it; people love you forever. That football down there, there is not another place like it. I saw it from the first game in all that rain.

Lance Smith was an All-America tackle in 1984. He was All-SEC as a sophomore in 1982 and as a senior in 1984. Smith was drafted by the Cardinals and played in the NFL for 13 seasons. He owns a distribution company for apparel, T-shirts, and hats in Charlotte.

DALTON HILLIARD

RUNNING BACK

1982–1985

A LOT OF PEOPLE THOUGHT I WAS CRAZY going to LSU. It was supposed to be too big for me. There was a challenge. It didn't faze me going to LSU and competing for a job.

I loved playing against the older kids.

I have always been an overachiever, size-wise. It's always been a major factor. LSU was the only major school that recruited me. Oklahoma recruited me some with the Selmon brothers, but I never heard from them with a scholarship offer. They visited, they looked at me, but I guess being 5′7″, 165 wasn't what they wanted.

Buddy Nix recruited me for LSU. I'm from Patterson, 65 miles southwest of New Orleans. Jerry Stovall was the head coach, but Coach Nix, who was the linebackers coach, was the one I developed the relationship with. I had offers from Tulane, Southern, Louisiana Tech. My high school coach, Coach Jack Andre, talked me into LSU and said if I wanted to play major-college football, then go to LSU.

I wanted to play major-college football.

When I got there for training camp, the summer workouts, I was probably eighth on the depth chart, but I knew I could play. We had good players at LSU. They moved a couple of guys to receiver, and I had a chance to play. I liked the challenge.

Few players in LSU football history did more with less. Hilliard was undersized and did not have breakaway speed, but he was named All-SEC three seasons—1983, 1984, and 1985—and is the second-leading rusher in LSU history with 4,050 yards.

My thing was a low center of gravity. My size and body shape, my lower body strength with my thighs, that was my strength. I had elusiveness, but I did not have speed. If I had had speed, I would probably be one of the best running backs around. I could turn, fake, create, but I was not blessed with that giddyup. I couldn't turn those 10-yard runs into 60-yard runs.

The first 10–15 yards, I had the acceleration, and I relied on my vision to see a hole. I could run up inside or bounce outside. I liked the quick toss. I felt if I was one-on-one with anyone, I should always win. Making linebackers miss is my responsibility.

We had Garry James as a running back, too, and what a talent he was. It turned out that he and I got to start as freshmen.

I started the first game as a freshman [against Oregon State] and started all four years. I was nervous as heck. Coach Stovall said I was the first freshman running back to start at LSU. Coming from a small school in Patterson, it was quite a rush.

The nature of how I played was to compete. After the first contact, the jitters go away and you play. It came natural for me.

The one thing I remember was coming out of that locker room and seeing so many people. It was unbelievable. The Hilton in Baton Rouge was the biggest building I had ever seen. The stadium was confined, people were close, but after a while I went to playing. Just shake and not let too many people touch me.

In that first game, Garry and I both got over 100 yards, I believe. We had a very good relationship. It was great having four years with Garry. He was a blazer, he could really run. I was his compliment in between the tackles.

We tried a few times to stay in the same backfield on plays, and we did more with Coach Arnsparger, the split backs. With Coach Stovall, it was more power I formation.

Florida my freshman year was my first nationally televised game. We went there and beat [No. 4] Florida. That was the first time my mom had seen me play on TV. The people were back home barbecuing and cooking up some stuff. That small town was lit up. I realize now how people really followed me in my hometown, and I am thankful for their support. I had no idea at the time, being a kid.

The big play for me was I blocked Wilber Marshall—he was a very good linebacker—and then caught a screen pass from Alan Risher, and it went for a touchdown.

The other thing I remember about that 1982 season is that we had enough talent to win a national championship. We were really good [8–3–1]. We went to the Orange Bowl against Nebraska, and they came back to beat us in the last three minutes or so, 21–20.

We lost three games by seven points. We had Leonard Marshall and nine or 10 other guys who could have played in the NFL. My freshman year it was amazing to see guys like Leonard Marshall and them.

That season in 1982, my freshman year, Coach Bear Bryant made the comment that Alabama should have recruited me, and they made a mistake. That was amazing, meeting him coming off the field.

In my sophomore year, 1983, I injured my ankle and missed three or four games. We had a lot of injuries that year and finished 4–7. We did not play up to expectations and could have played better than we did. The injuries had something to do with that.

It was after that season that they fired Coach Jerry Stovall, and none of us saw it coming. The injuries had a big influence on the season we had; it wasn't all his fault. None of the players expected it, and none of the players blamed him.

We adjusted with the coaching change. There was no player animosity. We handled the business of the coaching change, and it helped that Coach Arnsparger was relaxed. If you did what you were supposed to do, things were fine.

149

The offense was changed, and we went from a power I to a more diverse scheme. Garry James and I started playing in the backfield more together. Now, we still had some fun with the offense my freshman year because coach Mack Brown ran the offense and he would try some things. But the bigger change was having Garry in the backfield more with Coach Arnsparger.

That junior season in 1984 we had a good team [8–3–1]. The big game was playing Notre Dame because you heard so much about them.

My last game was against East Carolina in Tiger Stadium and the last chance to become the all-time leading rusher. My family came out, and my brother was taking pictures. It was a big day because all the offensive linemen who were blocking for me wanted me to break the record. It was held by Charles Alexander, and he was a great back. Curt Gore and the rest of the offensive linemen fought hard to get that record accomplished.

I was an overachiever in people's eyes and wanted to prove people wrong. That happened in college and in the NFL. I was a second-round pick of the

Saints. Watching my brothers perform on the high school level and how they were recognized and how they handled themselves helped me achieve what I did.

I watched my brother, Curtis, and all his popularity, and to achieve that recognition you had to work hard. That was my drive. When a lot of people tell you that you can't do something, you're eager to prove them wrong. I have a son who is playing football. He's a small back, and he will go through the same scenario where people say he can't do something. A lot of people are going to regret they didn't get him, I promise you.

It is a remarkable feeling to have been a part of the LSU program. It should be a treat for any kid coming out of Louisiana to play for LSU. I was not as aware of it as a high school kid, but what it does is strengthen your surroundings, your networking, for future endeavors in the oil business. It is a tougher environment in the oil industrry than on the football field.

The business side has been helped. I own an oil field company, Southland Energy Services, and my connections through my time at LSU have helped me. It's a blessed scenario, having that LSU background. It was the best decision I ever made, besides marrying my wife.

Dalton Hilliard was named All-SEC three seasons, 1983–1985, and is the second-leading rusher in LSU history with 4,050 yards. Hilliard had the fourth-best rushing season in LSU history with 1,268 yards in 1984 when he averaged 115 yards per game for the Tigers. He is the third-leading rusher in the history of the New Orleans Saints. Hilliard lives in Louisiana and works in the oil business.

MICHAEL BROOKS

LINEBACKER

1983–1986

THERE WERE A LOT OF GOOD GAMES I was a part of at LSU, a lot of wins, but what stands out is how the defense rallied after I got hurt the third game of my senior season [1986]. They still had a good season, even without me, and I was supposed to be the All-American. It showed what kind of talent LSU was recruiting back then that they could go out and win the SEC championship without me.

The knee went out in the first quarter at Florida. Guys on the sideline said they heard it pop. Crawford Ker was their big offensive tackle, and I came off the edge and tried to go back underneath him and fell down.

Being a tough guy, I thought I could play. I tried to stand up but couldn't, and I knew it was all over. I waved to the sideline and told them to come get me because I knew my college career was over. I tore my ACL. We still went on to win that game.

We had a good year because there were a lot of good players on that defense—Eric Hill, Ron Sancho. I was preseason All-America, there were big things expected of me, and then I got hurt. The guys won that game and rode me the rest of the year and said they were going to win a championship for Michael Brooks. So I still had a part to play in that season.

I could have been a two-time All-American, but I was still a third-round pick of the Denver Broncos and played in two Super Bowls.

Michael Brooks is considered one of the best linebackers to come through the program, even though his senior season was cut short by injury. He was an All-American as a junior in 1985.

When I did play a full season in 1985, one of the things about our defense that season was Bill Arnsparger, who was a great defensive coach. A lot of players respected him, and he gave me a lot of insight and knowledge. Where he helped me most was in giving me freedom as an inside backer where I could pretty much take the inside move, if I felt like I could get there, or take the outside rush.

That freedom gave me a lot of flexibility and helped me get sacks. He let you go out there and play football, and that's why a lot of guys excelled under him. Just go play hard and use your instincts.

I loved him so much as a coach that when he came to one of my NFL games when we played the Eagles, I had one of my best games a Bronco linebacker ever had. I think I had 21 tackles just to show Coach Arnsparger that he helped me get to where I was.

We were all disappointed when he left for Florida to become the athletic director. He was the one who brought Steve Spurrier to Florida. We thought a lot of him at LSU.

I wore No. 94 because of Lyman White. He was an idol of mine. When I went to LSU, I wanted to be the next Lyman White, and that was his number. Even though Lyman was a defensive end, sometimes I got to line up in a three-point stance like Lyman White. I could stand up and rush the passer or I could get down in a three-point stance. Bishop Harris, who coached me at LSU, used to tell me, "Boy, you are going to be the next Lyman White." It was an honor for him to say that.

They used to talk about Lyman White's forearms, how he would literally knock people out with them. I wasn't able to do that. I had my share of knocking people out, but I was more known for being kind of fast and also strong. I wasn't the biggest of linebackers, but I was one of the strongest, and I could fight off the big tight ends while still being able to run with some backs.

I was 6′1″ and weighed 220. When I left LSU, I weighed 235. I put on 15 pounds of muscle. LSU helped me do that and get ready for the NFL.

In 1984, my last full season, there were tough games all over our schedule. Kentucky was a tough team for us because they would play an eight-man front and get after it. Mississippi was good, and then there was Alabama and Florida.

Alabama was good, and I remember they had Cornelius Bennett. He and I were always being compared as outside linebackers. When we played them, I always tried to play well to match anything he could do for Alabama. I knew if I played well, the guys around me would play well, too.

I had a chance to come back and use my redshirt year in 1986, so I went in and talked to Arnsparger before he left, and he introduced me to A.J. Duhe, who played at LSU. I asked them what I should do, and they said I had proved everything on the college level and that I was ready to play in the NFL. A man like him telling me what I should do—I didn't second-guess him. I went into the draft.

When I went to LSU, we had great talent at linebacker, guys I grew up watching in high school like Ricky Chatman. LSU was getting all this talent in north Louisiana, and I felt if I went there and we kept getting all those players, we could keep LSU as a solid program. I looked up to all those north Louisiana guys and knew I had to go to LSU. I wanted to be on the field with those guys, and they influenced me.

I thrived on the competition at LSU. There were a lot of schools from the SEC recruiting me—LSU, Ole Miss, Arkansas, were coming after me hard. You had to have the competition. Toby Caston and I talked about it all the time; he signed with LSU first, and I signed after him.

We didn't start well my freshman year in 1983, but we had flashes. We ended up beating Washington. They were No. 9 in the country when they came in, and we beat them. We showed in spurts we could be pretty good. When Bill came in, he had some respect because he was the coach of the Miami Dolphins defense. I think guys thought if they had any intentions of going to the NFL, they better listen to this guy.

When he walked into a room, you could hear a pin drop. He had that much respect. He wasn't the type of coach who yelled at you, he treated you like a man and had the same format he had in the NFL as far as weight and training.

154

We played an attack-style defense, and then we had Dalton Hilliard and Garry James. Instead of just starting one guy, Bill would have two guys in there, Dalton and Garry. Coach Stovall would put one or the other in, but Bill had a good knack for utilizing their talent.

We started off my sophomore season tying Florida 21–21. I remember flying off the corner and knocking off Kerwin Bell's helmet. They had Lomas Brown, who was a great offensive lineman. We didn't win it, but we didn't lose it. I still remember how hot it was on that turf, 100 degrees on the field and your feet were burning up. Guys stepped up to the challenge. That was one of the best games we played together, and it gave us a lot of confidence for the rest of the season.

It was scorching hot, and being from Ruston, that was the first time I played on that turf and got those cherries on my arm from running and tackling. You slid on that turf and your skin came off. I wasn't used to that. When you went in to hit the shower, that water really burned. Being a country boy from Ruston, that was different.

That defense was very good with Henry Thomas, who had a good career in the NFL. We had Roland Barbay and Karl Wilson, who had a long career in the NFL. We were very physical. We had a love affair with each other.

We had that 3–4 defense, like what New England plays right now. I was on the outside and had to learn how to drop in the flat and how to cover. I stayed in Baton Rouge during the summer working on flat drops and zone drops to prove I just wasn't an outside rusher. LSU helped me be a complete player because I learned the technique.

Kurt Schottenheimer, Marty's brother, came in and really coached me up. He did the same for Carl Banks when he was at Michigan State, and Banks went on to become a great NFL player for the New York Giants. Without him, it would have been difficult for me to make it to the NFL. Arnsparger brought all of these coaches in that helped my game and other players, too. Mike Archer was a very good coach at defense.

There is no other feeling like being an LSU Tiger. I go down there now and sometimes they let me on the football field. I say to myself, *I wish I was playing now*, because the stadium is bigger now that they added that upper level. When I was playing, they had 70,000 and it was Death Valley. Now it's 90,000 and it is really Death Valley.

The thrill is still there. Running out of the tunnel always fired me up. Guys just loved playing in Tiger Stadium. There was no other feeling like it. You were ready to knock somebody out. Nighttime made it better. Teams knew when they came in there, they were probably going to lose. We hardly ever lost at home. Opponents couldn't hear the snap count, so it helped me coming off the corner.

I think I had 20 sacks without playing much my senior year. I started off great with three sacks against A&M, but then I got hurt. I wanted to break the sack record, but the knee injury stopped that.

One of the most disappointing losses was to Miami of Ohio because that's where Bill Arnsparger was from and where he played college ball. I don't know how we lost to Miami of Ohio. They had a big running back, it was muddy, and they just came in and beat us. We should have won that game, but they outplayed us.

Bishop Harris is retired now and he used to tell me I had the best talent of any linebacker he had ever seen. I hear this all the time, that if I had not gotten hurt and kept all my speed I would be in the Pro Football Hall of Fame.

Coach Arnsparger would say I was just like Lawrence Taylor, just a smaller version.

It took me a couple of years in the NFL to get all the strength back in my knee and get back to that high level. I didn't have all the explosiveness. I still made All-Pro even with this brace on my knee. It took a lot of work in the gym. I only played 10 years in the NFL; I thought I could play 14, but I was still having problems with my knee and the swelling playing on that turf in the NFL.

I had a great time at LSU and still visit with my old teammates. The one thing I always wanted to do was be the guy who made the big play for our teammates. I remember hitting the Arizona quarterback in one game when they were driving for a touchdown, and we won 27–26. It was plays like that I wanted to be known for at LSU.

Playing for LSU, I thrived on being a player who could be depended on. I wanted to be the leader of the Tigers.

Michael Brooks was an All-America linebacker in 1985 as a junior. A knee injury early in the 1986 season cut short his LSU career. Brooks was drafted in the third round of the 1987 draft by the Denver Broncos and played 10 seasons and appeared in two Super Bowls. Brooks lives in Ruston, Louisiana, and is a member of the Louisiana Hall of Fame.

JOE "NACHO" ALBERGAMO
CENTER
1984–1987

I'VE TRAVELED ALL OVER THE WORLD. I still have family in Germany and Italy. Mostly in Sicily and Milan, and I have cousins in Germany. I've been to see them all. My parents came over from Italy right after they were married. My maternal grandfather, whose last name was Montagino, was born in America and came down here as a child, worked here a significant number of years, and went back to Italy.

The "Nacho" nickname—I'll tell you that story. Joseph is my middle name and what I go by. My first name is Ignazio with a *z*, which is Italian. In Spanish it's "Ignacio" with a *c*. In Spanish culture, if you have that name, you're nicknamed "Nacho." It's not Italian. But I was maybe in the fourth grade and had a teacher who was Brazilian. She started calling me "Nacho," and the nickname stuck. I'm Ignazio to my parents. Some people call me Iganzio, and some people call me Joseph.

But I prefer Joseph. Enough is enough.

There's been a lot of talent to come out of Marrero. You've got Garry James and Norman Jefferson; Skyler Green came out of Westwego, which is right near Marrero. Traditionally, a lot of talent has come out of the West Bank of New Orleans.

From Shaw High School, I was recruited by Alabama, Auburn, Ole Miss, Texas A&M, Texas, those were the regional schools. I wanted to stay close to home. There were others, but I didn't give them much consideration. I was going to LSU, although I did give Alabama serious consideration.

They were still the premier program in the South and were making a big push into Louisiana that year. I was real impressed with Alabama, but it came down to staying where my parents could see me play.

At LSU, my first consideration was that I was going to graduate. There was no question that academics were important to me, and there was no doubt I wanted to start. I wanted to start as a freshman, but we all think we can. It didn't happen, but I got to start as a sophomore and started three years. I had a great time. I accomplished all I hoped for at LSU. I really didn't expect to be All-SEC or All-America, that just kind of happened. A lot of that is luck. You've got to be on a good team, you've got to be noticed and play on TV. So it turned out then when I left LSU I was fulfilled with what I'd done, and looking back it was probably the best years of my life.

I had Eric Andolsek playing to the right of me. He went on to the pros and probably would have had a 15-year career and been All-Pro for 10 years if he hadn't been killed. Our quarterback was Tommy Hodson, who played in the NFL for a number of years. We had a bunch of pros. Wendell Davis, Brian Kinchen, and Ralph Norwood, just to name a few. Dalton Hilliard was there my sophomore year.

158

One of the things that helped me was that Henry Thomas was our nose guard, and I thought he was the best nose guard in the country. He played for the Vikings, Lions, and Patriots for 14 years and was All-Pro. Practicing against him really made me better.

I was with [Bill] Arnsparger for three years and [Mike] Archer for one year. When Arnsparger stepped down to take the athletic director's job at Florida, we as players knew the coaching staff and thought we were going to have a pretty good team coming back. I'll never forget our going to a board of supervisors' meeting and making a pitch for Archer. Really, it was only because we wanted continuity. He was a very likeable guy, and I thought he was a good coach. We finished fifth in the country his first year [1987].

That year we tied Ohio State 13–13. We should have never tied Ohio State. We were much better than them. And we lost to an Alabama team because we had several starters who got hurt. If the ball had bounced right for us that year, we could have been playing for a national championship. We should have been playing for a national championship. And I don't think that would have been the case if we had hired any other coach. Because when you come in

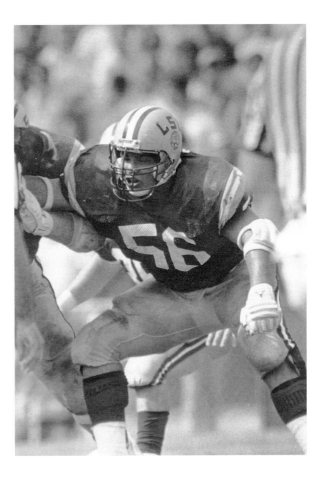

Joe Albergamo was a consensus All-America center in 1987 when he was named to eight All-America teams. He was one of eight Tigers named to the All-SEC first team in 1987.

and change schemes and change personalities, you just don't have that continuity that first year. You don't have that chemistry.

Our offensive line coach was Pete Mangurian, and [defensive line coach] Pete Jenkins recruited me. We had some good coaches, we really did. Pete Mangurian was a great Xs and Os coach.

I had several favorite games, but two come to mind: playing the Crimson Tide in 1986 when we beat them in Alabama and then won the SEC championship. That's when they had Bobby Humphrey. We probably should have never beat them, at least not at Legion Field, but Bobby Humphrey fumbled twice going in to score, and that allowed us to win the game.

I would also say our 21–19 victory over Notre Dame in 1986 was a favorite. We had a goal-line stand where we held them in the south end zone to win the game. They had a first-and-goal and we held them.

We offensive linemen tend to have team-oriented goals, and when Dalton Hilliard set the LSU rushing record our sophomore year, that stands out. That takes a lot of teamwork. It takes good blocking. Half of it was Dalton Hilliard, half of it was us. That came late in his senior year. He thanked us. He took the game ball, and we all signed it.

That 1987 Gator Bowl, South Carolina had Todd Ellis, Sterling Sharpe, and that great blitzing, attack defense, which fed right into our hands. We had Davis and Hodson, we knew we could protect, and they just tore them apart.

It ended perfectly—with one regret. I think we were good enough that year to play for a national championship, but the ball didn't bounce our way.

I had lukewarm feelings about playing in the NFL. As it turned out, I didn't get drafted. I went up to Green Bay for a mini-camp but I got accepted to med school and thought I would come back. It was time to move on.

I first thought about becoming a doctor my second year at LSU. I was in the engineering college, but after my third semester at LSU I had taken some anatomy and biology classes. I really liked it and decided to switch. I enjoy what I'm doing. It's better now, after med school and residency—that eight-year stretch is pretty tough.

When you get recruited, one of the well-known pitches of these college coaches is, "If you're going to live in Louisiana, the best place to go is the university in your home state." And it's for obvious reasons. You build connections, you build name-recognition, and it's easier for you to enter the business world or the labor force. It was kind of a natural. It's helped me out. Every day patients will come by and tell me they remember watching me play.

I go to the games. I'm not as emotionally involved as some of the fans are because I had the ultimate athletic experience. But I'm still friends with so many of the guys—Ron Sancho, Jamie Bice, Ruffin Rodrigue, Tommy Hodson, Jimmy Goodrum. On a regular basis and during football season, 10 or 20 of us get together.

Joe "Nacho" Albergamo was a consensus All-America center in 1987 when he was named to eight All-America teams. Albergamo was one of eight Tigers named to the All-SEC first team in 1987. The Tigers had 4,485 yards total offense in 1987, which led the SEC.

WENDELL DAVIS
WIDE RECEIVER
1984–1987

IN 1984 I WAS PRETTY MUCH an add-on to the recruiting class. I was not heavily recruited by LSU until the end of the recruiting period. I had been recruited by Northeastern, Northwestern, USM, Grambling. A lot of the local universities and Division II schools. LSU came in at the end of the recruiting season. Wanting to play at that level, I made the choice to go to LSU.

I went to Fair Park High School and was a receiver and was used at running back sparingly. I wasn't a speedster, and that probably had something to do with the big schools not looking at me hard. I was a consistent 4.5 in the 40. I ran a 4.4, but not consistently. My biggest strength was ball speed, running precise routes, and catching the ball in traffic. I was more of a possession-type receiver.

I was 6′, but back then being tall wasn't part of the criteria like it is today. You didn't have a lot of tall receivers. When I went to LSU, I was as tall as the other receivers, like Rogie Magee and Herman Fontenot. But after I got out of LSU, it exploded with 6′2″, 6′3″, 6′4″ receivers running 4.2 and 4.3. Before, the tall guys were just Al Toon and Harold Carmichael.

So I was there in 1984 when they let Jerry Stovall go, and in came Bill Arnsparger. I was thinking my scholarship was going to fall apart. But the new coaching staff still offered me a scholarship. Arnsparger was a defensive genius, and he was a coach who taught guys to work at their position and not

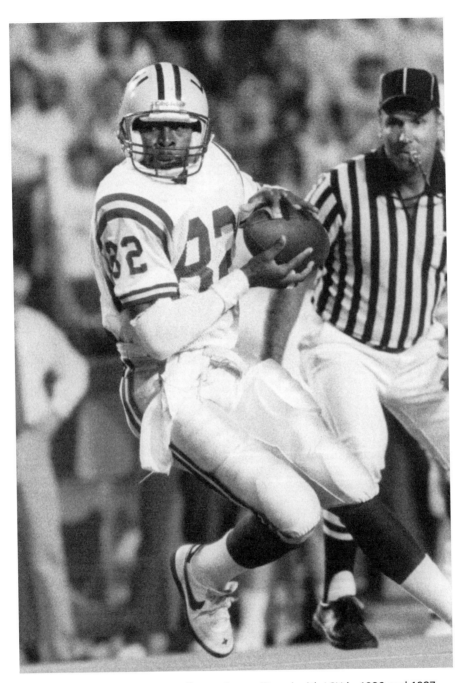

Wendell Davis was a two-time All-American split end with LSU in 1986 and 1987 and, 30 years later, is still LSU's all-time leading receiver with 183 catches.

to worry about any other position. His biggest thing was to know what you were supposed to do and don't worry about other people, do your job. I liked Bill.

He was coach at LSU for just three years, and it was a shocker when he went to Florida. I was in the first class he recruited, so we got to our senior season, and he was leaving. Our class took it upon ourselves to step it up that year [10–1–1]. We won a bowl game and finished ranked in the top 15.

We decided to take it upon ourselves to win. We fought for Mike Archer to be the coach because we didn't want much to change. We had a recipe for winning in 1987 in his first year. We lost one game, to Alabama at home. We could have been in a big game, a national championship scenario. One loss back then and we were done. We got up to No. 5 in the country and lost to 'Bama [No. 13].

The big game for us was winning that season opener at Texas A&M [No. 13]. That really boosted our confidence. We were off and running after that. We had a young kid by the name of Harvey Williams, a running back who had been heavily recruited by Texas A&M before he chose LSU. He was big for our team.

Another big game was when we played Notre Dame my junior year [1986] and beat them at home [21–19]. We got down to the last minute of the game and had to hold on to the ball to keep it from them. It was third-and-13, and I had to stretch out and catch a pass to keep a drive going.

163

There was a point in time when we bonded as an offense and started holding hands in the huddle. We did it one time, and it wasn't scripted. We just grabbed each other's hands in a tight situation and started winning. We kept doing it and kept doing it, and we kept winning.

It is things like that that show you how special a time it was for me. That started my junior year. We won nine games that season and beat some good teams: Notre Dame, Alabama, Texas A&M.

I remember I scored my first touchdown at Florida, which was my junior year. That was really just the second season I played. My freshman year I probably should have redshirted because I got in just a few times.

When I got to LSU, coming from Fair Park, I looked at some of the guys, just their size, and wondered, *What am I doing here, little me?* I got down there and saw guys like Nacho Albergamo, Ralph Norwood, and Eric Andolsek, and I thought, *Boy, these are freshmen!* This was the next level, and maybe I'd bitten off more than I could chew.

Then I found out they had brought in a guy named Glenn Holt from Miami. He was a heavily recruited receiver, and I found out I was going to be playing behind him. He was fast, a great talent. So, during my sophomore year, I was behind him on the depth chart when we were in training camp.

Unfortunately for Glenn, he started having injuries and developed this itching problem, this disorder, and it took a toll on him. They couldn't find out what it was. They thought it was all in his head. They thrust me up into a starting spot, and I stayed there.

This guy, Glenn Holt, was a legitimate 4.3, was strong, and could catch. He was the real deal. He left after the 1985 season. He had a host of injuries and left and went to Western Kentucky. I think he has a son who plays for Cincinnati.

I ended up playing split end. My favorite route was the choice route, where you ran to the middle of the field and had the choice to turn inside or out. That was my bread-and-butter route. It depended on coverage. If zone, you sat down in the zone. If man, you ran away from the guy. Tommy Hodson and I perfected that thing. When it was third down, we would run the choice route or the out route.

So I started my sophomore year with Glenn having problems [injuries]. After staying there over the summer and working out with the team, I got rid of those feelings that maybe I didn't belong there. I got stronger in that summer between freshman and sophomore year. I got pushed by Glenn and other teammates and felt I could make a difference on the team.

When I was a sophomore, I wanted to contribute. That was my thing. I had bought into the team thing in high school and as a Pee Wee player, and what I wanted to do more than anything was win.

As far as being on those All-America teams, I didn't think I could do that until after my sophomore year. My ultimate goal was just contributing to the team; the personal stuff started coming after that.

In my senior year, people started paying attention to me and bracket me with two players and take certain things away from us. We did a good job of calling plays with Tommy and the receivers we had brought in, like Tony Moss. We had guys who could catch the ball, Moss and Rogie Magee, and they had to defend all of us.

We had started that two-quarterback thing with Mickey Guidry and Tommy Hodson. That started with Bill Arnsparger. Tommy would have a great game, and they would bring Mickey in. People didn't understand it, but it worked. Mickey was ready any time to play.

The game I remember was Ohio State my senior season, which was a 13–13 tie. We were both ranked high [LSU was No. 4, Ohio State No. 7]. It was a big, televised game. We were driving on them and were about to score when they called my favorite route, the choice route. We were down in the red zone, near the goal line. That was the one time Tommy and I were off mark. I went inside, he threw it outside, and the guy intercepted the ball. It was one of the few times we were not on the same page, and it cost us.

We were 10–1–1, and the great part about the season was winning the bowl game. The previous three years we lost bowl games, two Sugar Bowls and a Liberty Bowl. Our goal was to win a bowl game.

So we had a chance to play the Gator Bowl against South Carolina, which had this blitzing defense, called the Black Death, I think. The one thing about our offense was we were used to checking out of things. We could do that all day. So they we were sending people and we were reading it, and Tommy was doing a good job checking off and making hot reads.

If you get a guy to miss once on a blitz, he's gone. I scored the first touchdown when we hit a hot read, and I took it up the sideline. They kept blitzing, and we kept making plays. We won that one [30–13], and I had nine catches.

165

Tommy was on point. You had a lot of time to prepare for a team in one of those bowl games, and we were ready for that defense. We were picking them apart with his passes, and he was protected.

They had Sterling Sharpe, and we stifled them. They couldn't get the ball off with their quarterback.

I really enjoyed going to the practice facility—the "Ponderosa," we called it—which was across the highway there. We would catch the bus from the locker rooms at the stadium and go over there. That was always fun to do. Now they have the big facility built on the Ponderosa and no more bus rides.

When we would board the bus, Eric Martin would always yell out, "Kick it in the ass, bussy." After he left, people would still say that. Once you got off the bus, you had to get off the bus running and you had to run around the field a couple of times.

I liked the training table. I'm from the northern part of Louisiana where there is more of a flavor of Texas and Arkansas and the meat and potatoes.

There was some Cajun, but not as much as in southern Louisiana. When I went south to Baton Rouge, I started eating the crawfish and gumbo.

We also had the athletic dorm. I'm still a fan of the athletic dorm because we bonded with those athletes. We could create memories and create chemistry.

It means a lot to be a Tiger. There is the LSU pride that you have. Being from the South, there is a pride. It does my heart good up here in Chicago when I see somebody wearing an LSU hat or shirt. My wife and my kids and I would yell, "Geaux Tigers!" and sometimes we would spell it out, G-E-A-U-X. And they understood.

The experience taught me so much about diversity. It was a melting pot of people. You learned to interact with other cultures. It prepared me for going out in the real world.

Wendell Davis was a two-time All-America split end with LSU in 1986 and 1987 and LSU's all-time leading receiver with 183 catches. He was named to eight All-America teams and was All-SEC in 1986 and 1987. Davis once caught 14 passes in a game (versus Ole Miss in 1986) and has the second-highest number of receptions for a season (80 in 1986). Davis had 13 100-yard receiving games, which is second all-time behind Josh Reed. Davis played in the NFL seven seasons (1988–1993 with the Bears and 1995 with the Indianapolis Colts). He owns a barber shop franchise called Big League Barbers in the Chicago area and is a partnership specialist with the federal government.

TOMMY HODSON

QUARTERBACK

1986–1989

MY GRANDFATHER ON MY DAD'S SIDE moved to Louisiana from Ohio when he was six months old. So my grandfather pretty much grew up in Raceland, Louisiana, and my dad is a native. My grandmother is a Robichaux, from Lafourche Parish. And my mom is 100 percent Cajun, from a Breaux and a Bourgeois.

At Central Lafourche, I wanted to play basketball in college, and I was really kind of holding out. You could take five visits, and I was saving a couple of visits for basketball. But in football it was Michigan, Tulane, LSU, and Stanford that recruited me. I ended up only going to Tulane and LSU on my visits, and at the end of the season I decided I just wanted to play football.

When it got close to deciding, the momentum of LSU and their popularity where I grew up in Lafourche Parish were key factors. LSU is king, and football is king, and I had such a great experience my senior year playing football. We were 13–1, losing in the semifinals, but the community just rallied around the team. It was a big deal. And Coach Arnsparger had just gotten to LSU, so there was a lot of hubbub about LSU and a lot of excitement about the program.

It just seemed like a good fit. They wanted me to come and they recruited me pretty hard. It was a good fit for me. I was just looking to have a good time in college. I didn't look that far in advance.

Tommy Hodson was All-SEC first-team quarterback in 1987. He still leads LSU in career passing attempts (1,163), career completions (674), career yards (9,115), and career touchdown passes (69).

It kind of worked out perfectly for me, the quarterback situation at LSU. [Jeff] Wickersham was a junior, and I redshirted my first year when Wick was a senior. Stan Humphries had left LSU, and it kind of left a void, so there was an opportunity to play as a redshirt freshman.

I wasn't concerned with the pressure. My day didn't revolve around what happened on the football field. I liked sports and prepared well, but I never was one to worry too much. I gave it my best, and if it didn't work out, I'd move on to something else.

I probably felt more pressure as a junior than a freshman, and I let that pressure affect my play. I just got back to not playing scared or playing to lose, and my senior year we didn't win, but I played better.

My freshman year I was surrounded by a lot of good players and teammates. It's always special, when you're an underclassman, you kind of look up to the older guys, and I'm probably closer to those guys than anybody still, even today. Like Roland Barbay, Shawn Burkes—he was a senior when I was a redshirt freshman—Jeff Wickersham, Dalton Hilliard, and Garry James. They played in that 1983 Orange Bowl when I was really following LSU in high school.

169

The class ahead of me was really loaded and really exceptional, and a lot of those guys didn't redshirt. Eric Andolsek, Nacho Albergamo, Wendell Davis, Sammy Martin—none of those guys redshirted. If they had redshirted, my junior year would have been a whole lot different. We would have been really loaded coming off a 10–1 season.

For every quarterback there's a defining moment where he takes control of the team, takes ownership, and earns the respect of his teammates. And you've got to do it some kind of way. It's different for everybody who's ever played the position.

For me it was in Kentucky when I bit through my tongue. I went out of the game, and they stitched my tongue up. Coming back in and leading the team to a couple of touchdowns and a halftime lead—that was it for me.

Keith Melancon was the guard, and we laugh about this all the time because he swears that Coach [Pete] Mangurian told him not to peel, not to come out and get the end or outside linebacker who was rushing. So he stayed in and I threw an outcut to the left, where the defensive end was coming from. I just took a five-step drop, stopped to the left, threw the pass, and he popped me right over the chin. Luckily, I had a mouthpiece in, but my bottom teeth when right through my tongue.

It happened so fast. I was dazed. I had a little concussion. It was in the first couple of series. Dr. [Sonny] Carona sewed me up in the locker room, and I came back out and was just standing there. I wasn't thinking I was going to go back in.

I wasn't thinking of anything, really, not going in, going out, I didn't care. And Arnsparger said, "You ready to go back in?" I said, "Sure."

We scored a couple of touchdowns before the half. My teammates really didn't know until after the game, I don't think. But then the reporters got a hold of it. Kid bites through his tongue. That doesn't happen every game. So the whole week they were talking about it.

My teammates could barely understand me as it was. I had a coon-ass accent—a pretty thick Cajun accent back then—and they couldn't understand me before. Johnny Hazard from New Orleans with his Yat accent said, "I couldn't understand him before, and now I gotta listen to him like this." My tongue had swollen, so they could barely understand me in the huddle.

I think we played North Carolina the next week at home, and I can remember taking the drop and being scared to get hit. And I was never afraid to get hit. I got tackled hard the first time or got hit as I was throwing, and it was okay, I was back.

My sophomore year we had a lot of guys who knew what they were doing, and we prepared well. Plus, when you're talented, it's easier to do well.

People who know me know I don't have much of a relationship with my coaches. I was never buddy-buddy with anybody—in the pros, college, not even high school. My dad was a coach, and he'd always say, "I'm your dad. I'm not really your friend, I'm your dad." So we had that relationship, and that's kind of the relationship I've had with most of my coaches.

Coach Arnsparger really taught me how to play error-free and manage the game. My high school coach [Bob Gros] had a big influence on me, too. He had a tremendous influence on me on how to manage the game, run the two-minute drill, and like that. But Arnsparger always told me it's not a bad thing to punt. Punting is not a bad play. And it's true. If you look at football, it's good to be flashy, but if a guy gets to where he starts making a bunch of turnovers, it's a different ballgame. Arnsparger made me understand that you manage the game, you prepare, and you're a professional.

Ed Zaunbrecher really kept that going. He was my offensive coordinator all four years and always prepared and had me prepared really well. He was probably more of an influence than the head coaches.

My junior year we lost a lot of players, and they started playing me differently. The first two years they blitzed, blitzed, blitzed. Man-to-man coverage and blitz. The third year people started playing cover 2. They tried to bang our receivers—we had small receivers—so it took me a while to adjust to all that. Our passing game was set up to block the blitz and pitch-and-catch against the blitz and man-to-man coverage. That changed our style and changed our offense. With the change in players, it had me reeling.

About midseason, we basically installed a bunch of different patterns, because everything we had was good against man-to-man but not against cover 2 or zone coverage.

My senior year we weren't really as talented as the year before. My class was pretty talented—we had six or seven guys drafted—but then there was a big dropoff. When I look back at that '89 team, we just didn't have the depth.

It was rough for me. I'm not much of a rah-rah guy. Never have been. Never one to call a meeting and get everyone together or say we're not spending enough time together. I always think if you want to be good and you want to correct the mistakes, you need to study more film, you don't need to hang out in the dorm room together and be like family. I don't buy into that. In pro football, I was on a lot of losing teams and always thought that, when the players called a team meeting, players only, that's when the team was headed for a downturn. That's been my experience.

The team's already in trouble, and I can remember having a team meeting at LSU. It's always funny to listen to the wisdom of 22-year-olds. You think back to the things that were said, and as an older guy now who's been around sports, that was the stupidest thing I've ever heard. Only a 21- or 22-year-old would come up with BS like that. It was just garbage.

I'll never forget, I was with the Patriots, and we were in a players-only meeting at the end of a 2–14 season. We were 1–11 or something like that at the time, and some rookie got up and said, "We need to go to each other's houses and watch movies and drink a couple of beers together and get to know each other." And David Howard stood up and said, "I don't care if none of you ever come to my house. Y'all need to get yourselves up in that film room and start watching film! And start preparing better." That was real wisdom right there.

My favorite game? Everybody wants to think it was the Auburn game, the 7–6 win, but it's not one of my personal favorites. I mean, I'm glad that Eddie

[Fuller] and I and the team in 1988 got to go down in LSU folklore, but when you're on offense and you only score seven points, only cross the 50-yard line twice, and get booed the whole game, it's not really that great. I would think from a personal end, the Tennessee game we lost at home my senior year was a game I really enjoyed playing. We got to throw the ball a bunch, and I threw for a bunch of yards.

But the [1987] Gator Bowl was probably the best game. We were prepared, we knew what they were going to do, and everything worked. Wendell Davis had a great game. Heck, everyone had a great game. That was a big one and was probably my favorite game.

Tommy Hodson was All-SEC first-team quarterback in 1987 as a sophomore and in 1986 as a freshman. In 1989 he was All-SEC second-team quarterback. He leads LSU in career passing attempts (1,163), career completions (674), career yards (9,115), and career touchdown passes (69). In a 1988 game at Tennessee, Hodson completed 12 straight passes in the rain at Neyland Stadium, which is fourth all-time for consecutive completions.

The

NINETIES

DAVID LaFLEUR

TIGHT END

1992–1996

OBVIOUSLY, GROWING UP MY WHOLE LIFE as an LSU fan and living in the state of Louisiana, I knew that nobody accepts losing—they don't accept losing anywhere—but it seemed especially true in Louisiana. When you start stringing along back-to-back losing seasons, things need to get fixed and turned around.

That first year I was there was the fourth straight losing season [two under previous coach Mike Archer], and we had the worst season in LSU history [2–9]. That did not go over well for Coach Hallman.

Like I said, we thought with a good class coming in we were going to get it turned around. Curley Hallman was in the second year of his tenure, and the attitude was still upbeat. We all thought Curley was the right guy for the job. The atmosphere was pretty good around there.

And then we were 2–9 my true freshman year. What made it worse for me was I fractured and dislocated my ankle and fibula about a week before the season when a linebacker rolled up on my ankle. It was ugly, and it was six weeks before I could put weight on it. I was redshirted and couldn't get on the field.

That was tough. It was a lifelong dream to be there, and then I got hurt. And then you see your team go through a season like that, and it was definitely the low point of my football career. It was a rough place to be that season.

So after that 2–9 season in 1992, we kind of faltered around as a program. We were close to turning it around in 1993. The way the conference worked out, the people from the CarQuest Bowl were there for the last game of the season with Arkansas, and we were 5–5. If we won, we got the bid to the bowl. That would have bought Coach Hallman more time to get things going in a positive direction. But we lost [42–24] and were 5–6. I thought that was a big game in Coach Hallman's tenure. It was a pretty disappointing day. If we'd beaten Arkansas, we would have had a chance to go to a bowl game. We had a lot of miscues on offense, they had three backs each get 100 yards rushing, and we were back to the drawing board again.

My redshirt freshman season in 1993 I got to start a couple of games. I was back from the injury and split time with Harold Bishop. It was a pro-set, I-back, one tight end and fullback.

The injury I sustained my freshman year was pretty serious, so I was still fighting through that my second year. I had never been injured before, and I was trying to get comfortable and feel my way through. I needed to see if I belonged there or not.

I had come in with a good class, and that second and third year we were still young enough to think we could get the job done. Jamie Howard, Ben Bordelon, Gabe Northern, and James Gillyard were in my class. We had a running back, Robert Toomer, who had broken Herschel Walker's records in high school in Georgia. We had Eddie Kennison. We had some good players.

175

After the 5–6 season in 1993, you could see a firing coming for Coach Hallman. It wasn't a fun place to be. There was a lot of backstabbing among the staff. It was everybody looking out for themselves.

I made All-SEC as a sophomore, which was my third year at LSU. I was back to playing 100 percent from the ankle injury and feeling more comfortable, and started to progress. I liked to think I could do a little bit of everything as far as running routes, but I was probably a better blocker than anything. I took a lot of pride in blocking in the running game and took a lot of pride in sitting up in zones. I felt like I could move the chains.

We were just 4–7 that season [1994]. It was disappointing. It was our time to be up there, we were representing the state, and nobody likes to lose. Our coach had just got fired, and we didn't know what the future held or who they were bringing in. Obviously, we thought we could compete because in '94 we were on the cusp of winning some pretty big games but never could get it right.

David LaFleur was named All-America in 1996 and All-SEC in 1994 and 1996, but back problems likely kept him from becoming All-Pro in the NFL.

The straw that broke Curley Hallman was losing to Southern Miss [20–18] at home near the end of the season. They fired Curley, and then we won the last two games against Tulane and Arkansas.

The stands were half full the day we played Southern Miss in Tiger Stadium. It was the first time I had a two-touchdown day as a Tiger. I thought we were going to win the game. But then we lost, and people were booing and throwing shoes out of the stands at us.

It's not what I'd signed up for. Shoes were being thrown at us, other stuff being thrown at the staff. It was pretty rough there. I was running relatively close to Coach Hallman, and a shoe bounced off the turf. I was hoping it was at him, not me. There were a lot of boos. It's not what I listened to on the radio as a five-year-old.

Coach DiNardo came in that spring and changed the whole culture of the place. A very tough guy, a smart man who demanded respect. He really pushed us to our limit and tried to break us down. There was a lot of moaning and complaining, but looking back it was the right thing to do.

He came in there and grinded on us. He came in and instilled a mentality in us that we were going to be tough and run the ball. Coach DiNardo had a solid offensive coordinator, Morris Watts, who knew the running game and knew play-action, and that is the team we became.

They instilled that we were going to run the ball on anybody, and we did. We had a good offensive line and we had Kevin Faulk.

In 1995 we won seven games. I remember Todd McClure came in as center and Herb Tyler came in as quarterback, both true freshmen, and they stayed in the lineup. Their first game to start was the Ole Miss win [38–9].

My junior year, 1995, toward the end of training camp, we were just beat down. I came into the meeting room one day, and there was an uprising. There wasn't much time before the first game, and we thought there was going to be a scaled-down practice. But there was a full scrimmage, a long practice, and I thought there was going to be a revolt.

DiNardo and the staff walked in, and what we were feeling was quickly told to the staff. DiNardo quickly nipped it in the bud. Basically, what he told us was that he didn't recruit any of us, he didn't ask any of us to come play here, and if we wanted to play here and be a Tiger, we do what he says. That was the bottom line.

We ended up with seven wins and finished with a win over Nick Saban and Michigan State in a bowl game. It was a huge win for the program because it was in Shreveport. We had six losing seasons prior to that, and the state was wanting to win so badly. We thought we were on the top of the world.

It was an unbelievable feeling because the Class of 1992 came in with a 2–9 season and there we were beating Michigan State [45–26]. It was a physical game, and we just ran the ball down their throats. It was a great crowd, and they brought in extra bleachers.

It was a great week for us because no one on the squad had been to a bowl game. We beat a Nick Saban team pretty handily.

The next year we won 10 games. There had been just five or six teams in the history of LSU that had double-digit wins, so knowing we had a place in history and made a mark was special. It was a great sense of accomplishment.

When our class left LSU, we thought DiNardo was the man to be there for the next 20 years, or however long he wanted to be there. We all respected him, and he was a great guy. We thought he was going to be there for a long time.

He came in there with a good staff—Morris Watts on offense and Carl Reese on defense—but they left for other jobs down the road. I don't know that DiNardo had the same talent coming in to replace them.

DiNardo got the most out of his players. He pushed us to our limit and kept pushing us to better ourselves. He pushed us to a point we didn't think we could go. He was a smart man and a good motivator. I have a lot of respect for the guy.

I knew I always wanted to be a Tiger. I remember being a young boy and sitting on my dad's lap, listening to the Tigers play Saturday night on the radio. That's when it was instilled in me that one day I wanted to be playing in that stadium.

I listened to the radio for names like David Woodley at quarterback, and Dalton Hilliard and Garry James running the ball. I listened to all of them. Steve Ensminger at quarterback. Back then the Tigers didn't play on TV as they do now—they didn't have the regional coverage or national coverage. Once or twice a year you got them on TV, the rest of the time it was the radio at nighttime. I don't know if we invented night football, but we sure like to think that we did.

I knew I wanted to go to LSU, but I went through the recruiting process and enjoyed it very much and got to meet a lot of great people. I was flattered that people had an interest in me, but I always wanted to be a Tiger. I visited Notre Dame, Colorado, Texas A&M, who were very good at that point and thought they had a chance to win the national championship. Colorado was not far removed from winning a national championship.

I was 6'7", 275 pounds, and a tight end all the way. The University of Houston recruited me as a tackle because they were run-and-shoot and did not have a tight end in their offense. But everybody else recruited me as a tight end.

I could run a little bit, and I loved to block. I had good feet, so you thank the good Lord and your parents. My parents instilled a work ethic in me at an early age.

You look at the talent that comes out of this state, and if you can get the right guy in here to recruit and capture the bulk of it, you can compete on a consistent basis.

It means a great deal to me to be one of those players who was recruited and had a chance to play there. It was a childhood dream, and I wouldn't trade it for anything in the world. The best friends I have are from those days. It will be with me forever. They were the best years of my career.

David LaFleur was named All-America in 1996 by Walter Camp as a tight end and was All-SEC in 1994 and 1996. LaFleur led the Tigers in receiving in 1996 and was part of an offensive line that led the SEC in rushing in 1996. LaFleur was a first-round pick of the Dallas Cowboys in 1997 and played in the NFL from 1997 to 2000, though his career was hampered by back problems. LaFleur works in Lake Charles for COL Management, LLC, which owns and operates medical outpatient facilities in the South.

CHAD KESSLER

PUNTER

1994–1997

THE PUNTING AVERAGE OF 50 YARDS a kick my senior season is still the NCAA record, but that needs a little bit of an explanation.

First of all, in the beginning of the season I was taking all the kicks—the pooch punts and the long kicks behind the 50, everything. Up through the Auburn game I was doing all the punting, which was three games into the season.

In the Auburn game I had some touchbacks where I kicked it too deep. We lost the game 31–28. The coaching staff wanted to let the No. 2 kicker get in some games to do the shorter punts and also to get him some experience. So I got to take the big boots, just hammer it while the backup did the pooch punts. That helped me out as far as my average, no doubt about it. Nonetheless, if you were just to go out and see what you could kick, averaging 50 yards a kick is still pretty hard. Ball flight is still 60 to 65 yards because you are standing 10 to 15 yards deep behind the line.

I was hitting every ball beautifully that year. Every ball I kicked had a tight spiral and turned over. It was all clicking. That might have been why I was having trouble gauging it down a little bit. It worked out well for both of us. Jeremy Witten got in the game for short kicks, and I was bombs away.

That senior season there were some tremendous ups and downs. We beat No. 1 Florida but then lost the next week to Ole Miss. The week before we beat Florida we almost lost to Vanderbilt at home.

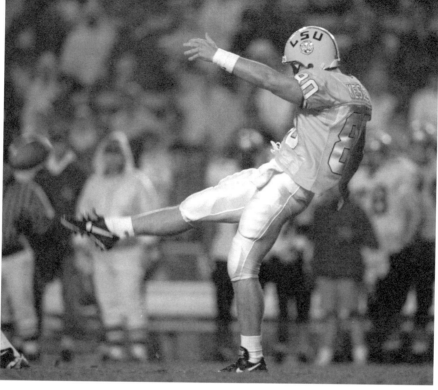

Chad Kessler still holds the NCAA record for punting average in a season (50.3 yards per kick in 1997).

We were doing well, and then Notre Dame came in, and we were just flat. There was a lot of hype around it, and it was a cold day, but we were completely flat. That was just after we beat Alabama 27–0. We always played well at Alabama, and then we came home and weren't very good against Notre Dame.

The recent LSU teams with Saban and the 2007 team with Les Miles had that consistency thing figured out. In 1996 and 1997 we were almost good enough to beat anybody, but it was, *Who is going to show up this week?* That was the problem.

I'm from the Orlando area, and during the recruiting process, being a kicker, you have to look far and wide at schools. The Florida schools were set, so I knew I had to get outside the state to get a scholarship. I looked at several schools, and LSU was the most prominent, the one with the most history. And it was in the SEC.

It came down to LSU and Princeton, and I committed to Princeton. My dad was into the athletic side of things, and he kind of pushed me in the direction of LSU. I thought it would be prestigious and great to go to Princeton. LSU said the invitation was open, the reporting date was such-and-such, and if you are here, you are here.

At the last minute, I decided to go to LSU and get the best of both worlds. I wouldn't have had a free ride at Princeton, but I had a scholarship at LSU. I showed up a day before reporting day and said I was on my way.

I redshirted my freshman year in 1993 and was ready to go in 1994, which was Curley Hallman's last year. That freshman year there was a senior who played. And then I went through spring practice [1994] and worked my tail off. But Curley Hallman didn't think I was much of a player. He called me up and said I wouldn't be one of the 105 players who was going to report to fall practice.

I was distraught when I heard this. I kept it from my parents for a while and finally had to tell them. My dad was furious and ended up calling Hallman. In the end, they said they would let me back; that was a last-minute thing. What did I do wrong? Nothing.

182

I was producing in school. I had a 3.9 or 4.0 GPA, and I knew I wanted to go into medicine. Coach Hallman played hardball with me, and I'm not sure why. I was adequate for a backup as a freshman when I redshirted.

So we started the 1994 season and had two punters, me and Mark Walker, whose brother was a big baseball star at LSU, Todd Walker. Sometimes Mark was first-string, sometimes he was second-string. Todd was a college all-star, and I felt like Mark got a lot of benefit of the doubt with Todd being an All-American in baseball.

Every game that 1994 season Curley would have Mark and I punt in pregame, and whoever was kicking the ball better in pregame would get to start. It was messed up. We were wearing ourselves out and then would get into the game and have to deal with it. I think I started nine out of 11 games that season. Mark ended up not playing after that.

Curley got axed, which was a godsend. I tried to do the right thing; I wasn't a bad kid. Could I have been better? Sure. My average was just 36 or 37 yards, it was pretty low. My longest punt of the season was my first punt. Curley wore out Mark and me.

The next year things got better under Gerry DiNardo. He respected the fact I was a hard worker in the classroom. All too often under Curley, the guys who just slid by with classes got a lot of respect from him, maybe because they were good football players. On the other hand, they weren't the best of guys.

DiNardo invigorated things, and I ended up making All-SEC my sophomore year in 1995. At the college level, you either go to camps to get better, or you do it on your own, and I went to camps and got better.

There are a lot of inexperienced special-teams coaches on the college level who don't have the experience to coach individual kickers. I went to see a guy named Ray Pelfrey, who taught me most of what I know. The longer I did that—went to camps—the better I got. I would go to his camps every year.

So in 1995, my sophomore year, I made a dramatic jump to 44 yards a kick. My junior year I slipped to 42 or 43 yards a kick. That junior year we were 10–2 and ended up playing in the Peach Bowl. These days a 9–2 team goes to a New Year's Day Bowl, but we ended up playing in a second-level bowl.

The big disappointment of that 1996 season was going to Florida and getting destroyed. They were off-the-hook good. They were so ridiculously good. They had those timing routes down, and Danny Wuerffel was on his game. Every time we went down there, they beat us badly. Florida ended up winning the national championship.

183

In 1997 we had a lot of talent. It was just inconsistent when we would play well. Maybe it was just the uncertainty of day-to-day life for some of those guys. What I noticed with Nick Saban is that Alabama never had a letdown with him in 2008. They were always ready to play and blow people off the ball.

My brother was at LSU when Saban was there, and he didn't care who you were, starter, all-star, or what. You would get your butt yanked as soon as someone acted out. You looked at LSU this year [2008], and there were players who took plays off on the offensive and defensive lines.

I liked DiNardo. He came in and changed the attitude and culture. His motto was "Bring Back the Magic" to LSU football and Tiger Stadium. The Auburn game in 1995 was the key game. We won it [12–6] when a pass was batted down, and that was a milestone for the DiNardo era.

As things went along, we started to lose assistant coaches, and I don't think those assistant coaches were replaced with equal quality. I don't know if there was a reluctance to go out and find a good hire, but the quality dropped, and DiNardo took a little too much upon himself. That was kind of the downfall of his era.

Maybe what happened was a product of his success. He thought things were smooth sailing and he could make any move and make it work, but things didn't work. That happened to Les Miles last year [2008] when he lost Bo Pelini, and Miles tried to hire from within out of loyalty. He got burned by that decision. If he doesn't win this year, it's the hot seat.

I think you are only as good as the coordinators and coaches under you because, once the head coach starts to intervene with too much stuff, that's trouble. It was obvious the quality of assistant coaches started to go down in 1997, and it definitely was an issue in 1998.

The 1998 team was a killer team that was stacked with talent. They should have cleaned up. They had Kevin Faulk and Todd McClure, Herb Tyler was back at quarterback, and LaBrandon Toefield was at running back. They also had a great player on defense in Booger McFarland.

LSU has never been short on talent. When you get quality coaches and quality assistants, like they have had the last four or five years, you can make a run at a championship.

I didn't get drafted in 1998. There were no punters and no kickers drafted. I thought my name was going to get called. I think I might have shot myself in the foot because whenever I was interviewed by teams, I told them I had a backup plan going into medicine. A lot of teams didn't think I was committed to football.

I signed as a free agent with Tampa, but didn't stay. I thought I would go through most of training camp and then get cut because I was in competition with Tommy Barnhardt, who was a veteran kicker. I finally asked for my release so I wouldn't miss a year of medical school.

I grew up a Florida Gator fan through and through. I lived two hours from Florida Field and would travel up there almost every weekend with my dad to Gator games.

And then I went to LSU.

When I went out there on Florida Field, The Swamp, as an LSU Tiger and got booed in the place where I had been as a kid, then I knew I had arrived as a Tiger. I was being hated and jeered, and that's when I realized I was a Tiger and hated Florida. I am now a Gator Hater.

I never thought Division I football, SEC football, was a level I was going to achieve. Things fall your way sometimes, and I am so glad I am an LSU Tiger. I am online every single day looking for LSU news, and I bleed purple. I am close to the program and love them. It drives me crazy that I'm in South Carolina because I can't go to Tiger Stadium more often.

The culture is so much different than what I grew up with. I carry the traditions with me, like the Louisiana cooking and the music. That is a part of me. Like turducken. People up here don't know what that is, but I do. It's Louisiana food.

The people made the football fun, and to run through the goal posts and play in that environment was special.

What does it mean to be a Tiger? When the games were moved from the nighttime to the day, it hurt. You lost some of the special quality because we are all about night football. The team fed off the energy in Tiger Stadium. It was a letdown to play during the day.

All in all, for me, I am so grateful I got to live the experience of LSU football. The people, the connections, the culture. I got my foot in the door with medical school because of LSU football, and I have tried to stay connected there. I would not have wanted to play for any other school.

Chad Kessler was the first player in college football history to average more than 50 yards per punt and still holds the NCAA record for punting average in a season (50.3 yards per kick in 1997). He was named to Associated Press, American Football Coaches Association, *The Football News*, Walter Camp, and *The Sporting News* All-America teams in 1997 and was All-SEC in 1995 and 1997. Kessler carried a 3.91 grade-point average in LSU in premed and was first-team Academic All-America. He is a doctor in Rock Hill, South Carolina, for Charlotte Eye, Ear, Nose, and Throat.

ALAN FANECA

GUARD

1995–1997

I COMMITTED TO ALABAMA THE NIGHT BEFORE signing day. I graduated in 1994, and this was not long after they won the national championship. I visited there, and people were showing off their national championship rings [from the 1992 season]. I got mesmerized by that. I committed.

It had come down to Alabama and LSU, and the LSU coach who was recruiting me was not happy. He cussed me out a little bit, and it stirred me up. It wasn't a dog cussing, just a shaking. I started thinking about it in my room, and I was looking around my room at all the LSU stuff on the walls. If he hadn't done that, I might not have looked around at all the stuff on the walls and how I had grown up in New Orleans and been an LSU fan all my life.

I said to myself, *What the hell am I doing? I have 30 things on my wall; I have a Shaq poster, an LSU shirt*. So I changed my mind the morning of signing.

I was at my house in Texas. I called my O-line coach at LSU, Larry Zierlein, and told him I'd changed my mind. Curley Hallman called five minutes later to make one last push, but he didn't know the whole story yet. He said, "Hang on, I will call you back." He called back and said, "Congratulations." I guess Coach Zierlein had not told him the whole story about me committing to Alabama, then going to LSU. He was out of the loop.

It wasn't over yet, because Alabama wasn't too happy. I know it wasn't the best timing. Gene Stallings kept calling and calling; he was pretty hacked off.

Alan Faneca was named All-America in 1997 as an offensive guard by the
Associated Press, Football Writers Association of America, Walter Camp,
The Football News, and *The Sporting News*.

Eventually, we had to take all the phones off the hook. We said, that's
enough, because at that point it was badgering.

I grew up watching the Tommy Hodson era and the successful teams they
had. I grew up on the west bank in Harvey before we moved to Texas prior
to high school, so I knew the LSU tradition and followed them a lot.

I was not on a lot of high school all-star teams, the All-America teams. My high school coach didn't do a lot back then for me to get my film out. I found out later a couple of coaches in my district in Texas had told some of the recruiting publications and other publications that I was a lot smaller than I actually was.

They said I was more like 265 pounds, but I was 295 pounds.

The big schools were looking for big offensive linemen. So all that got out, and that shied a lot of people away. My coach wasn't inviting, and it was a slow process. He told me before the season he would make sure the schools I was looking at got the tapes. Well, he asked me in October, two months later, whom I was considering because he still had not said anything to colleges about me.

Then we were at an event right after the season, and he asked me again where he wanted me to send the tapes. I said, "What?" The last day of school before Christmas break he called me in and said he sent all the films out. This was December 20.

I got up and walked out of his office, straight to where we kept all of our tapes, and took all of the game tapes for the season home with me. I didn't have a car, so I walked a mile and a half home from school and made a tape of me playing. I mailed them out myself.

LSU was recruiting me at the time because Larry Zierlein's son lived in Houston and would help out with the stat book at games. He called his dad and said, "How is the recruiting going of Alan?" and Larry said, "Alan who?" LSU didn't know who I was because the LSU coach in charge of our area was on his way out and quit doing his duties. A day later, Larry Zierlein came out to see me.

Then I started getting feedback from the schools where I sent the tapes. I had heard from some schools earlier, but they were not the schools I was interested in looking at. Alabama started calling. Other big schools had gotten all their commitments early, and they don't back out of those commitments because it looks bad. Schools said they wished they could, but they couldn't. They said if something happened, they'd call me. They had numbers and had to keep their word to in-state prospects.

I got to LSU and did not play my freshman year, which was Curley Hallman's last year [1994]. They ran two offensive lines that season to keep everybody fresh. I almost played, but they were a little wishy-washy about it. When we got to Week 6, they were thinking about playing me, and I said,

"Let's not do this." I wanted to finish my redshirt season and not just go out there and get spot duty.

We weren't looking the greatest. We were 4–7. The older guys wanted to play, and we had some depth. I ended up being a four-year junior. I did not use my last year of eligibility. I ended up going in the first round to Pittsburgh.

The first game I played was at Texas A&M, and it was hot. There were stories of previous games there where guys had to change cleats at halftime because the cleats were melting and sticking to the turf.

That was Gerry DiNardo's first season. We had a brutal training camp where he mixed three-a-days into two-a-days up until the first week of the season.

We had a little mini-coup that failed. We had a bunch of older guys who started talking. They were saying we had to get ready for Texas A&M but we were still doing double days. Coach DiNardo came into the meeting room, and a couple of older guys said something to him that we needed to back off, but then nobody backed them up. He said to everybody, "I don't want to hear this, go to your meetings." And everybody started filing out.

The next practice he beat us down for even thinking about it. We were all standing at the back of Eddie Kennison's truck, which was parked outside the front door of our stadium. People were getting up on the truck talking and saying the coaches needed to back off. You try and get 100 guys up on a truck talking, and half of them are saying they are just happy to be there, they just want to go to practice. It's hilarious when you think back about it now.

So we went into the first game at A&M, and my first game I was lined up against a preseason All-American. We were tired and beat down. We did a good job early in the game, but we were a young team that could not finish.

We had one of our coaches get an IV on the sideline, it was so hot at A&M. Their team had about 14 guys get IVs. That was the kind of training camp we went through. We didn't need the fluids because of the abuse we had been through. We were practicing right in the middle of the day in Baton Rouge in training camp, so we knew the heat.

That 1995 team [7–4–1] won its last three games and beat Arkansas [28–0]. They came in with their heads shaved, all fired up—they were ranked pretty high [No. 14]—and we put it to them. It was a day game, and the stadium was half filled. It was Thanksgiving, we had lost four games or so, and they were bad times.

We were playing for each other in that game. We knew the work we had put in with the training camp and where we had been since July. There was a core group of guys who wanted to put their mark on LSU football and turn things around. You have to win some games to turn things around. You have to grind it out, and DiNardo kept that up with us.

Things got moving that next season [1996] when we won 10 games. We set the stage for what is going on now because there had been six losing seasons before we got there. That team my redshirt freshman year was very talented. It was a great group of guys, and if we had another year together it would have been a nice team the following year in '97. It was a hell of a team. It was the most talented team we had while I was there, and we could have played for it all.

The one bad game of 1996 was against Florida, and they killed everybody. They beat us [56–13] and won the national championship. I have a picture from that game of us breaking the huddle. It's the only picture I have of us. Nobody else would know, except for us guys, that we were getting the crap beat out of us. You can kind of see it in the picture of us breaking the huddle. It is hanging up in my basement in New Jersey.

The next season we beat Florida at night in Tiger Stadium when they were No. 1. That was one of the craziest nights ever. Fans stormed the field. The game was insane, too. I heard stories later that night that the fans had tried to get the goal posts out of the stadium so they could parade them around outside the stadium.

We came in Sunday morning to do some stretching and cardio—our Sunday routine—and the first thing I did was go out and look in the stadium to see what it was like. The goal posts were torn up and at both ends of the stadium where the fans had dragged them to the top of the stands. They were trying to throw them out. They said it took every cop they could find to stop these people from throwing the goal posts out of the stadium.

There was another wild night when we beat Auburn in Tiger Stadium. They were ranked pretty high, and we won [12–6]. A buddy, Mark King, and I jumped up to collide with each other, and all of a sudden there was a big pile of us. We were underneath it and couldn't breathe. This is players and students. It was one of those things where you are thinking, *Okay, time to get off, time to get off.* We were under the pile looking at each other eye to eye, and he had the same thing going on, like were we going to be smothered to death. Finally, they got off.

We had a good run in three seasons. The last year I was there [1997] we had something good going on but slipped up and lost to Ole Miss. We were ranked in the top 10 [5–1] but could not get our minds right. We had a players-only meeting that week and told each other that we were in a good position. There were teams above us that had to play each other, and we could climb in the rankings with a win, but we still lost.

DiNardo had mapped it all out. He said, "Take care of our business and let everybody wipe each other out, and we'll be right there." We lost [36–21] and we shouldn't have lost.

It was an awesome experience to play for LSU. Nobody had more fun as a group playing football. I know guys on other teams at other universities had a good time, but I have a hard time believing they had as much fun as we did, on the field and off the field.

It was hard to leave school early without playing that last year I had left. The stars were aligned to where I had to go out to the NFL. Looking back and landing in Pittsburgh and playing there for 10 years was probably the best thing that happened to me. I got a Super Bowl ring.

I always keep the SEC rivalries going in the NFL locker room. I'm always talking trash to the guys in the locker room about LSU and the national titles. Everybody wants to point back to a game where we played each other and, if you went to LSU, you can always point back to your share of wins. That's what it means to be a Tiger.

Alan Faneca was named All-America in 1997 as an offensive guard by the Associated Press, Football Writers Association of America, Walter Camp, *The Football News*, and *The Sporting News*. He was the first Outland Trophy finalist in LSU history and LSU's first winner of the Jacobs Trophy (given to the best blocker in the SEC) since 1978. Faneca led an offensive line that helped LSU lead the SEC in rushing in 1996 and 1997. Following his junior season, Faneca chose to enter the NFL Draft where he was selected in the first round by Pittsburgh and went on to win the 2006 Super Bowl with the Steelers. He now plays for the New York Jets.

KEVIN FAULK

RUNNING BACK

1995–1998

IT WAS CLOSE BETWEEN LSU AND FLORIDA. Steve Spurrier versus the family, the home state, the high school friends. In the end, family made the difference over Coach Spurrier. For one thing, I wanted to be close to the family so they could go to games. My girlfriend at the time, who is now my wife, had our first little girl, and that was a key factor.

People here in Carencro wanted me to stay so they could see me play. But Coach Spurrier, wow, what a guy. It was really hard to say no to him because that was when Florida had it going under him. He was telling me how he could design things for me as a running back and football player, and it was appealing.

So we decided that for my official visit to Gainesville, we all would drive. My dad, my little sister, my girlfriend, and I got in the car to drive, just to see what it would be like for them to come see me play. We needed the car ride, the highway, things along the way to get a feel for what it would be like for them for years.

When we got back home from Gainesville, it was 10:30 at night. Then, a few hours later, maybe 3:00 in the morning, we had to take my girlfriend down to the hospital. She had our little girl. I looked at that baby, held her in my hands, and said, "I can't go to Gainesville." My girlfriend and the baby needed to stay here with family. That next day I called Coach Spurrier and told him thank you for everything and that it was a tough decision, but I had to stay home. Coach Spurrier wished me luck and thanked me for letting Florida recruit me. The baby made a difference. When I see Coach, we still talk.

My freshman year was the season right after Curley [Hallman] was fired. Coach DiNardo was hired and introduced, and then he walked off the podium and came straight to my house. It was 45 minutes after his press conference. He came to the high school, we jumped in the car, and drove home to meet my parents.

Guys I played with included Anthony McFarland, who played in the NFL, Herb Tyler, and Rondell Mealey. We had some good players coming in at LSU and won some games, 10 one year, nine another year. We had some good talent.

Senior year it fell off a little bit, and we did not have a good year. We had good team chemistry, but then assistant coaches got good jobs elsewhere, and we lost that continuity. Coaches understand players and players understand coaches so, of course, you are going to have some issues getting it together all at once. It was hard to adjust with so many coaches coming and going. You don't want to make excuses for losing, but there were some things that weighed on that season, and we won just four games.

I tried to make sure I was working hard and tried and lead by example. I wasn't a vocal leader, I just wanted other people to work hard.

I had a good career there and a big reason was we had good offensive lines, guys good enough to play in the NFL. My favorite play was the zone play, where I would read off the lineman's leverage and make one cut and then go.

There was no pressure, even with all the expectations on me, because I was a young kid coming out of high school playing football, and that's what I loved to do. I never thought about the pressure; that was the furthest thing from my mind.

Now that I'm older, I understand there had to be some things on the line and some pressure. I was just too young at the time to see it. I got a few jitters before games, but it wasn't overwhelming pressure.

How did they use me when I got to LSU? Our coach had a saying that Bill Parcells used to say, "When you are going to do something, don't just stick your toe in the water." So I didn't stick my toe in the water, I dove right in. I ran back kicks, punts, played offense, catching the ball, running with it. I got on the field a lot.

My first big play I remember was a 12- to 15-yard run down there at College Station against Texas A&M. It was 110 degrees on the turf, my feet were

Kevin Faulk is LSU's all-time leading rusher with 4,557 yards and is the all-time leading scorer with 318 points.

hot, and they were a real good team [No. 3 in the nation]. We lost that game [33–17], but it was the first good run I had in college. It was hostile and crazy. The atmosphere was unbelievably crazy. That was a game where I thought, *Okay, I belong here.* That was a good team we were playing against, and I had that "you can do it" mentally. That was my first game, and I was able to have a good run.

My first big game was the first game of my sophomore year against Houston, which we won [35–34]. I ran for 246 yards, and we were on our way to a good season. We won 10 games that year.

What was big about that game was I was not supposed to play. I was suspended for something that happened in my hometown that got blown out of proportion. A week or two before the game, the district attorney dropped all the charges because the charges were bogus. Coach lifted the suspension, and I got to play.

That was exciting for me because I got to see all the fun in the stadium and help the team. It's fun outside the stadium for the fans, not just inside for us. They started showing up Friday in those RVs. It was about 3:00 o'clock, and they were pulling up to the stadium getting ready for Saturday. I thought it was great that they were coming Friday afternoon.

The night football in Tiger Stadium was the best. We didn't like it when TV moved our games to the afternoon. We had something special at night in Tiger Stadium.

Playing there was big, especially when you are coming out of that tunnel and going through the goal posts and the band is playing. It still gives me chill bumps. Now that we're in the league, guys who played there against LSU talk about the noise and how it affected them.

Coach DiNardo was a disciplinarian. If you did what he told you, when you were supposed to do it, you didn't have any problems with him. He wanted you to go to school and graduate and work hard for the team. Some guys decided to go the hard way with him.

My position coach was Mike Haywood. He just got the coaching job at Miami of Ohio. Cool guy. He coached Cedric Benson at Texas and went to Notre Dame. He taught me about using my eyes, trusting my vision. He said your eyes are better than you think they are. He did not want you second-guessing yourself—make a move if it is there and then go.

There are times when you have to be patient and wait, and the one thing I wanted to work on a whole lot was making that quick move to the hole. He had a big impact on me and ended up at Texas with Mack Brown after the coaching change at LSU.

One game I remember was playing Notre Dame in South Bend my senior season. Notre Dame was one of the recruiting trips I took. It was awesome to play there with all the history in the program. You had to be crazy if you didn't want to play in Notre Dame Stadium.

The reason I remember it was I fumbled the ball, and they picked it up and returned it for a touchdown. They had to kick off to us, and I returned it for a touchdown. It was about 88 yards.

I was on the field for a lot of snaps, but I worked in practice, kept my body right, and stayed in shape. I was young, and that is what I loved to do. And we also had some other backs who were pretty good, so I probably wasn't on the field as much as other people think.

It means everything to be an LSU Tiger. You hear about all the schools that have so many guys drafted in the first round, but what you tend not to hear about is the staying power of players. LSU has guys in the NFL who have stayed in the league.

Look at our team with the Patriots. We have had five or six guys from LSU on our teams at New England.

We have guys who weren't drafted, got free-agent deals, and are still in the league. What does that tell you about the kind of guy coming out of LSU? There are a bunch of guys like that. We work hard, guys know what it takes. And to see the undrafted free agents in the league says something about LSU.

I don't know how it happened, but for some odd reason there was one game where I ran out in front of our guys at the goal posts and I would raise the roof, and the whole stadium would get loud. It got to be a little tradition. People got in sync with it.

I had not heard a lot about the traditions of LSU football where I grew up, but when I got there, I heard about all the great players like Billy Cannon and how the stadium rocked so much it registered as an earthquake. You hear about this stuff and you want to be part of it.

Kevin Faulk is LSU's all-time leading rusher (4,557 yards) and was named All-SEC three times. He is also LSU's all-time leading scorer with 318 points. He led the SEC in all-purpose yards and ranked No. 2 in the league in rushing as a sophomore. Faulk was an AP All-American as an all-purpose player in 1996. His 246 yards in the season opener against Houston in 1996 set an LSU single-game record. Faulk was a consensus All-SEC choice in 1996, 1997, and 1998, and the SEC Freshman Offensive Player of the Year in 1995. He led the SEC in rushing during both his junior and senior seasons and led the league in scoring as a senior. He was selected by the New England Patriots in the 1999 NFL Draft and was a member of their 2002, 2004, and 2005 Super Bowl champion teams.

ANTHONY McFARLAND
DEFENSIVE TACKLE
1995–1998

THE BIGGEST THING I TOOK AWAY from LSU was a sense of accomplishment. It was accomplishing a couple of things. One, it was graduating in four years. Two, LSU had lost six straight years before our class of 1995 got there. That class got it pointed in the direction it is headed in today. Every year hasn't been perfect, every year hasn't ended in a national championship, but we went from a culture of losing to a culture of winning. That should give you a sense of accomplishment.

I took advantage of the opportunity. I was a small-town kid coming to the state university, and my first semester there I had fun. It was enjoyable. It was the first time in my life that I got to make my own decisions, not report directly to anybody, and do my own thing. I had a head coach and football obligations, but nobody to report to directly. That first semester was too enjoyable, and my grade-point average suffered.

I had a talk with a buddy of mine back home, and he reminded me that, you know what, football is not promised. Sure, you want to play football, but take advantage of the education. LSU is going to get four years out of you regardless, so why not get something out of LSU? It was very rewarding to walk across that stage and get that degree; I want to say it was May 17, 1999, the School of Business.

It was mostly southern schools that wanted me. I got a couple of hits from Notre Dame and Penn State. But mostly it was schools in the area—Arkansas,

Tennessee, LSU. I tell people all the time, being a defensive lineman, I wanted to go to Miami and play in the legacy of Russell Maryland, Cortez Kennedy, Warren Sapp, Jerome Brown. But, when that opportunity didn't come, I was forced to choose between LSU, Arkansas, and Tennessee.

Tennessee wanted me to play offense. They wanted me to play center, and I didn't feel like having a guy stick his hands under my rear end 60 or 70 times a game. So that threw Tennessee out the window. It came down to Arkansas and LSU. And why get it eight hours away in Arkansas when you can get it two hours away in Baton Rouge?

Once I got to LSU and linked up with Kevin Faulk and Herb Tyler, we started that trend of freshmen playing early. We changed the whole culture around there. Kevin graduated, Herb has since graduated. Todd McClure graduated. Guys changed the culture as to what you do as a college athlete at LSU. It changed the culture of what it meant to play football at LSU. It was not *if* we win, but by how big a score are we going to win? That's how you prepared, to win on the field and get things right in the classroom.

I give Gerry DiNardo credit for starting that. He wasn't able to get it over the hump, but he started the process. If you go back to 1993 and 1994, the team was split. The defense was dynamite and the offense struggled. Jamie Howard took a lot of heat as the quarterback. What we were able to do was be one team. I was in McClure's wedding, and I was a defensive player. Tyler is one of my closest friends, Faulk is the same way. There was no dissension.

You look at that opening game our freshman year when we played Texas A&M. They had six All-Americans, they were good, and we hung with them in College Station. They were No. 3 in the country, and we started six or seven freshmen that day. They ended up pulling away, but that told us we had a chance and had some players. Football is a fourth-quarter game, and we had to get better athletically and understand how to play.

That day, it was so hot. I had on every pad they gave to me, and I kept thinking this college football thing may not be for me. At the same time, there has never been a game since that game where the conditions have been worse. My first college game prepared me for the rest of my career in college and the NFL. That was a baptism into the game; I was just 17 years old.

I started 44 out of 46 games. One I didn't start because I was hurt, and the other was when DiNardo and I had a little bump-in, and I got benched.

How I am built—300 pounds—enabled me to get the leverage playing inside. I was blessed with athletic ability. The hardest thing I had to do when

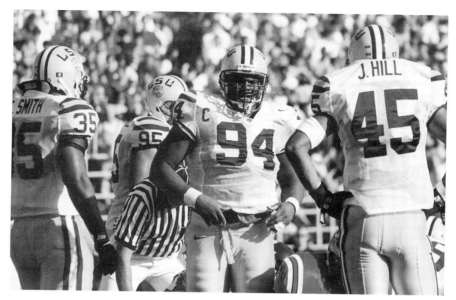

Anthony McFarland was a true two-way defensive lineman who could stuff the run and rush the passer. He was a four-year starter for LSU and finished his career with 17 quarterback sacks.

I got to college was get in shape. It was having fun and having the will not to quit.

We played a 4–3 under Carl Reese, but we didn't stay on the line of scrimmage, we tried to penetrate and get in the backfield and do some things like that. We played left and right, meaning when it was an over front, I wasn't on the nose tackle, I was a 3 technique. I got a chance to play both ways; I wasn't always in there eating up double teams. When they did double-team me, we made them pay with somebody else making a play.

After we lost to Texas A&M that freshman season, we beat Mississippi State and then we played Auburn under the lights at Tiger Stadium. It was the first time I got to run out of the tunnel and play under the lights in front of the home crowd. From Winnsboro to Tiger Stadium. That's a big jump for a kid.

Auburn was in the top five and had Stephen Davis. It was some experience. We won [12–6] and played very good defense.

It was a good measuring stick for us. That was my first SEC test to see how I was going to match up. Defense played lights out that night. There were some good players there before us, so we just wanted to come in early and help out by playing early.

If you wanted to win the conference, you had to win the west. And if you wanted to win the west, you had to match up with Auburn, and we did that.

We had a decent year [7–4–1] and finished strong. We beat Michigan State in the Independence Bowl, and they had some good players. We thumped them pretty good, and the program was on track.

The next year [1997] we got to 10 wins, went to the Peach Bowl, and got that thing rolling. We started to get some more help through recruits.

My junior year the big game was beating Florida, which was No. 1. It was the wildest atmosphere in Tiger Stadium. I have been in two Super Bowls, and I tell anybody the night we beat Florida is still the most unbelievable atmosphere I have ever seen. We beat Florida the way a lot of people didn't think we could. We played a lot of zone coverage, made Doug Johnson, the quarterback, throw the ball in spots instead of against a lot of man-to-man. Spurrier use to kill man-to-man.

But that was the pinnacle. DiNardo kind of maxed out after that season. There is a different kind of football in the Southeastern Conference than he was used to coming from Colorado and Vanderbilt. Off the field, how you relate to your players, is where he kind of bottomed out, or topped out.

200

The program went down, and we won four games and then only three the year after I left. Nick Saban came in, and the program shot off after that. If you are able to relate to kids in Louisiana, the kids will come. It is the people and relationships you build.

The big game my senior year, a decisive game, was playing Georgia at the House. We were ranked in the top 10 [No. 6], and they were ranked pretty high [No. 12]. We were down 21–14 and were at Georgia's 14-yard line going in. But we got a false-start penalty, and it crushed us. We had a toss play, and there was so much room to run I could have scored. It was the Red Sea parting, and there was a false start. We went for it on fourth down and didn't make it. That was the game and the drive that stopped that season.

It was one of those made-for-TV games and was unbelievable. We lost [28–27]. After that, we won just one game the rest of the year. There were some bad breaks, and we didn't play well.

DiNardo tried to bring that old Bill McCartney philosophy of relating to coaches and players, a kind of Upstate New York philosophy, and it just didn't mesh. He didn't understand one thing, that you have to have relationships with

The Nineties

players and coaches. What happened was the coaches who could leave left the program.

When we left, people started to understand what DiNardo was all about, and they fired him. I had a conversation with someone in the administration who told me that Louisiana has some of the best high school players in the country, and that if you get somebody in there who can get those players to LSU, then LSU will be one of the best programs in the country.

If LSU could get the top 20 players out of Louisiana for four years, you would never have to leave the state to get another player. There are too many guys who left this state to go play elsewhere, guys like Warrick Dunn and Eli Manning and Peyton Manning. I firmly believe that. You have to dominate that state in recruiting, and anything you get extra is lagniappe.

They know that, and that is why they went after Nick Saban. He was regarded as a master recruiter and a player's coach. He was a hard guy on coaches—he worked coaches like crazy—but the players loved him and played for him. Saban changed the entire relationship between coaches at LSU and high school players in the state. Things have changed down there, and they are now a national powerhouse.

For me, it means a lot to be a Tiger. In order to understand where you are, you have to understand where you came from, and I saw where it came from. It makes me very proud to look on TV and see where they are right now. Over the last 15 years, I have seen LSU at the bottom and now I have seen LSU on top.

This spring I am going to get inducted into the Hall of Fame at LSU, and that makes me proud. To have been a part of that is wonderful and makes me feel proud every day.

Anthony McFarland was a 1998 Associated Press and *Football News* All-American. A four-year starter and a defensive co-captain as a senior, he finished his career ranked sixth in LSU history in quarterback sacks with 17. He was a first-team All-SEC pick as a senior, a second-team selection as a sophomore, the Defensive MVP of the 1996 Peach Bowl, and the 1995 SEC Freshman Co–Defensive Player of the Year. McFarland was drafted as the 15th overall pick in the 1999 NFL Draft by Tampa Bay. He won two Super Bowl rings, one with the Buccaneers and one with the Indianapolis Colts.

The
NEW
MILLENNIUM

BRADIE JAMES

LINEBACKER

1999–2002

IT WASN'T EASY GOING TO SCHOOL, trying to get good grades, and playing Division I football where there are a lot of demands on your time. My first thought, though, when I entered those doors at LSU, was to use the football scholarship to get a degree.

My mom, my dad, my family—the only thing on their minds was my getting that degree. It wasn't football. How I handled it was by taking the competitiveness of the field to the classroom. I didn't make As all the time, but I damn sure tried.

I got my degree in criminology/sociology. My dad was a welder, and my mom worked in the school board office, so put those things together and you see my background. Work hard, believe in education. I come from a long line of educators on my mom's side.

The other thing about my story and getting that degree was that I lost my parents while I was at LSU. Both of them. My dad had kidney failure, my mom had breast cancer. They passed three months apart. That's why it was so important that I complete my degree. I wanted to honor them. My mom was so big on that. That's why I continued and kept at it.

Then I started to get a little good at football. People kept saying I might have a chance to play in the NFL. I never dreamed of playing in the league until I got into my college career.

Both of Bradie James' parents died while he was at LSU. He went on to an All-America career and received his degree in their honor.

My dad died just before the Peach Bowl where we beat Georgia Tech [28–14]. I got Defensive Player of the Game and dedicated it to him. Three months later, my mom passed.

I was at school, and they did not tell me from home how severe it was. They didn't tell me until it was time. I went home, and she passed in February. That's where the family picked up, and the LSU community. My release was football and my help was the people at LSU.

I never did think about the NFL until they passed. When it happened, I still had football, and I played hard and worked at it. After my junior year, people said I had a chance to come out early. It was a no-brainer for me to come back because I wanted the degree. But I wanted to see Coach Saban sweat a little bit about my going pro or staying in school. After some of the stuff he put me through, I had to get him back.

I got a second- to third-round grade following my junior year. Then I got moved to middle linebacker when Trev Faulk left early for the NFL. That was a big adjustment for me.

When Saban first got there, I couldn't stand him. I called him the mini-tyrant. He was crazy, but after my dad passed, our bond got closer. He came to me and said he lost his dad about the same age as me. Nick Saban helped me in the transition from a teenager to a young man. He had his favorites. If he liked you, he liked you. If he didn't, you fell into the same pot as everyone else.

Here is the one thing I really learned at LSU about football programs. You don't ever go to a school because of a coach, because it can all change the next season. I got there with Coach DiNardo, and the next season here came Coach Saban. I tell recruits, "Don't go for the coach, go for the school." The attrition rate is so high.

I was thinking the guys who sat in my living room and talked to my mom and dad would be there my whole college tenure. It wasn't even one year before they were gone. I signed in February, and nine months later those guys were gone.

Coach Saban came in with a different philosophy. He tried to weed out the guys who were weak and didn't want to go to class and didn't love football. If you didn't represent the traditions at LSU and didn't do things his way, you got in trouble. I didn't agree with the way he went about doing that, and he and I bumped heads. I never heard so many curse words out of somebody's mouth.

I didn't like the way he addressed some guys, I didn't appreciate it. Saban didn't have trouble with me, because I did what I was supposed to do. He will say what he has to say and then forget about it.

So I kept going to class. I was not the most intelligent guy there, but I stayed with the program, and it gave me a better opportunity in life to stick with it. I didn't care what he thought really. I was there for me and my teammates.

My position coach my sophomore year was Sal Sunseri, who is now the D-line coach at Carolina. He helped with that transition from coaching regimes, and then my junior year Will Muschamp came in. I will never forget him.

He came in and looked so young, I said, "Dude, you're so young there is no way I can call you 'Coach Muschamp.' I'm just going to call you 'Will.'" He said, as long as I did what I was supposed to do, I could call him anything I wanted.

Will related to us. He had just gotten through playing. I felt like I could talk to him. We hit it off from the start. He taught me how to play the game the correct way, how to study and how to anticipate.

Sometimes guys try and make the game complicated, but he kept it simple. He just told me, go get the guy with the ball. Now, the system some people say is complicated, but Trev and myself, it wasn't tough for us. We were like quarterbacks on the field, and we were prepared.

One of the things about Nick's defense was he would adjust. At halftime we might throw out the whole game plan and do something different. Trev and I talked to each other and helped each other through the adjustments.

I started some games as a freshman in 1999. There was a game where I thought, *Okay, I belong here*. We played Georgia, and I sacked Quincy Carter. Carter had not been sacked all year long. I got the picture.

Quincy was with the Cowboys when I got here, and he would talk stuff about how he tore us up. They beat us by one point, and I said, "I got to you a couple of times and caused a fumble." I said, "I have the picture." And I still have that picture. People after the game asked me about sacking Quincy when I was just a freshman, so I felt good about that.

That was the game where I got a new pair of cleats, so I felt like I could do anything. You know how you are as a kid. I called those cleats the "Quincy Killers."

Then we played against Florida the next week in the rain and got killed [31–10]. They beat us up bad, but we kept playing. We all kept playing. A few weeks later Coach DiNardo was out the door.

That next year we got some good guys in the program. Chad Lavalais, Justin Vincent, Mike Clayton, and a bunch of others. We took off. We won 10 games my junior year and beat Tennessee. They were No. 2 in the country and were going to play in the national championship game, but we beat them in the SEC championship game [31–20].

That game had to be the biggest game in my college career. All you heard about going in was Tennessee going to play for the national championship after they beat us. I kind of talk to Jason Witten [Tennessee's tight end] about that, him and Kevin Burnett. We had Matt Mauck and the quarterback draw. That was the game where Rohan Davey, our quarterback, got hurt and Matt came in and led us.

We stopped Travis Stephens, who was Tennessee's big-time running back. We stopped their running game, they had to pass the ball, and we won. They overlooked us.

The next season we were 8–5. That was my senior season in 2002, and I took it pretty hard. I wanted to go back to the SEC championship game, at least. If we had beaten Arkansas, we would have gone back, but they had a last-second pass that beat us. I remember that game. Corey Webster went for the interception, and I was yelling at him to knock it down. We lost that game 21–20.

During that season Mauck got hurt. Marcus Randall came in, and he got hurt. We finished by losing to Texas 35–20 in the Cotton Bowl. They were just better than us.

The scouts were taking a tough view of me that senior season. I was in the middle and had to take on more blockers. When I was playing outside, I could run around people. But I had to play middle—there was no one else but me after Trev left. Nick gave me a choice, but it wasn't really a choice. He needed a veteran in there, and I had to bulk up a little.

The other thing that happened was that I lacerated my kidney during spring ball and had to sit out. I don't think I even played much in the training camp before my senior season, maybe some. I had thought about sitting out my senior season and coming back, but I felt like I had a duty to the guys to be out there because we needed someone in the middle.

That senior season was the first time I ran into Ronnie Brown of Auburn. We lost 31–7, and they were really good. He ran all through us. We had beaten some teams, we were in the top 10, and then we fell down. Cadillac Williams didn't play that game, but I remember I had hosted him at LSU, and he could have been playing for us.

The next week we had the Blue Grass Miracle with the win at Kentucky, but then we got beat bad by Alabama [31–0]. We lost to Arkansas, or else we could have played in the SEC championship game and made it a better season. But Matt Jones threw the pass to Richard Smith, and we lost. We lost four of the last six games, including the game to Texas in the Cotton Bowl, and they were better than us.

The draft that spring was a disappointment for me. The Cowboys picked me in the fourth round. I was embarrassed because I was supposed to be the big man on campus.

Maybe I could have gone higher if I had dropped out of school to get ready for the draft. There are plenty of guys who dropped out, left school, and I know some of them regret it. I couldn't leave school; I had to finish for my folks. So I didn't train hard, I studied hard.

I didn't get drafted very high, but I wouldn't have changed anything because there was no way I could go back to school now. I got to walk across that stage. It was my personal national championship. I'm in my office at home right now looking at the trophy, my diploma.

Everybody has a story to get there, and there is nothing like the camaraderie you feel in college around a football program. My Tiger family stepped in for me when I needed them. It is about the relationships you form. The people never forget you.

Bradie James was an All-America linebacker (2002) and was named National Scholar-Athlete by the National Football Foundation. He finished his college career with 418 tackles, which included a school-record 154 stops in 2002. James, who is from West Monroe, Louisiana, was named the 2000 MVP of the Peach Bowl. James was named All-SEC in 2001 and 2002. He is a standout linebacker for the Dallas Cowboys.

STEPHEN PETERMAN

DEFENSIVE/OFFENSIVE LINE

2000–2003

Not many people thought much about our recruiting in 2000. We might have been rated No. 50. The biggest thing I remember about the national championship we won in 2003 is that on paper, four years earlier, no one expected too much out of our class.

What was interesting was how guys came in playing one position and then were moved around by the coaching staff and succeeded. I was recruited as a tight end, then played defensive end and on the kickoff return team my freshman year, and was back to tight end the following spring.

Then, after the spring game, Coach Saban asked me to move to offensive line. It needed some help, and I said, "Whatever," and moved there. I met with Coach Yarno, worked with him that offseason, and the second week of training camp I won the job.

There were other examples like that in the program. Jack Hunt came in as receiver and moved to safety. Devery Henderson moved from running back to receiver.

The other thing that was key to winning that national championship was losing that game to Arkansas our junior year on the last-second pass [21–20]. We went to the Cotton Bowl and lost to Texas, and then that group of rising seniors got together the first week back in school in January. We said we weren't going to let the next season end like that.

We made a commitment, the whole team bought into it, and we ended up winning the national championship. On paper, like I said, that class was not supposed to accomplish that.

What made it better was that, on paper, Oklahoma, the team we beat for the national championship, had won all the awards that season [2003]. They had the Heisman winner and all these other award winners. It was that way for a lot of that senior season; other teams were supposed to beat us—Georgia, Auburn, Oklahoma.

I could not think of any guys who were not good teammates that year. They got along and worked hard together. They bought into the whole team thing.

Going into the season we won the national championship, Saban had a team meeting with the seniors to go over team goals. In the years prior to that, the goals were mostly statistical, how many wins, how many rushing yards, etc. Rodney Reed, other seniors, other guys, and I said our goals needed to be more team-oriented and positively affect people. We set goals to outwork opponents every day and work hard in practice toward a goal. There were a lot of things that were not related to stats. Everybody took a leadership role themselves.

211

We won some games our junior year and went to the Cotton Bowl, but we thought we were better than 8–5. That was the season of the Blue Grass Miracle when we beat Kentucky. We lost some games we didn't think we should have lost. We got committed to winning all the close games the next year.

I got better because it was so tough in practice. I was working against guys like Chad Lavalais. We beat on each other and made each other better. By the time you got to the games, that was the easy part.

By the time the season came along, we said to each other, relax a little, we've done a lot of work. Perform on Saturdays. Saban looked out for the kind of stuff we did in practice where we went half-speed one play, then picked it up a little if he saw us.

But we never had guys who did not want to go out and practice and get better. We always wanted to practice and work on things. It was all the hard hitting that we took a little break from once in a while.

Saban ran practices like he wanted the offense beating the defense, and he wanted things very competitive out there. Guys were talking trash in training camp; we got after it. We all wanted to be remembered. We wanted to leave our mark at the university.

The seniors had a dinner at the end of the year, or maybe it was a luncheon with the Bengal Belles before the last game of the year. The seniors got to speak, and I was in tears. It was the last game in Tiger Stadium. It was coming to an end.

In that lunch, every one of the seniors said our greatest memory was yet to come. That was with the Arkansas game left, the SEC championship game with Georgia, and the national championship game. Guys really believed we were going to win three more games.

The last game in Tiger Stadium was special because, when I first went inside Tiger Stadium at a football camp when I was younger, I fell in love with the place. I'm from Mississippi, and I had other schools that really wanted me. Mississippi State was one, and people said I should stay in Mississippi and play, but Tiger Stadium kept pulling me.

I guess the big game to remember is Oklahoma in the national title game. I really studied their All-American Tommie Harris because he was supposed to tear us up. He is a great player. I turn my motor up and give it to him every game I can in the NFL.

212

His main thing was he is quick off the ball and tries to make you miss. My main thing is to stay back on him and let him make his first move and then get my hands on him. On run blocking, he was a little bit lighter, and every time I tried to come off the ball and push him on the ground, I did.

The first play of the national championship game we busted for 60 yards behind me and Rodney Reed, and that was a good feeling. They had all these award winners, and people said our O-line was a weak part of the game and a reason why we would lose. Coach Jimbo Fisher said the way we were going to beat Oklahoma was to run the ball right at them.

I first came to LSU at a camp before my sophomore year in high school. My dad owned a grocery store in Waveland and would take me over to camps. He said, "Save up your money, and I will match your money. Then you can go to some football camps around the country."

LSU was one that I picked. Coach DiNardo was there and Coach David Kelly was the tight ends coach. There was something about Tiger Stadium on that first trip, and I said, "I'm going to play there." I came from Waveland, Mississippi, and I was looking over at Tiger Stadium telling myself how much I wanted to play in there one day.

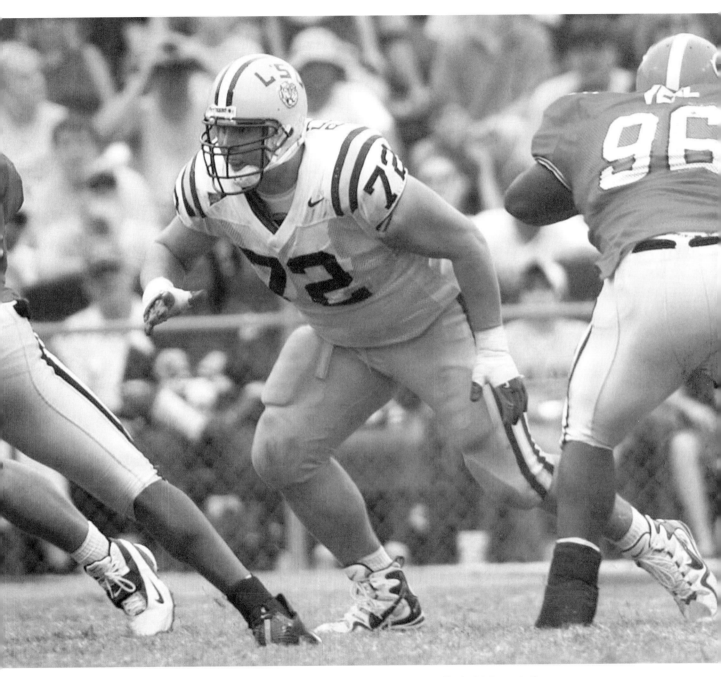

Stephen Peterman was part of an offensive line that controlled Oklahoma's fierce defense in the 2003 national championship game.

It always felt cool to be around that place. Once I started getting recruited, I got game tickets, and they invited me to come to the home games. Coach DiNardo would come talk to me, and the band would play the "Salute" while I was standing there on the sideline. I sat there and thought it would be unbelievable to play in front of that much energy.

I never got that feeling from any other place I went, and I went to camps at Auburn and Ole Miss. I went to Notre Dame and Mississippi State. I went to the Florida-Tennessee game at Florida, and there was never a place where I said I wanted to be other than LSU.

It was the greatest decision to go there. I met my wife; we had our first son the summer before we started the championship season. My whole time at LSU was a blast and a blessing.

I was going to be at the last game of the DiNardo regime, but he was fired and Coach Hal Hunter took over. Sam Nader called me and said it would mean a lot to the program if I would show up anyway, and I told him I wanted to be there. I had a good relationship with those coaches. They won that last game, so I was happy for them.

They had offered me a scholarship and said once a new coach was there they would be in touch. I always fell back on the fact that I loved Tiger Stadium. I loved every time I came there. It didn't matter who the coach was; I was going there.

Through all the time playing here in the NFL, Texas Stadium in Dallas, all the other big stadiums in the pros, I never got the same feeling in those places as I did walking out of the tunnel at Tiger Stadium. You slap the crossbar and come out of there, and those people get you ready. You feel like you are a gladiator and something more than you are. Unless you experience it, you can't understand.

Every home game we got on the buses to come down to the stadium, and the passion started as we were walking down the hill. It was just alive.

The game that stands out was when ESPN's *GameDay* was there and we played Georgia early that 2003 season. There were fans everywhere. People were high-fiving us and we walked through all that.

We built confidence off that Georgia game. A week or two later, we lost to Florida [19–7], and I remember guys saying that day, we worked too hard, put in too many hours in the off-season to let this one game get in our way. Don't lose again!

Georgia had a good team, a lot of NFL guys like David Greene and Thomas Davis. They had David Pollack, and he and I did not get along well that year. I never really liked him that much. He was a trash talker. Every chance I could, I would get a hit on him.

What always got me through and helped me the most was being physical and tough and fighting to the end. That will get you through. Even in high school, I was like that. No matter what, I'm going to turn it into a fight and make you quit. I just try and bring it every play, the whole game. A lot of my career, I was able to do it.

Once I moved to offensive line before my sophomore year, I was fine with it. Coach Yarno played 11 years in the NFL, so every chance I could, I was in his ear trying to learn stuff. We still have a great relationship. He is the assistant O-line coach at Tampa Bay. He took me under his wing and showed me everything.

Then Coach Stacy Searels showed up at LSU. He was a technician and cleaned my game up. He saw how hard I played. He stayed on me about little bitty things like a foot step here, a hand placement there. I was blessed to have two good offensive line coaches at LSU.

The greatest thing about the O-line is that it is all five guys, and if one guy is not on the same page, it makes you all look bad. Saban would run hundreds of blitzes at practice, and we would pick those blitzes up. Matt Mauck or Rohan Davey would stand back there at quarterback and make a good throw or a back would break through to the secondary. I got a good feeling and felt like I had something to do with that.

Saban would try out different defenses on us. It was more than you would see in a game, and he was experimenting on us. He would get pissed at the O-line because after a couple of years there, Rodney Reed and I would listen to his calls, figure out what he was running, and change our slides. Coach Saban would get all mad at us.

Sometimes we would make his calls for his defense. We would hear the defensive back make the call, and we would yell it out. The defensive end would slant inside, and the guy off the corner would be coming. You would get down in the middle of the drill and make calls for them, any call—not the right call—and the guys in front of you would get mad.

Saban was very tough on everybody. There was nobody he was not tough on. It was what it was. He got the best out of you. I was always trying to prove him wrong. If he told me I couldn't do something, I wanted to make sure I proved him wrong. He didn't give many pats on the back. If you didn't hear anything, you were doing okay. If you weren't, you heard it.

It was weird to see him go to a rival school like Alabama, but that's where my admiration for him stops. There is no way I would root for Alabama, even if a coach I respect is there. It was tough to see LSU lose a great coach, but they picked up a coach like Les Miles and won another national championship.

When people are talking up their teams in the NFL locker room, I will pop out my ring every once in a while. Then I will put on the purple and gold, and you can never miss that. It's fun to bring out the LSU stuff.

What it means to be a Tiger is building the friendships I will have for a lifetime. We did it. We won a national championship. Along the way a boy grew into a man in that stadium, and I won't forget it.

Stephen Peterman was a first-team All-American named by *Sports Illustrated*, ESPN, and *The Sporting News*. He was also named All-Academic by the Southeastern Conference and was first team All-SEC in 2002 and 2003. Peterman was drafted by the Dallas Cowboys and now plays with the Detroit Lions.

CHAD LAVALAIS

TACKLE

2000–2003

THE FIRST TIME I VISITED TIGER STADIUM, Death Valley…crazy. I mean, it was nuts. We upset No. 1 Florida, and it sold me. I had offers from Louisville and Mississippi State and Auburn, but I was going to LSU after that game.

And then things started happening, and I almost didn't get to play a game there.

I didn't make my ACT score—twice—and I just threw my hands up and said, that's it, I'm not going back to school. I had no intention of going back to school; I gave up. I was just going to get a job. Man, I got some crazy jobs. I was a prison guard for a while.

So Coach DiNardo, the head coach, stopped calling. My position coach stopped calling. They were moving on. But one guy kept calling, Sam Nader. He stayed in touch with me. He's been there since the dinosaur age. He is one of those guys that when they get rid of the whole staff, he is still there.

Coach Nader kept telling me to give it one more shot and not to give up. So when Coach Saban came in, he met with Coach Nader, who explained my situation. On one of Saban's first visits, he came by my house, we laid out a plan, and decided to give it a try.

I made my score, and that was it. I was on my way. That was January 2000. While I was sitting out, I had offers from other schools. I took a visit to a

Chad Lavalais' college football career had a rough start, but he developed into the SEC Defensive Player of the Year in 2003.

junior college in Texas in 1999, and it was horrible. I was there for two days and then just walked out.

I lied to the coaches so I could leave. I told them LSU was going to sign me, and the Tigers wanted me bad. The coaches there at the junior college tried to call the football office at LSU to check my story, but they couldn't get through because they were having a football camp at LSU and no one was in. So then they called my mom.

My back was against the wall, and I didn't think my mom would lie for me. No way. But she covered for me. She said LSU called and told him to come home. That junior college ended up winning the national championship in their division, but I'm still glad I left.

I wanted to have four years at LSU. I didn't want to be in junior college. You go to a game in Tiger Stadium like I did in high school, and it sticks with you.

Marksville is one and a half hours away from Baton Rouge, and it's back roads mostly. Saban came up there in January 2000 and said if I went to junior college, he would have a scholarship waiting for me. He is a guy who likes to recruit his own guys and check them out and evaluate them, and I guess he liked me. Coming from Michigan State to LSU, Coach Saban had to do a lot of backtracking in January to see the guys who were the recruits from the old staff, and he came by to see me.

That first year in 2000 I played every game, but I didn't start until the middle of the season against Alabama. I got a lot of playing time that season. They weren't going to redshirt me, so I played.

When you got to put the jersey on, it was even better than when I saw the upset of Florida. When you are growing up in Louisiana and you are being recruited by LSU, it's the best. There should not be any competition in the state for players.

Things happen for a reason, but I was finally there, and it was topped off by a Peach Bowl victory and the end of the 2000 season.

We had a good season in 2001 [10–3], were 8–5 in 2002, and the next year we won the national championship. It sounds like a cliché, but it was just hard work. Everybody says that, but it's true.

That 2002 season was my junior year, and I blocked that out because that's when we lost to Alabama 31–0. The best team in the conference was Alabama, but they were on probation and couldn't go to the SEC championship game. So we were co–division winners. We didn't look like co–division winners; we got it by default.

That 2002 season we finished with a loss to Texas in the Cotton Bowl. The starting time was horrible, something like 10:00 AM, and then we got crushed. The final score was 35–20, but it was worse than that. It was the Roy Williams show. He was the Texas receiver, and he just put it on us.

That next season, my senior season in 2003, we had a lot of people back on the defensive line and a lot of players back on the offensive line. The strength of the team was the D-line and secondary and the O-line. We had something we could build on.

When we beat Georgia, a top 10 team, and held down their offense, that showed we could play. They had a fast tempo to their offense, and they got a lot of yards, but we kept them out of the end zone. We hit the quarterback, David Greene, a ton of times. We built on that game throughout the year.

The game where I first thought I could be a decent player was against Alabama in 2000, my freshman year. We won [30–28], and I had something like eight tackles and one and a half sacks. I got player of the game for that.

The thing that made me good was that I went against Stephen Peterman every day in practice, just the battles we had. It got to the point where we said to each other, let's calm down, and we would ask each other, "What are you doing on this rep?" I would say, "I'm doing this." We were killing each other for two or three years, and finally we just said enough. We still went at it hard sometimes, but there was a time where we had to save our bodies. It's the same thing guys in the NFL do, too.

Saban caught on, and he would yell. And then you would just pick it up a little bit, be a little more convincing. It's something you learn.

As for Coach Saban and his style, if it was something that needed correcting, you corrected it. You took the relentless way he went about his business with a grain of salt. That's who he is. I respect him much more now. My freshman year I was just happy to be there and didn't care if he yelled at me. When he would go off, it didn't bother me. I know I told myself, *If I can handle this guy, I can handle anybody.* He's a great Xs and Os coach.

If you make a mistake and keep making it, you will hear about it. But he will make you better. You have to learn to take criticism, whether it is in sports or business. I have a lot of respect for him.

I had some quickness. I wasn't the biggest or the strongest guy, I just tried to utilize my quickness to get in and get off the block. I wasn't one of those guys who could bench press O-linemen all day. My footwork and quickness, things like that, I used to my advantage.

When I was named Defensive Player of the Year in the SEC [2003], I didn't hear about it until right before the national championship game with Oklahoma. One of the coaches finally gave me the trophy. I didn't even know. I was going to a lot of banquets for this award and that award, but that one I didn't know about.

I was very grateful, very thankful to be named Defensive Player of the Year in a conference like the SEC. I had seven sacks as a tackle. I had a decent season.

We went into that national championship game with Oklahoma, and we were looking forward to that. They would sit back there and try and throw 30 to 40 passes a game. And, honestly, we thought, *You're losing if you think you can do that*. Oklahoma could not run the ball. I know they ran through their conference, but they could not run the ball against us.

The SEC championship game was the second time we played Georgia that season. Georgia slowed down and made David Greene a pocket passer. They huddled up and gave us time to set up and get things together how we wanted them. In the first game with Georgia that season, they had over 300 yards rushing with a no-huddle. The second game with them was much easier.

Oklahoma was not fast tempo. If they wanted to huddle up and give us time to see what they're doing, okay, we're going to destroy them. Oklahoma tried to huddle up and throw deep routes to receivers. It was not a complicated game plan for us, just stuff we did all year.

The defensive playbook Saban has can be complicated, but it is not the number of blitzes, it is the audibles. That's what gets you. When he lays out the playbook, the basics, it is simple. But when you get to the audibles, that's a different story.

For example, when I played for the Falcons, if you called a blitz in the huddle, we ran that play. We didn't change it. We might change one part of it. With Saban, if we called a blitz in the huddle and they changed the formation, we changed the blitz.

221

So within a play, if they changed somebody, there would be an audible, and the blitz would come from a different side. Now our linebackers would call out the audible, but in the SEC you can't hear because of the crowds, so you have to know the audible yourself, you would have to know what to do.

If they went to a different front, then it was off. If there was a blitz called, you had to be ready. You never really heard the audible. My first two years, wow, it took me two years to get the whole concept. I knew why it was called, and if I saw a different front, we would change it up. Oh, my goodness, the first two years it was like chickens running around.

So you imagine what was in store for the Oklahoma quarterback. We were seniors, we had it down. Jason White was a quarterback who couldn't scramble and could only throw the deep ball, playing against a team that gets after you. We loved to hit quarterbacks. It was an easy game plan, and he did not have a good day [13-of-37]. I can talk some smack now. It was much harder preparing for Eli Manning and Ole Miss than Oklahoma and their Heisman winner.

It's funny because when I was in Atlanta and we played the Miami Dolphins and Coach Saban, they would line up and Coach Muschamp, who was at LSU and went to the Dolphins, was calling in some of the same plays. I was calling them out on the sideline. It was the same. Saban is smart, I'm sure he has changed some things up by now.

We were a 4-3 defense, but I saw this season at Alabama he went to a 3-4. As far as confusing offenses and quarterbacks, the 3-4 is the best. But you have to have the personnel. He had a bunch more linebackers at Alabama this season.

When Alabama lost to Florida in the SEC championship game [2008], I really thought Alabama would win. That's how good a coach he is. I talked to some coaches up there at Alabama, and what they are doing now they expected to do next year or the year after. A good coach will get the extra out of a player; an average coach will get what he gets. Saban got a lot out of a lot of players.

We laid the foundation for LSU's return to the national scene when a lot of guys stayed in state in 1999, 2000, and 2001 to play for the Tigers. We had lost guys like Peyton Manning to Tennessee, Eli Manning to Ole Miss, and Warrick Dunn to Florida State. When you win, it cures everything, and there is a lot of talent in the state of Louisiana that is going to stay. You need to get them to stay in your state and have them say, "You know what, I don't need to go anywhere. I can stay right here and play for the national championship and make a name for myself here."

We were the best team in school history in 2003. Rohan Davey and I got into an argument about the 2001 offense versus the 2003 defense. I'm sure Glenn Dorsey thinks the '07 team was better than the '03 team. Glenn's team was a nice team, but we were better, and we were national champs.

Chad Lavalais was named All-America by six publications and was the SEC Defensive Player of the Year in 2003. Lavalais was named National Defensive Player of the Year by *The Sporting News*. He was drafted in the fifth round by the Atlanta Falcons. Lavalais lives in Baton Rouge.

MATT MAUCK

QUARTERBACK

2000–2003

I GREW UP IN SOUTHERN INDIANA and signed to play football at Michigan State. But I got drafted by the Chicago Cubs and played baseball for three and a half years. I wasn't having fun, and I wanted the education, so I decided to go back to school and play football. I contacted Coach Saban when he was still at Michigan State.

The year I retired from baseball, he went to LSU and said right away I could come on down to Louisiana. My education was being paid for as part of my contract with the Chicago Cubs, so I joined the team for summer workouts in 2000 as a non-scholarship player. I was technically a walk-on with the Cubs' money.

I played baseball from 1997 to 2000. The Cubs drafted me as a pitcher and third baseman, and then Terry Kennedy moved me to catcher. Jim Hendry, who is now the GM of the Cubs, was the guy who drafted me. He and I talked, and we thought I had a future in it. But I didn't want to be 28 or 29 and find out I wasn't good enough after all and not have any back-up plan. It was hard enough going back to school as a 21-year-old. And you also get to a point where you can't play football anymore.

When I got there, the quarterbacks were Josh Booty, Rohan Davey, Craig Nall, Marcus Randall, and myself. Four of those guys actually played in the NFL. After Josh left for the pros early and Craig transferred, Rohan was the starter, then me. Then we recruited JaMarcus Russell and Matt Flynn.

I did not get in any games in 2000. In 2001 I was the backup to Rohan the whole season. I played against Florida in the second half [of a 44–15 loss], and then the next game I played was the Tennessee game in the SEC championship.

In that game, I guess I'm known for the quarterback draws we ran. We didn't have it in the entire year. It wasn't until Tuesday or Wednesday the week of the game when Jimbo [Fisher] came in and put it in the offense.

At that time Tennessee had one of the best defensive lines ever in the SEC—John Henderson, Albert Haynesworth, Demetrin Veal, and Will Overstreet. Jimbo put in that draw in case their rush was too much. We practiced it 20 or 30 times all week.

Rohan ended up going down with an injury in the game. We ended up running it 10 or 12 times and got two touchdowns out of it.

When I came in, in the second half, we ended up playing with an empty backfield so Tennessee didn't know if we were going to pass or run the quarterback draw. We spread out their defense by putting a running back in the slot.

The other thing is I played just one half that season before that game, so they knew nothing about me. I ended up throwing 23 or 24 passes in that second half and running the quarterback draw.

Tennessee was playing for the national championship, and they brought all kinds of fans to the Georgia Dome. Jimbo and I walked out of the tunnel before the game, and it was all orange. LSU has crazy fans who are willing to go anywhere, but we were outnumbered. Tennessee orange was everywhere at what was supposed to be a neutral site.

It looked like a Tenneessee home game. They were ranked No. 2 and had booked their tickets for the national championship game.

We'd lost our starting quarterback to injury and our starting running back, and we were playing an away game against the No. 2 team in the country. It was one of the greatest moments I ever had at LSU, not quite the night we won the national championship, but right behind that.

It's funny now, but Rohan got hurt running into John Chavis, who is a pretty big guy and was the Tennessee defensive coordinator. Now he is the LSU defensive coordinator.

The next season, in 2002, I started the first six games [going 5–1]. I got hurt in the Florida game in the fourth quarter. It was actually a quarterback draw.

Matt Mauck said an
injury helped him
develop into a better
pocket passer, and
that helped LSU win
the national
championship in
2003.

I tore all the ligaments between the first and second metatarsal in my foot and was out for the rest of the season. There was some question whether I could play football again. They put some screws in my foot for a while.

That injury actually turned out to be a blessing because I couldn't run in spring practice, and so I had to learn to be a pocket passer. I had to sit there in shotgun and take snaps and look downfield. It made me a much better player and was a big factor in the run to the national championship.

The big game in the regular season in 2003 was the Georgia game. We had some success in 2001 and 2002, but we didn't quite have the respect in 2003 until that 2003 game with Georgia. They were highly ranked [No. 7], and it was a big game.

When we got out of the busses to walk down the hill to the stadium for the Tiger Walk before that game, you could not see the pavement there were so many people there. The stadium holds 92,000. They estimated there were 120,000 people around Tiger Stadium that day with 92,000 having tickets and the rest without but still there because it was a big game.

It was a big game for us, for respect and also for recruiting.

They tied the game late, and then we won it [17–10] with a long pass to Skyler Green. It was supposed to be a rollout and a five-yard out to just get the first down, but Skyler got confused about the route and broke deep. I got a glimpse of him and threw it up. It was a busted play, but it turned out to be the winning touchdown.

We had to beat Georgia again in the SEC championship game and went on to play Oklahoma in the national championship game. We were ranked No. 2, and most people thought Oklahoma was better. They had every major award winner on their team, like Jason White, the Heisman winner. They also had the No. 1–rated defense, and people were saying all season they were one of the greatest college football teams of all time.

We had the No. 2–rated defense, so we knew what kind of game it was going to be. We had to protect the ball, and I didn't want to do anything to mess it up. Sure enough, Justin Vincent broke off a long run early in the game for us, and then I fumbled the snap at the 1 and lost the ball.

Our defense played great, though. Corey Webster made a big play, and Marcus Spears had an interception return for a touchdown. Skyler Green had a big play for our offense, and we won it.

I grew up in Indiana and had always heard about the Big Ten and dreamed of playing Big Ten football. But I couldn't imagine playing football anywhere but the SEC and LSU. It is really something to be able to tell people that I was a Tiger and I played at LSU.

Matt Mauck was the quarterback of the 2003 national championship team. He was also the quarterback who came off the bench to lead the upset of No. 2 Tennessee in the 2001 SEC championship game, which was LSU's first SEC championship since 1988. Mauck was on the SEC All-Academic team in 2002 and 2003. He was second-team All-SEC quarterback in 2003. Mauck is in dental school at the University of Colorado.

MICHAEL CLAYTON
WIDE RECEIVER
2001–2003

I CONSIDERED OTHER SCHOOLS because there's so much politicking at LSU and word got out that players from Louisiana might end up transferring to Southern U with a coaching change. There wasn't as much success as the community wanted with the coaches that were there before Coach Saban.

All that turned me away from LSU for a while. Coach DiNardo did not recruit me hard when I was in high school. So I looked at Florida State and wanted to follow behind Warrick Dunn, who was from Baton Rouge. I also looked at Miami, too.

Then I watched Coach Saban come in and take them to a bowl game his first year, beating Georgia Tech in the Peach Bowl. He was recruiting me, and I paid attention to him. The biggest thing he said to me was to make a 40-year decision, not a four-year decision. He came off as a guy with whom—if we believed in his system—I could succeed. I felt he was a coach who could put me where I needed to be in terms of being a football player.

I graduated in 2001 from Christian Life Academy. Marcus Spears and I took some visits to colleges and we were going as a package deal. We took a visit to Miami. We took a visit together to Florida State. We have been best friends our whole lives. To be top high school players in the state, we wanted to go somewhere together. And once Saban came in, we made a conscious decision to make it work at LSU.

Michael Clayton is second all-time in receptions at LSU. He is still playing in the NFL, and when he retires he wants to devote himself full-time to his businesses in Baton Rouge.

We were invited to a high school All-America game and went out to Dallas. There were six LSU signees in that game. We all sat around in a restaurant in Texas and watched Rohan Davey come in, in the second half and lead LSU to the win in the Peach Bowl. It gave you a sense of confidence in the program that in the first year Coach Saban could succeed like that.

When he came here, Coach Saban told us it was important that the Louisiana guys stay home and we be his guys, that he was going to build around us. It had not been that way before him. There were guys like Warrick Dunn who went off to other schools. Saban boosted the program by having local guys stick together.

Besides, when I went down to Miami and saw all the stuff going on down there, all the ways you could get distracted, I knew I didn't want to go down there. No way I could concentrate on football.

Saban came into my high school a few weeks ago [December 2008] for the retirement of my jersey, and he talked about building the program with local guys. The one thing he preached was to get everybody to follow exactly what he wanted with his plan. I became one of his guys because I would pass his word, his way, on to younger players.

He made you better with the mentality of the game. That's what it was, a mentality. He gave me a chance to play special teams and defense, as well as wide receiver. There were some people who thought I might be a better safety in the NFL than wide receiver, so I got to play some defense.

Coach Saban was a great judge of talent. He could see guys coming in, like Corey Webster, who was a receiver and move them to defense, where they could become stars. We became a No. 1–ranked defense in the country with his moves.

The most memorable game was the win over Oklahoma for the national championship because it was my last game, and we also saw a plan work out. We played in the Superdome in front of our fans, and it helped create the program that you see now, a program that is very good. It was huge for Louisiana. The guys from Louisiana were very proud because now guys from Louisiana were not going to leave; we helped create a powerhouse.

I did not have a big game against Oklahoma, it was a running and defense game. We opened up that game with Justin Vincent going 64 yards on a dive off tackle. It was a great feeling to beat them because they had the Heisman winner, and they had Tommie Harris, the All-American. They had guys who had won all these national awards, and people wondered how we could stay on the field—that's how I remember it. They had all the accolades.

SEC football is real physical, and we put them to the test. One of Coach Saban's mottoes was playing hard for 60 minutes and being physical. He used to tell us that, win or lose, that other team you played should say this about you every time, "We just played a hell of a team." We had that respect every game we played.

Coach Stan Hixon also had a lot to do with me improving as a player at LSU. He was the wide receivers coach, and the one thing he preached was being physical as a wide receiver. He recorded knockdowns on blocks. He would yell at us, "G-A-T-A!" Get after their ass.

Every day after practice we would have to catch 20 balls before we left. That was every single day. Then I would have to line up against Corey Webster, who is playing in the NFL. I would have to go against him, and that made me better. We made each other better.

If I had to go by stats, my best game was against Kentucky on October 13 my freshman year. It was my birthday. I think I had two touchdowns, 105 yards, and we won the game. It was the only game my parents did not attend, and it was because of a hurricane. I asked them to stay home. I caught a slant in the end zone from Rohan Davey with 13 seconds left. I might have caught four or five balls on the last drive because their defense was all over our All-American, Josh Reed. I was around a great group of guys. I was able to come in and fight my way in as a starter, and Rohan Davey was throwing that thing back in the day. Josh Reed got double coverage, and I ate everything up.

The next season we played at Kentucky in the Blue Grass Miracle. I was the guy who jumped and tipped the ball to Devery [Henderson]. He caught it and took it in for the score. It was trips right, rebound pass.

To start the drive, I caught a pass on a dagger route to about our 25- or 30-yard line. Then we threw the pass that shocked the stadium. It was quiet except for our fans screaming. Devery was the speed guy, and the idea was for me to jump—I'm 6'4"—and try and tip the ball to him. I tipped it, he grabbed it. I was in the middle, and Devery was lined up right. I was the jump guy. The Kentucky guys were trying to catch it, and Devery grabbed it. My back was to the goal line.

The fans charged the field while the ball was in the air. They drenched their coach with water, celebrating. They were thinking they had the won the game, and then their fans just stopped and had that look of "What the hell just happened?" We piled up in celebration. We ended up winning an ESPY for that.

You never needed much to get hyped for an LSU home game. Just running out of that tunnel was enough. The stadium was always rocking, the moment we stepped off the bus and walked down the hill. Our opponents knew what kind of atmosphere it was going to be. Our fans, hands down, are the best in the country, and Death Valley is a dynamic place to play.

Still today there a ton of SEC guys who say it was the worst place, the loudest place, to play in the SEC. They are pretty rowdy in there. And rightfully so, because we made them proud. Even away games we would have a great turnout from our fans. When we played the SEC championship against Georgia [2003], they had a lot of red in that Georgia Dome, but our fans were heard.

We beat them pretty good, 34–13. I remember getting close to 100 yards and making a one-handed catch, a 43-yard touchdown. Then we went on and won the national championship.

My decision to go to LSU has turned out to be a 40-year decision, not a four-year decision, because I came back to my hometown and my home state to be an entrepreneur. Things worked out at LSU, and there is an opportunity for me in business after I am done with football.

231

I have a clothing store in Cortana Mall, 80 Stitches, an urban clothing store. It is a direct reflection of playing football at LSU. I have LSU pictures up; it shows a lot of good times, and I have a lot of support from people.

I have part ownership in a bank, Business First Bank, where Buddy Roemer, the former governor, is the CEO. Going to LSU is truly going to be a 40-year decision for me and a great thing.

Michael Clayton was an All-SEC receiver in 2003 and one of the key players in LSU's national championship run. He had 12 receptions in a game against Alabama in 2003 and finished his career second on the all-time receiving list with 182 catches, just one behind all-time leader Wendell Davis. Clayton is fourth all-time at LSU in receiving yards [2,582]. Clayton was drafted in the first round of the 2004 NFL Draft by Tampa. He owns a clothing store in Baton Rouge and is in a partnership in a Baton Rouge bank.

COREY WEBSTER
WIDE RECEIVER/ CORNERBACK
2001–2004

HERE IS WHAT IT MEANS TO BE A TIGER: when you line up at practice, you have somebody across from you who can make you a better player. I had Mike Clayton, wide receiver. Great player. We went at it every day. We're still good friends, but we battled and fought each other.

We worked out together and made each other into players who could play in the NFL. On the practice field, you could not tell that Mike and I were good friends. That was every day at practice. Coach Saban let us go at it, and it made us the players we are today.

That's what it means to be a Tiger.

Mike is 6'4" and a physical guy, and I had come over to play defensive back after always playing on the offensive side of the ball. I played quarterback in high school and receiver my first year at LSU. So to go against one of the best receivers in college ball like Mike made me a physical corner. I am a guy who likes to get his hands on a receiver and throw the timing off between the quarterback and receiver.

Coach Saban loved that kind of stuff at practice. He worked with the DBs, and we won our share of battles with Mike and them. We won more of the battles than the offense did.

Corey Webster has two championship rings, one for LSU's 2003 national title and the other for the New York Giants' 2008 Super Bowl win.

When Coach Saban moved me over to the defensive side of the ball, my dad and I were not too thrilled about it. He sat down in our house when we were making the switch and told my dad he would much rather I played cornerback. He said he thought I could be a better player. He saw me play basketball and how I stayed in front of people. Coach Saban told us we had to trust him and to trust that I was going to be a corner who was All-SEC and All-America, and that I would never look back at it.

I'm not going to lie. We still weren't thrilled about it after that conversation. We just looked at each other and said he was just saying all this stuff, no way I should switch. He made two trips to my house to try and talk to us about it.

But everything he said was exactly what happened. He still calls me, and I call him. I congratulated him [in 2008] for winning Coach of the Year at Alabama.

Coach Saban tells you what he is going to do and goes out and does it, whether on the field or off. When he came from Michigan State, he said he was going to bring the graduation rate up, build this kind of academic center, and do this with academics—and all of those things happened at LSU. The graduation rate went up 20 percent when he was there.

The guys I was close to at LSU, we all graduated. He also wins and is a competitor. He demands excellence, and as long as you give him that, he is good with you.

One thing he teaches is kick-slide. It is a big, big thing for him. Cut off the wide receivers. A lot of guys like to turn and run and think that is the best way. But you have to trust and believe the kick-slide works. It's all legal—nothing is illegal—you just have to work at it. It is beating the wide receiver to a point and giving the quarterback less room to work toward the sideline.

Coach would tell Travis Daniels and me that we did a great job of taking wide receivers out of the game and allowing us to blitz the way we did. We always had different packages. LaRon Landry was young when he started playing with us, and we took a lot of pressure off him by knowing the defense the way we did. Jack Hunt was another guy back there who was an intelligent guy calling shots.

I remember Oklahoma having the best of everything. They had the Heisman Trophy–winning quarterback, they had Tommie Harris, an All-American on defense, and [Teddy] Lehman at linebacker, who was also very good. They had the best corner in Derrick Strait.

We came out and showed them we were much more physical than they were. I know a lot of people talk about the SEC having speed, but we came out and showed them we could play with some muscle. We bumped the wide receivers off the line of scrimmage. We threw off their timing.

They tested me on the first play of the game with a deep ball, and I got an interception off of it. We wanted to impose our will against them. I matched up with Mark Clayton and followed him around. On that first play of the game for them, they motioned him inside, I bumped outside to a wide receiver, and they took a real deep shot on us.

We didn't believe in help over the top. We pressed receivers 85 to 90 percent of the time. There wasn't a whole lot of help going on. You only got help if you were tired after running down the field on some long passes a few times in a row. We could get into a cover 2 then if we needed a breath.

We also had those guys like Marcus Spears, Kyle Williams, Chad Lavalais, and Marquise Hill. Glenn Dorsey might have even played as a freshman. If you sat in the pocket too long, we were coming. We put pressure on the quarterback like there was no tomorrow.

That junior year, when we won the title, I played well because I didn't give up any big plays. But I would have to say my best game was in my sophomore year, just after I switched to corner, when we played Florida.

We played in the Swamp against Rex Grossman, who was up for the Heisman, and I had three interceptions, one for a touchdown. Being a young kid and playing in a game like that was unbelievable. They had Taylor Jacobs, and he was really good. It was my sixth game as a corner. I think my dad and I started believing a little bit that Coach Saban knew what he was talking about when he moved me to defense.

We were 8–5 that sophomore year, and going into the 2003 season, my junior year, I knew we could be good, but I wasn't sure how good. Coach Saban was turning things around. We took a lot of pride in getting better, and I remember nobody wanted captains because we all knew what had to be done. We didn't need captains telling us.

Once that season started, we didn't have any trouble. People just wanted to go out and play. We got to a point where we didn't think we could lose. We lost to Florida that year, but we still thought we had something special.

We went up against a lot of good quarterbacks, guys like Rex Grossman and Eli Manning. Our whole motto was that these guys were not going to pump up their stats for the Heisman Trophy on our watch. They weren't going to make their names against our defense. We were trying to pull them out of the Heisman race.

Eli would just find every open receiver that season. It didn't matter what the name was on the back of the jersey. If you were open, he found you. We beat them [17–14], but we had to work to stop him because he was scoring it that season.

We worked extremely hard at LSU, and I still go back in the off-season to work with the younger guys and pass some things on to them. Joseph Addai comes down; Mike Clayton will come down. Joseph, Travis Daniels, and I go back, and Les Miles said it is important for us to keep that up because the young guys need to see that it works.

It builds a lot of character to work hard together like that. I tried to work with Byrd and LaFell, guys on the team now [2008]. Jai Eugene, I worked with him. The guy from Florida, Patrick Peterson, we're going to take him under our wing and work with him.

The success at LSU gives us a lot of bragging rights in the NFL locker room. That's a good thing. The people at LSU bleed purple and gold, and to go out there and win two national championships in the last few years is big for the players. But it is really big for the people down there because of all the support they give the program. They appreciate us, and it means a lot to me.

I took a few visits to other schools, but I think I was always going to go to LSU because I wanted to be a part of turning the program around. It never really was good when I was coming up. They had good players, Kevin Faulk and those guys, but they did not have the great teams.

I'm from Louisiana and know everything about LSU, the traditions and the history. I was rooting for them in the late 1990s when I was coming up, and they gave me a headache every weekend because they could not get it going.

To be part of the transformation process was fun because people said we were not going to do this, we weren't going to do that. We ended up winning a national championship.

I'm most proud of the degree, though. My mom is an educator and always preached to me about getting the education. To see the look on her face and how excited she was to see me walk across that stage was tremendous. She was happy when we won the national championship, but she was really happy when I got that degree because they can't take that away from you.

236

Corey Webster was a starting cornerback for LSU's 2003 national championship team and a two-time All-American. Webster was named first team All-SEC in 2003 and 2004. He was part of the Giants' 2008 Super Bowl championship team.

RUDY NISWANGER

CENTER

2002–2005

M Y JUNIOR YEAR IN HIGH SCHOOL I was leaning toward Florida State. They were the first ones to offer me a scholarship out of high school, and they had just won the national championship, so I was in awe with them.

I went to their spring game my junior year on an unofficial visit, but their facilities were not as nice as I expected. I kind of got a feeling of arrogance. My thought at the time was, *Wow, if this is the national champion, LSU has nicer stuff than this.*

LSU was coming off a 3–8 year in 1999, and Nick Saban had just gotten hired and was there one year in 2000 when I was recruited by LSU. After I crossed off Florida State, it was pretty much all LSU.

One of the big things Saban talked about was discipline. Going to a small school, it was something I could identify with. That was one of our big issues. He told me coming in that LSU had become an undisciplined team, not only with things on the field, but off the field.

He had the fourth-quarter program in the off-season, which was finishing out the fourth quarter of games. I believed him. He had that kind of personality where I knew discipline was going to be a big issue for him.

When people ask me about combining the academics and the athletics, for one, I tell them the Good Lord blessed me with the intelligence to do it, but it was also about priorities. You will find time to do things that are important to you.

Rudy Niswanger won the academic equivalent of the Heisman Trophy in 2005 when he was named the winner of the Draddy Award, given to the top scholar-athlete in college football.

238

My first semester, my academic counselor challenged me, and I met the challenge with straight As. I said if I can do it once, I can keep doing it. It became a pride thing to continue to get good grades.

I debated about physical therapy school versus med school my second year. I talked to physical therapists I knew, and they said if you are going to go through all that stuff, you might as well go to med school. A lot of people go into biology, microbiology, chemistry. I went into kiniesiolgy with human movement.

I graduated from Ouachita Christian School in Monroe in 2001. I was a A/B student and played football through high school. I didn't quite put the emphasis on academics in high school that I did in college.

I played center my first two years in high school, and junior and senior years I played guard. I was 6′5″, 260 pounds, so I was on the lean side.

I was recruited by all the SEC schools and got scholarship offers from all of them plus Texas, Texas A&M, Northwestern, Colorado, and Nebraska.

We started to build a very good offensive line at LSU in 2001. Being in the NFL now, I see even more how important the offensive line is to a team. If you have a good offensive line, you can hand the ball off to people. If you can protect the quarterback, and if he is halfway good, you can get things accomplished.

Saban had some big dreams for LSU. He came in to recruit me and laid out his ideas. He was not just visualizing his ideas, he actually did these things at Michigan State. He said, "This is what the facilities looked like at Michigan State when I got there, and this is what they looked like when I left." LSU, from what I understand, had one of the worst graduation rates in the SEC. It wasn't good, and those things were going to get turned around, he said.

When I got there, the coaches did not say to me, "Okay, you're a center." They were big on putting the best pot of guys on the field. Unless you were a starter, you played every position—guard, tackle, center. If you never played a down at right guard, well how do you know he couldn't play it? A guy might turn out to be the best right guard to play the game. Saban was big on everybody learning all positions, so if you had somebody get hurt on game day, you would have that sixth man.

I was redshirted in 2001. In 2002 the majority of my snaps was at right guard. I didn't start any that first season, I was back-up at center, guard, and I think I even played some tackle.

In the national championship season in 2003, I started four games at left guard: Alabama, Auburn, Louisiana Tech, and Arkansas. Then I was a reserve in the other games. I played in every game.

We had a lot of talent. Ben Wilkerson was the starting center; Stephen Peterman was our starting right guard; our right tackle was Rodney Reed; the left guard was Nate Livings; and our left tackle was Andrew Whitworth. I was the sixth man, the back-up to all five positions. I had a lot to learn that year.

Obviously, it was disappointing. You don't play the game to be a backup; everybody wants to start. But LSU and the team were bigger than I was. The important issue was getting wins on Saturday. It made me work harder, and I had something to prove to get on that field and be a full-time starter and not just be filling in gaps.

Once you get to college and major-college ball, there is no ego-boosting by the coaches. We are in a performance-driven business. You have to perform if you want to play.

239

Looking back on it now, I don't think I was mentally mature enough to be a full-time starter. I think I could have done a good job, but I think at that point I was too up and down with how I played. If I made a bad play, I was down in the dumps. One thing I have learned in the NFL since then is to stay at an even keel. You have to put the play behind you, whether it was good or bad. I worried too much.

I felt I had good feet. I used my intellect and tried to learn what the defense was doing and use their gap schemes against them. I tried to set them up for things, and I was relatively quick for a big guy, as I was one of the lightest offensive linemen at 300 pounds. I tried to out-quick guys and run my feet. I tried to outwork them.

I tried not to let anything in football interfere with academics. My offensive line coach my first two years, George Yarno, talked about intensity and described it as total focus and concentration on the task at hand and not to let that bleed over into something else.

When I was at football, I wasn't worried about schoolwork. When I was studying, I wasn't worrying about football. When I was out with my girlfriend, who is now my wife, I was with her. That's where my mind was.

That 2003 season, the finish to it, was amazing. We were down in New Orleans for the national championship that week, and the streets were filled with fans. It is practically a home game for us. Then they went nuts after the game when we beat Oklahoma.

The next season, 2004, I had a good year. It was a crazy year. I started six games at left guard, one game at right guard, one game at right tackle, four games at center. We had a guard get hurt, then a right tackle got suspended at the start of a game where he couldn't play the first quarter, and then I moved to guard.

Then our starting center, Ben Wilkerson, got hurt, and I started the last four games.

My senior season I was All-SEC, and that was with Les Miles. I liked him, he was a very personable guy. He took over right after the Capital One Bowl, and the impression to me and my teammates was he was a guy who would listen to us and was player-oriented.

Les Miles got there five or six days before my wife, Patricia, and I got married, on January 8. In my wife's dressing-room suite, just before the wedding, somebody delivered a huge bouquet of flowers from Les Miles. He won my wife over immediately. It was a perfect gesture to win her over.

At the time, we were trying to decide to come back for the fifth year of football or go on to med school. I had already been accepted to med school but decided to come back. The flowers didn't hurt.

My senior season I was second-team All-SEC, and we had a good season. We were the first team in LSU history to beat Florida, Auburn, and Alabama in the same year.

One of my best games of the season was early against Tennessee when we lost to them in overtime, 30–27. They had some very good players on the defensive line, NFL guys, and I played pretty well against them. The night before I had a 104° fever. I was sick as a dog and was worried about the game. I came out and played one of my best games of the year.

We were up 21–0 at halftime, and they come back to tie it 24–24. Our offense was moving the ball, the defense was getting turnovers, we were demolishing them in every phase of the game. The second half it was like another person took over calling the plays, and a different set of players took over running the plays.

Rick Clausen was the Tennessee quarterback. He had transferred out of LSU; they booed him out of Baton Rouge. I felt bad for him; the media didn't like him. Our fans were pretty mean to him. It was a big deal for him to come back into Tiger Stadium, and it added an interesting dynamic to it. That game moved to a Monday night because of Hurricane Rita, so it was some kind of setting with all those things happening.

241

Another big game was Alabama and beating them in overtime [16–13]. They were highly ranked [No. 4], and I remember going into Tuscaloosa and their fans screaming at us and throwing things at our busses. They were undefeated, and the talk was they were playing for the national championship. The newspapers, radio, and TV up there had talked about how Alabama wins a national championship every certain number of years, and this was one of those years. But we beat them.

We went to overtime tied 10–10. They kicked a field goal to take the lead, 13–10. But then JaMarcus Russell threw a pass to Dwayne Bowe for the winning touchdown. We went nuts celebrating in the end zone.

We had to hold on to beat Arkansas the next week and win the west division of the SEC. We were beating them 19–0 or 19–3, and they came back and made it 19–17. It was a close game that should not have been a close game.

We had one loss [10–1], and then Georgia just beat us good in the SEC championship game [34–14]. They did to us what we did to them in the conference championship game [a 34–13 win] the year we won the national championship.

We had worked out all the scenarios about how we could play for the national championship. We were No. 3 in the country, and Texas and Southern Cal were undefeated and ranked No. 1 and No. 2. We still thought that we had a little bit of a chance. We were holding on to hope from the computers, but then Georgia beat us.

That loss was a huge blow to us. Andrew Whitworth and I were talking after that game, and I told him I had never wanted something so bad in my life and not gotten it. Everything else in my career had worked out, except that game.

To not win the SEC championship in our last year was a pretty big blow to all of us. Andrew, Coach Miles, Stacy Searels (the offensive line coach), and I were on the bus coming back from the game, and all of a sudden our bowl options, instead of the Sugar Bowl, were the Independence Bowl or the Peach Bowl. We weren't even in a New Year's Day Bowl.

We drew Miami in the Peach Bowl. All week of that game, we heard how Miami was going to kill us. We had a lot of bowl functions with the Miami players, and they were extremely arrogant. Their players didn't like us for whatever reason. It was a different environment.

The game was over right after halftime. We beat them pretty good [40–3]. There was a fight after the game in the tunnel. Dwayne Bowe, who is from Miami, was teasing them after the game, took a ball or something, and then it got out of hand. Guys from both teams think it's a fight, and the next thing you know, a punch is thrown.

I went into the stands to kiss my wife. I decided to let the young guys fight. All this fighting stuff was for guys who didn't play in the game.

LSU gets a lot of players who don't have the measurables that people look at for football players, particularly the NFL guys. Let's face it, guys can get drafted if there is a lot of buzz about them. They draft on ability, but also what people are saying and that sort of thing.

If I had to take a guess at it, LSU has a lot of guys in the NFL who were not drafted because they don't have the measurables the league is looking for, but when they get in camp, they open up eyes, they make an impact. The guys that slipped through the cracks of getting drafted, when they get on a team, and the team gets to know them, they see the impact an LSU guy can make.

There is a lot of pride in being a Tiger. It is a big fraternity. It's just a big group of guys who have one thing in common, and that's LSU football. I'm not talking about the stadium or the locker room. I'm talking about the tradition.

I once had an LSU coach tell me that I was not out there playing for myself, the name on the back of the jersey, and I was not there playing for my parents. What you are playing for is that helmet and the logo that is on that helmet that has stood for what LSU has been for 100 years. You are playing for the guys who came before you, the guys next to you now, and the guys who will come 100 years after you.

In 2002 we played Kentucky in the game that came to be known as the Blue Grass Miracle. The night before a game, Jimbo Fisher would run a one-reel tape about the game plan and then finish it and give us a speech before we went to bed.

Before that game he said, "You remember one thing tonight. If any one of you guys had a scholarship offer to go to Kentucky, you wouldn't have gone. You think you would have chosen Kentucky over LSU? We're LSU, that's who we are, and you remember that tomorrow."

He just kept repeating it. Winning that game the way we did drove home that point. It takes confidence and knowledge of who you are as a team to go into that situation and say, "It's cool, we're going to win. We're LSU, that's what we do."

Rudy Niswanger won the academic equivalent of the Heisman Trophy in 2005 when he was named the winner of the Draddy Award, which is given to the top scholar-athlete in college football. Niswanger also won the Wuerrfel Award, which is named for the former Heisman Trophy winner Danny Wuerffel. It is based on community service. Niswanger was the seventh player in the history of LSU football to be nominated for the National Scholar-Athlete Award, which is presented by the National Football Foundation. Niswanger was an undrafted free agent in 2006. He became the starting center for the Kansas City Chiefs for the 2008 season.

CRAIG STELTZ

SAFETY

2004–2007

WE NEVER HAD BACK-TO-BACK LOSSES at LSU when I was there. That shows you some of the mentality around the program. You lose, you circle the wagons, and you come back harder.

That happened with the Kentucky game my senior year. We lost in triple overtime and came back with some big wins against Auburn and Alabama.

Then we lost to Arkansas but came back to win the SEC championship and beat Ohio State for the national championship. That's what happened around there in the four years I was there. Guys fought back when we lost and did not let any bad feelings build up. We kept our confidence.

That's what LSU football is all about.

There is a chemistry around the program because 80 percent or more of the guys are from Louisiana, and they have grown up around the program. My brother, Kevin, played there. We grew up an hour down the road from LSU.

A guy who ended up being one of my best friends on the team, Jacob Hester, was someone I played against in high school for three years. I lived with him up here at LSU, played on the same team, and we developed a bond.

So it doesn't matter for a lot of guys who the coach is, Saban or Miles. We are going to uphold the traditions of the program. We're going to wear the white jerseys and gold pants at home. We're going to run through the goal posts and walk down the hill. The tradition is what has to be upheld through the years.

Craig Steltz joined his brother, Kevin, at LSU and went on to be an All-America safety for the 2007 national champions.

You can tell how much guys want the program to succeed because when they come back from the NFL to work out, they are not just using the facilities, they are hanging around with younger players and teaching. They're showing guys, hey, we're in the league, this is what you have to do to get to the next level.

Some of the guys have been out of the league for a few years and are still around working for the school. You see Joe Addai and Kyle Williams helping out. It's amazing how jacked up guys get working for their colleges.

When I say it doesn't matter who your coach is, it means something about the tradition of the school. Now, with Coach Miles and Coach Saban, it matters because you knew both of those guys were the leaders, the guys you followed into the games. I played for Coach Saban one year and Coach Miles three years.

They are different people, except when it came time to recognize who the team leader was, and then they were the same. You knew whom to follow. You have to know who your leader is. They both knew how to circle the wagons.

Coach Miles was a blast for three years. He always has some type of saying. The first year he was there he was all about "chopping wood." We would always say something about chopping wood and get on him. Just work, that was his message. Guys would joke about what kind of axe they were chopping with, but we kept working.

He kept the atmosphere fun, and I guess when you are winning 11 games one year, 11 the next, then 12, you can have some fun.

When it got serious, like after the loss to Kentucky in triple overtime, Coach Miles got us ready for the next weekend to go get a win. We had some long practices to get over that loss. When you play that many plays in a game and lose, it's tough, and you want to get a win back. Like I said, we never had back-to-back losses. We had a mentality after losses. It happened over and over.

The team that won the national championship my last year had some trouble in the red zone keeping people out, and we lost a couple of games. Seemed like we always had our backs to the wall. I'm not sure why that happened. That red-zone efficiency was a huge stat against us. I don't know if we had the same intensity, but when you play in the SEC, it is against great players who make plays.

In the national championship game against Ohio State, our defense gave up the big run to Bennie Wells, and then we stepped it up. Somebody missed a gap on his run, I don't think anybody ever touched him. It only takes one player to be out of their gap, and a guy is running free.

I don't know how many times it happened during the year that something like that would happen and then we would shut things off. It was an exciting season. Playing in the SEC against unbelievable competition, you are going to get tested and you have to rally.

The game that stood out for me was the Florida game [2007]. Any time you get a chance to play the Gators at home, it is a big game. It was our defense against Tim Tebow and their offense. Percy Harvin was a tremendous player, too.

They moved the ball a little bit, but we got some turnovers. That kind of team does not get shut down. You have to take the ball. We got a fumble and an interception and won the game [28–24].

Personally, I had some big games thanks to pressure from our defensive front. You get guys like Glenn Dorsey chasing quarterbacks, and they are going to throw it up for grabs. I had two interceptions against Ole Miss and three against Mississippi State. We might have had six interceptions against Mississippi State [45–0]. It was exciting getting interceptions.

Our defense was about getting turnovers. It started with our defense on the corners with guys like Chevis Jackson. They were out there on an island and kept fighting.

I was always going to LSU. I had an older brother, Kevin, who was on the national championship team in 2003. He was a fullback. To have an opportunity to go play with him and to experience things in Baton Rouge was big for me and our family. Some other schools wanted to recruit me, but I was too close to the LSU program to go anywhere else. It was a no-brainer. My brother was here to teach me things. Mom and dad came up to every game for seven years. They never missed a game.

Before Kevin got up here, I might have come to just one LSU game. But now I'm into it. Once I heard the inside view from him, I was coming here.

You start out your freshman season and it all looks far away, your chances of starting. You saw who the leaders of the team were and just wondered when you might get out there and be a leader. That's what you look out for.

I started maybe four or five games my sophomore year, maybe four my junior year, and then all of my senior season. The starting term meant nothing to me because it all depended on the package. I wouldn't start, but I played more than the guys who started in the game.

My favorite tradition was the walk down Victory Hill. You could see family and friends and walk down the hill with friends and with your brother.

When Coach Saban left after my first year, it opened my eyes that you do not go to a school for the coach, you go for the school and what the school is all about. As a senior coming out of high school, you have no idea how things are going to work out, so you better like the school. You want to play for LSU, not for Coach Saban or Coach Miles. It is a business, and guys move on. You are extremely lucky if you are with a guy who is there five years.

You play with the guys in purple and gold. From the time I signed my name on the scholarship paper to the time I left, there was only one coach still there, and that was Coach Moffitt, the strength coach. Same as the NFL—they just cleaned house on the defensive side with my NFL team in Chicago.

The passion of the fans at LSU is a constant thing, even if they are changing coaches. When you run out that tunnel, there are going to be 92,000 fans there. You can't hear yourself think. The good news is there was more stress on the other team with the noise. The noise goes straight down to the field.

You could attack an offense with that noise. It was something every team was worried about. The quarterback has more plays with checks they can make, but we can make some calls on defense—not as many as them, but we could get to them. Coach Pelini's big thing was attacking an offense and making plays. That was a huge thing, attack an offense and make some plays.

Having an opportunity for both my brother and I to win a national championship is a pretty special thing. Having that chance is what it means to be a Tiger.

If you just closed the borders and kept all the great players in the state, it would be a very strong program. That's what makes LSU a national power—all the football players in the state that we can recruit. That was a huge thing that Coach Saban started to do and Coach Miles has done: keep guys inside the border and don't let them go to Florida State or Tennessee or Ole Miss.

Craig Steltz was a first-team All-America safety in 2007. He was a finalist for the Thorpe Award and started 14 games for the Tigers' 2007 national championship team. Steltz was one of seven LSU players named first-team All-SEC in 2007. He was selected in the fourth round of the 2008 NFL Draft by the Chicago Bears.

HERMAN JOHNSON

OFFENSIVE TACKLE

2005–2008

I REALLY DIDN'T WATCH A LOT OF LSU football because we didn't get a lot of the SEC games in Texas. It was all Big 12 games where I was, so I grew up watching those teams and was a big Nebraska fan. I watched a lot of Texas A&M, but I didn't see myself at Nebraska or A&M. I wanted to see myself close to family.

I was being recruited by Oklahoma, Oklahoma State, and the University of Houston. And then LSU came into the picture, and it was the only school where I thought I would be comfortable because I was going to be close to family that was still in Baton Rouge. I have ties all in Louisiana.

Coach Saban and Coach Stacy Searels showed up at spring practice before my senior season in high school, and everybody was shocked. People just got excited he showed up, the coach of the LSU Tigers, and that's when it hit me I had a chance to go to LSU.

The other schools, Oklahoma, Oklahoma State, sent scholarship offers, but Coach Saban was the first coach to come visit. I would get a call from head coaches, but he was the first coach to come and meet me personally. As a kid in high school, it was some feeling that the head coach at LSU would come all that way to see me.

It was exciting for me because all the time I was growing up, people were saying I was a big guy and it was highly possible for me to go play college

Herman Johnson said a "good luck" card from students at his former elementary school in Texas inspired him before the national championship game in January 2008, which LSU won over Ohio State.

football. I really didn't like playing football growing up. I liked watching it, but I didn't like playing it, because I was too big to play.

That's one thing that turned me away from it. They would not let me play because I was too big. If I did play, they said I would have to play in the older group, and my mom didn't want to see me playing with the older guys and risk getting hurt. When I first started playing, we weren't winning games, and that turned me away, too. I thought, *This is tough.* I got to a point where I didn't want to play.

Finally, in ninth grade I got to play. I was junior varsity, and it was a good program at Denton High School. I was playing with older guys and fit right in. They showed me the ropes. So that's how I finally got started into football.

I committed to LSU on my birthday in my senior year, January 29, 2004. I was one of the last to commit in my class. My mom and I had a long talk about it, and she wanted to make sure I was close enough so she could drive to my games. I had narrowed it down to Oklahoma and LSU, and the big thing was that if I had gone to OU my family would not have been close by, so one of my main reasons for coming to LSU was family.

My first start was on the road at Vanderbilt my redshirt freshman season. I started off as a right tackle and then moved to guard.

My favorite play was elephant left, Nike left, a formation where I would line up in the backfield, fourth-and-inches or third-and-short. They would call that play, and we always got a first down. Of course, I was the elephant. The Nike was the quarterback. This year [2008] they brought in somebody else for that, but that's all right.

One of the most memorable games was the Ole Miss game at home my sophomore year, where we had a fourth-quarter drive and ended up winning in overtime. When you are playing on the road, people expect the visiting team to get down, but when you are at home, they expect you to win.

The crowd was upset with us. We came to the sideline and heard boos in that game. When you hear that, you want to do all you can to get those boos to stop and get those cheers back. It's crazy. They will boo college kids at LSU. Fans, in general, whether LSU fans or other team's fans, they are going to be upset when things are going bad, happy when they are going great. Then you have those true, dedicated fans who are going to be with you winning or losing. Those are the fans the teammates care about. The boos are not helping us out.

The other game I remember, of course, was the national championship win over Ohio State. After that win, it took me a while before it hit me.

I didn't sleep for three days. I was so jacked up, I stayed up the whole night. I packed that night and got on the bus the next morning back to LSU. My mom called and picked me up. I stayed up all that next night, too.

We won the national championship, and there are so many young guys who want that, and work for it, but they are on teams that won't even come close to that type of recognition. For me to be forever ingrained on the list of players who won a national championship, there is no greater feeling.

All my friends back in Texas started calling me, guys I grew up and played with as a kid. They were all saying, "We're so proud of you." They all said I was doing the right things and was a positive influence on kids.

The one thing that really touched me was the elementary school I went to made me two greeting cards. The first one was a good luck card before the national championship game. I got this big card, a huge card, from Robert E. Lee Elementary with all the kids' signatures on it. They all wrote words of encouragement, and it was great.

Then they sent a card after the game saying congratulations and we're looking up to you. A lot of the kids were saying we want to be football players, we want to be LSU Tigers, and this is from kids living in Texas. It just blew me away. They were having purple-and-gold days at the school where the kids and teachers wear LSU colors to school. I didn't know I was having that kind of impact. They were having purple-and-gold Fridays.

You are always going to be part of one of the greatest families in college football. You are going to be one of the guys who put on that purple and gold uniform and ran out of that tunnel. Everybody who puts that uniform on does so with the utmost respect. And if they don't, they should.

There have been a lot of battles on that field at Tiger Stadium, and that is hallowed ground as far as I'm concerned. Every time we step across that line, we have to do our best, not just for the fans, but for all the Tigers who came before us. There is pride involved with it, LSU pride. No matter what the circumstances, injuries, whatever, you are upholding traditions.

There are a lot of veterans that come back, and you don't want to disappoint them. You want them to brag and talk about LSU. You don't want LSU to be the type of school where people say, "Hey, they were this type of school, but now they are just going down the drain." You want LSU to be a dominant school all the time.

If we keep up this winning, the veterans will come back and keep talking to the guys, and that is going to help our recruiting. Everybody has to play their part in keeping this tradition going. If you are an All-American, it is your duty not to just go away and get on with your life, but to come back and play a part.

I saw guys on television playing for LSU the few times I could watch them, and when I came to school here, even though they had graduated, they were still coming back to teach us. LSU is real good about having guys coming back to train. Joseph Addai comes back, Marquise Hill comes back, guys like that. Kyle Williams is another NFL guy who comes back. They run 110s with us. It is going to make you train harder when guys in the league come back.

You need to be the type of guy who comes back and helps with a football camp and teach and educate. It's a huge support group. That's what it means to be a Tiger.

Herman Johnson was born in Monroe, Louisiana. His family is from Olla, Louisiana, and moved to Denton, Texas, when he was two years old. Johnson graduated from LSU in 2008 with a general studies degree with minors in communications, sports studies, and African American studies. Johnson was named All-SEC and All-America in 2008 as a left guard. He was selected in the fifth round of the 2009 NFL Draft by the Arizona Cardinals.

HONORABLE MENTION

SKIP BERTMAN

BASEBALL COACH

1984–2001

ATHLETIC DIRECTOR

2001–2008

I'M PROUD OF WHAT WAS ACCOMPLISHED in football at LSU while I was athletic director. There's no question that football is No. 1. No question. You have to fill the stadium with 92,600 every single game. Seven or eight at home. There is no alternative to that.

Winning the championship, I was happy for me, but I was happy for them, too. Great bunch of coaches and a great bunch of players. I was really happy for winning it and winning it handily.

We were 3–8 in football, and Nick Saban was brought in the next year.

I get a lot of phone calls telling me he's not the nicest guy in the world, but the best football coach you'll ever see. I was still coaching and I got a phone call from his secretary, Ja'el, who told me, "Coach Bertman, Coach Saban wants to talk to you." He'd only been there like two weeks.

A voice came on, and he said, "This is Coach Saban."

I said, "Hey, Nick, how are things going?"

"What?" he asked.

"How are you doing? How's your family getting along?"

And he said, "Skip, the reason I called was to let you know that I'm okay with baseball players playing football and coming to spring football."

So I told him thanks. I got such a kick out of that. Well, I knew after watching him some he'd be successful because he had a system.

When I took over as AD, he already had a contract. After he beat Illinois [in the 2002 Sugar Bowl], we wanted to give Saban a new contract. I met his agent, Jimmy Sexton, and I tried to present something to Sexton that's a little different. I offered this "rabbi trust," which is a retirement where the government allows you to put in as much as you want, and it's tax-free. Jimmy Sexton didn't know what it was—it was brand new and was eventually outlawed. The government said no, it was too good.

But I went to Jimmy and said, "Listen: instead of a $300,000 bonus for winning the national championship, let's just make sure Nick makes more than Bob Stoops at Oklahoma." Stoops was the highest-paid guy at $2.1 million or something like that.

He didn't win it that year, but he did the next year, and what break. That was the year I put in the sideline fee of $400, which is a ridiculous fee—but to Dan Radakovich and Herb Vincent and Verge Ausberry, I give a lot of credit. They researched and found out that everybody paid to sit on the sidelines.

257

I was hoping he'd win nine games, but of course he won it all. Before the game, I went to Jimmy Sexton, and we worked it out. He would be the highest-paid coach whether he won or lost that game, which is the right thing to do, because one game shouldn't decide it. And he was getting that $300,000 anyway. Now everybody does it.

But the problem with Nick was he was always looking to the pros for the next challenge, and the chancellor was really fed up with it. They had to get permission, so Sexton would call and say, "Carolina Panthers are calling. Is this okay?" Yes. "The Chicago Bears are calling, I'll fax it over right now." Yes. You couldn't say no.

The Bears offered like $3 million. There was always a call. By then it was like, who the hell cares if he goes to the Bears? He did his time and he was killing us with this stuff. So, naturally, he turned the Bears down. The next year he was coming with the Dolphins. Nick called me, because this was serious. Not Jimmy. Nick said, "You're from Miami. You know what it's like."

It got to the point where [Wayne] Huizenga flew up in his 22-passenger, customized DC-3—this thing had to cost $50 or $60 million. Jimmy didn't want him to go, but they just keep coming at him, giving him whatever he wanted—being assistant general manager, getting more coaches, getting more money—to where finally he got to where he couldn't turn it down. He said to me, "I may never get another shot at the NFL."

I didn't want him to go because I knew my life would change because I'd have to hire a new coach. And whomever I got wouldn't be accepted at the beginning. Steve Spurrier had already signed, Urban Meyer had already signed.

I knew the people wouldn't understand. When Miles was hired, they went nuts.

Anyway, I asked Nick if he was going to take the job, and he said yeah, but he didn't want to announce it until Christmas at the Capital One Bowl in Orlando. Meanwhile, I went out and started searching.

We went and saw some coaches. We saw many coaches. One of them was Les Miles. Some of them were untouchable. For instance, Kirk Ferentz. No. Butch Davis: "I promised my wife I would take a year off." Frank Beamer's agent said he was interested, but he had a $3.5 million annuity coming up in July and then had a buyout.

258

I liked Rich Rodriguez, but he had a buyout of like $2 million and said, "Don't worry about it." I had to worry about it. But, then again, LSU went through this with DiNardo, when they paid a small buyout. But I chickened out because it was too high. I eliminated Rodriguez. We spoke to Houston Nutt. He's a great coach, but I didn't like the problems he had. And his AD, Frank Broyles, as soon as we asked permission, he called the newspaper and said, "LSU's speaking to my coach." Was Jimbo Fisher ready?

So we spoke to a lot of coaches. Les had several things working for him. No. 1 is there's no professional football in Les's future. He doesn't like professional football. Does he want to go to Michigan? No. But we put it in the contract anyway. But he wasn't going to Michigan. And he's not going to another university. You have to know what I knew. When you come to Baton Rouge and work at LSU, you don't go to another university.

In addition to a good football record, he has something that LSU needed badly, and that was the ability to communicate mixed with the ability to be nice. He's very, very nice, a great family man and very nice. People needed that. Not knocking Nick, but LSU needed that. People love working for Les, the players love playing for Les, and the community loves Les. In the interview, he struck me as a guy who would fit and be here forever.

Skip Bertman, the athletic director who hired Nick Saban, won five national titles himself as LSU's baseball coach.

He's had a better record than Saban. When Les came in, we helped him with some of his shortcomings, which were media relations and public speaking. I helped Nick a lot with that, although Nick was very good at it. And Les, to his credit, accepted all the help. None of the help had anything to do with football.

On the other hand, if he needed help with football, I, as the AD, would get it. No matter what it cost, if we needed it for football, we would get it. I would say we were very generous to assistant coaches and other things LSU wanted.

He's a great recruiter. Saban was a good recruiter, but Les is going to get them all here in Louisiana, and he's going to battle the others because he has the facilities and his personality is so good.

A lot of coaches do well their first year. Les did, but he had two hurricanes. I mean, it was serious. It was the most serious distraction in the history of college football for any coach. He handled it with dignity and was terrific.

That year, they went to the bowl and beat Miami and finished 11–2. And that wasn't good enough for some of the fans. But now they've finished the operations center, and it's beautiful. Like when Nick saw me in Destin [for the SEC meetings] after his first year at Alabama, and he said the culture and necessary facilities are there, they just didn't have the athletes. But now at LSU, we have them both. There are no facilities we don't have. You can always get better, but the truth is, we have them all.

When given time and avoiding injuries, Les can prepare for and beat anybody. He's got all kinds of terrific records. He's been labled lucky. If the right TV guy doesn't give you thumbs up as a coach on ESPN or Fox or somewhere, he doesn't get that.

He gets "Mad Hatter" because he's a gambler. But Les is much better than Saban as a team coach and team leader. That and the way he handles team things. And we all respect that.

J. Stanley "Skip" Bertman was the LSU baseball coach from 1984 to 2001, and his team won five national championships in 18 seasons. The Tigers won seven SEC baseball championships under Bertman. He was the LSU athletic director from 2001 to 2008 and managed an upgrade in athletic facilities, which included the construction of an academic center and new football facility with indoor practice space. Bertman currently works as a fund-raiser for LSU.

SAM NADER

FOOTBALL OPERATIONS
1975–Present

W E MOVED AROUND LOUISIANA. I went to high school in Lake Charles and Shreveport. My dad was a Methodist minister, so we moved every few years. We lived in Jennings, Houma, Lake Charles, Shreveport.

I went to LaGrange and then Byrd. I was a quarterback. I was okay. I went to Auburn. I wasn't particularly good—I mean, LSU didn't recruit me. Ole Miss, Auburn, the military schools did. I graduated in 1963. I liked Auburn. I didn't have that many choices. Actually, the way I got recruited by them was there was a guy named Lee Hayley, and Lee had played at Auburn and was coaching at McNeese when I was in Lake Charles. He went to Auburn from McNeese when I was a senior and came back and recruited me.

I was a special-teams player my last couple of years, just because I worked hard and would get my nose bloody. But I wasn't as good as the guys who played ahead of me. We had a couple of very good quarterbacks when I was there, one was an All-American, Jimmy Sidle, and another was All-SEC, Loran Carter, who was there my last year. Shug Jordan was the coach. A great man, I loved him.

I was a backup player and special-teams player, but I was there five years because I redshirted my first year, so I almost got through my master's. I went to work in Columbus, Georgia, which is only 30 miles from Auburn. I was coaching there, but I kept going to Auburn.

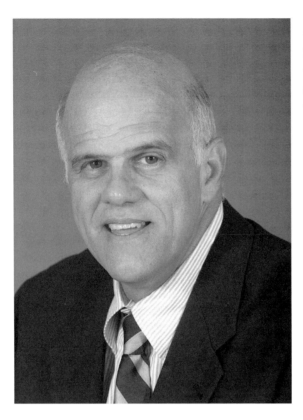

Coaches come and go, but Sam Nader has been with the LSU football program since 1975, which spans the regimes of 10 coaches.

262

I came to LSU as a graduate assistant, and one of the reasons I did that was to finally go ahead and get my PhD. I figured, after six years of high school coaching, I was going to be a G.A. and get a taste of college coaching and finish that degree.

I came here in 1975 as a graduate assistant. Coach McClendon was here. Coach Mac was wonderful to me. He gave me the tight ends to coach and let me learn by doing. It was a great experience. Then, of all things, after my second season one of Coach Mac's coaches left, and I just happened to be in the right place at the right time.

He hired me, and it worked out great. I finished my PhD classwork in those first two years, but once I became a fulltime coach I didn't start on my dissertation until three years later. So I ended up actually getting my degree in 1982 in kinesiology.

Coach Mac used me as an on-the-field coach. I stayed with Bo Rein and went recruiting with him for a month before he was killed in the plane wreck. Then Jerry Stovall took over, and he and I had coached together on Coach Mac's staff. I coached spring that year as an on-the-field coach, and going into his first year, we didn't have a recruiting office or a recruiting coordinator. All the big schools were getting recruiting coordinators, and he really wanted to do that. So he gave me a choice. He asked me, "Do you want to keep coaching on the field? I'm getting ready to create a position as recruiting coordinator, and it's going to be a better job." In other words, he wanted me to do that.

I was really interested in it because I thought the way things were going in college football, recruiting was becoming more and more important. I was keen on the idea, and I did it. I was the recruiting coordinator and did not coach on the field any more. My whole job was recruiting. That was 1980 when Jerry started, and that went on until the mid-1990s when the NCAA made a new rule. It was kind of a cost-cutting measure to reduce the size of coaching staffs. They put a limit on the staffs and said the recruiting coordinator had to be one of the on-the-field coaches.

Well, fortunately, the schools in our conference took care of their recruiting coordinators and gave them some more administrative duties and a different title, either administrative assistant or football operations director. I'm sure some schools just eliminated that position. Fortunately, here they let me stay and gave me a different title and some more administrative duties. So I continued and was able to do on-campus recruiting but not off-campus recruiting. But I could still do the planning for when kids came on their visits, and there were recruiting things that I did that I continue to do to this day.

And now my title is assistant AD for football operations. But I'm doing the same thing I've always done. But mainly what I do now is on-campus recruiting and acting as a liaison for the support system for our team, academics, dorm and eligibility issues, getting our freshmen in school and eligible, and those kind of things.

Going from Coach Stovall to Coach [Bill] Arnsparger was hard because Jerry and I are still friends. I've got a lot of respect for the guy.

I could say that anytime a coach was let go it's been very difficult, because you lose friends and you lose continuity. Even though a good coach came in here and was a guy that I love, it's still hard, a hard thing. All those transitions are hard things in a personal sense. You see guys having to job hunt and their families crushed, and it's a hard part of our business.

But it went okay. Coach Arnsparger was a good man and really did a good job. One recollection from that transition that was funny in the end but not at the time, was that Bill and the Dolphins were in the playoffs. So when he first got the job, he didn't come for good, he came on a weekend when they had played a playoff game on a Saturday and Coach [Don] Shula had let him off for a few days to come over and recruit. He kept Pete Jenkins on staff, and Pete and I were helping him recruit. That weekend he flew into New Orleans. So Pete picked him up, and they recruited the New Orleans area, and then he brought him up here. The next morning Bill and I started out early with about five in-home visits to make in South Louisiana. I think we were in the first home at 8:00 in the morning, which was unusual. Anyway, we were on the way to Eunice, and I think we were going to the home of Todd Coutee, who played center for us. It was about 3:00 that afternoon, and I was driving us down this two-lane country road and coming up on this old country gas station. Bill looked over and said, "Maybe we could pull into this gas station and get a pack of crackers or something." And I realized I hadn't fed the guy breakfast, lunch, nothing—and here I am lucky to be around, retained by the new coach, and I'm just killing him.

And he was so nice. Just a pack of crackers.

Mike [Archer] and I had been working together. He was such a good person. He kept most of the staff intact, and we were coming off an SEC championship year when Coach Arnsparger left to be AD at Florida.

A lot of it was the nature of the job I was doing. Usually, it helps a new coach to have someone who knows what's going on with recruiting. It helps with the transition, and I was always willing to stay and help out whether the guy retained me or not.

For example, Bill Arnsparger came in and didn't bring in another recruiting coordinator from another college because he was coming from pro ball.

Curley [Hallman] was hired, and I really think Joe Dean, who was athletic director then, talked to Curley on my behalf to say this guy can help you with the transition and at least keep him around for that and see how it goes. Nobody told me that, but I think Joe put in a word for me with Curley because Curley brought in a guy in an administrative position who could have done what I did. Curley was nice enough to hear Joe out and keep me and then keep me after the transtion.

I enjoyed Curley and I enjoyed Gerry [DiNardo]. Gerry's a really smart guy who had a lot of great ideas and did a great job here. We had some outstanding seasons right off the bat. Things were going really good, but they slipped away from us a little bit, and by that time the people who run college football were getting to be a fairly impatient lot—as we see in college football today.

I think with Nick [Saban] I got a little help from Joe Dean, too. I think Joe mentioned to him I could help with the transition, and he gave me a chance. He came from another university, but most of his old staff stayed at Michigan State. That left an opening for me to be able to stay, at least through the transition, and I was able to stay. I was glad for the opportunity. He was very good to me, and I treasure having worked with him.

All the guys I worked with, I wish everybody could know them behind the scenes, because they're all genuinely good, albeit tough, people. If you're not tough in that spot, the football world will chew you up and spit you out. So they have to be tough. But they all had heart. I enjoyed them a bunch and am grateful for the opportunity to have worked with all of them.

And the guy I'm working for now is as good a person as I've ever met. Les Miles has a big heart. He's a tough old-school football coach, but he's got a big heart, and I'm just enjoying the moment.

For the away games, I'm down on the field at the end of the bench. For the home games, I sit with the recruits and manage that part of what we do.

265

Winning the championship is the ultimate. That's what you shoot for, whether it's an SEC championship, which is close to the national-championship level of emotion and feeling. It's the ultimate level of accomplishment and satisfaction of being part of a team.

The greatest thing for me is to be able to share with my family all of this, because there's always a sense of guilt for a coach of robbing his family of a dad because of the way we work. At the same time what's comforted me is my family's gotten to grow up in a great town with a great university setting, which is wonderful for raising kids—and to share the victories, because it's meaningful to them, too. It really is, because they're into the team and love the team.

I didn't think we'd ever see two championships. To hope for one is something. To even dream that two teams could win it, that's pretty special.

The relationship with players and coaches and all the people we work with, that's edifying to me more than them, I'm sure. The benefit and joy to me has been a blessing. I tell people all the time, this is not a job. It's something that you live. People aren't in this kind of business if they don't want to live it, if it's not that important, because it's not fair to your family. It's not worth it.

You have to love being a part of a team, and I've grown up being a part of a team and being a part of a team like LSU. What a blessing, what an opportunity. I've been blessed by all those kids and coaches we've worked with. It's something you love doing, and I'm sure anybody who had a chance to do it would do it as good or better.

Dr. Sam Nader is going into his ninth season in 2009 as the assistant athletic director for football operations at LSU. Nader is responsible for overseeing day-to-day administrative duties for the program. He joined the LSU staff in 1975 as a graduate assistant and was made a full-time assistant in 1977 by Coach Charlie McClendon. Nader has now worked on behalf of nine LSU football coaches, including the late Bo Rein.